POWER OF WORDS

Some other books by Stuart Chase

ROADS TO AGREEMENT, 1951

THE PROPER STUDY OF MANKIND, 1948

MEN AT WORK, 1945

DEMOCRACY UNDER PRESSURE, 1945

WHERE'S THE MONEY COMING FROM? 1943

THE TYRANNY OF WORDS, 1938

RICH LAND, POOR LAND, 1936

THE ECONOMY OF ABUNDANCE, 1934

MEXICO: A STUDY OF TWO AMERICAS, 1931

MEN AND MACHINES, 1929

YOUR MONEY'S WORTH (*with F. J. Schlink*), 1927

THE TRAGEDY OF WASTE, 1925

POWER OF WORDS

by Stuart Chase

IN COLLABORATION WITH

Marian Tyler Chase

HARCOURT, BRACE AND COMPANY, NEW YORK

Contents

Part Two APPLICATIONS

Foreword

This book grew out of my earlier work, *The Tyranny of Words*, published in 1938. I had first thought of a revision, but so much new material had come in that the project turned into an entirely new work. Meanwhile my interest had expanded from semantics and the problems of meaning, to the whole broad field of communication.

The *Tyranny*, as its title indicates, was chiefly concerned with the misuse of language. The present book, as its title indicates, deals with the positive as well as the negative; power runs to both poles. Words are what hold society together; without them we should not be human beings. At the same time, words are responsible for untold and unnecessary conflict and misery. Consider the verbal aspects of the Inquisition, the political consequences of *Das Kapital*, the career of Adolf Hitler.

The author is not alone in his growing interest in communication. Administrators, educators, engineers, physicists, students of labor relations, psychologists, medical men, all sorts of people, pay increasing attention to it. The subject is urgent because of growing problems in television, telephony, radar, atomic energy, cold-war propaganda, and dealing with allies in the free world. The United Nations can be defined as an experiment in communication. All this new attention serves to intensify the continuing problems of how to improve teaching in the schools, how to say what we mean, how to evaluate what we hear.

A writer is supposed to understand the behavior of language, for his working life is largely spent in deciding the sequence in which one word follows another. In the *Tyranny* I said that writers search their memories for a better word to use in a given context, but are no more accustomed to question language itself than to question the weather. "We assume," I said, "that we know exactly what we mean, and that readers who do not understand us should polish their wits."

That was in 1938. Perhaps some writers are still in this confident mood, but I think not so many as there used to be. Some of us have begun to question the structure of language itself, which quickly dispels any complacency with one's powers of communication. Dostoevski was no technical semanticist—the subject was unknown in his day—but he had a firm grip on the idea when he said in *The Brothers Karamazov:* "If people around you are spiteful and callous, and will not hear you, fall down before them and beg their forgiveness; for in truth you are to blame for their not wanting to hear you."

When the audience turns away, there is something wrong with the writer's communication line. He should look to his tools. This holds for anyone who has something to say to others. It is primarily *his* lookout that the message gets through, not theirs.

Thumbing over some old scrapbooks, I was surprised to find that one of my earliest articles to escape a rejection slip, published in 1923, contained a bitter complaint about abstract terms. I cited "democracy," "liberty," "individualism," "Wall Street," "human nature," "metaphysics." Such words, I said, should be employed with caution, for no two people mean the same thing by them. Bandied about as they usually are, they tend to reduce an honest truth-seeker to despair.

I have been uneasy about the meaning of words ever since I began to write. For the past fifteen years, however, I have had the help of good men digging ever deeper into the subject. Sometimes they dig so deep that I cannot follow, except in a general way—for example, Dr. Shannon in his mathematical theory of communication. The more these students turn up, the greater depths they reveal.

The communication process is as vital, and almost as unconscious, as the circulation of the blood. When Harvey observed and demonstrated that process, physiology and medicine took a great step forward. Similar grand discoveries can be expected in communication. Only the preliminary hurdles have been cleared. An infant Harvey may even now be learning the phonemes of his native tongue in San Francisco, New Delhi, London, or Tokyo.

Research into communication is already scattered so widely, from cybernetics to group dynamics, that no one mind can hope to cover it all. Yet someone must try to integrate it, even if the level of abstraction may at times be pretty high. I am reasonably familiar with semantics and economics, but for the other sciences brought together in this book, I can pretend to no especial competence.

As the sciences become more specialized, the need for integration grows, if the intelligent layman is to keep track of his world. *The Proper Study of Mankind* and *Roads to Agreement* sketched such interdisciplinary charts in the social sciences. These books were well received, and now I attempt to connect some of the diverse disciplines touching on communication. From another point of view, the integrator is like a walkie-talkie operator, a communications man. As a writer I am helping myself in this quest, but also, I hope, the reader. What one of us cannot use better tools for sending messages and decoding them; for evaluating our world?

I am indebted to many co-workers, known and unknown. In the bibliography, credit is given to a hundred or more. In addition, the following have been of great assistance in reading part, or all, of the manuscript, and in giving me their criticisms and advice (which I have not always followed): Ernest Angell, Arno Bellack, Lee Deighton, Roma Gans, Dr. Kenneth Grevatt, Dr. Edwin Grace, Dr. Douglas Kelley, Edward Kennard, Eugene Reynal, James Saunders, Henry Lee Smith, Jr., George Trager, Armitage Watkins. Dr. Gans was the first to read the manuscript as a whole, and her encouragement and careful criticism were most helpful at a strategic moment.

My wife, Marian, and I worked together as an executive team, with a division of labor in research, writing, and editing. Without her help this book would have been severely crippled, if indeed it could have been done at all. We were fortunate in having two able secretaries in our neighbors Lola Donnell and Christine Loring.

Stuart Chase

Redding, Connecticut
November, 1953

Part One FINDINGS

... All linguistic processes derive their power
only from real processes taking place in man's relation to his surroundings.

BRONISLAV MALINOWSKI

A change in language can transform our appreciation of the cosmos.

BENJAMIN LEE WHORF

Chapter 1

EVERYBODY'S TALKING

We live in an ocean of words, but like a fish in water we are not often aware of it. There are close to two and a half billion of us on the planet today, and practically every one of us, except very young children, is constantly talking, listening to talk, learning to talk. Even a hermit talks to himself. The 50 per cent or so of the world's population who are more or less literate will also be reading words and, less frequently, writing them. Until relatively recent times, literate people were so rare as to be practically abnormal, and the ocean of words was almost entirely vocal.

Words link together all human activities, and form a connecting bond in every human relation. They have a physical existence on stone, paper, and microfilm, and probably in flesh and blood as well, by virtue of verbal habits built into the brain and nervous system.

Nobody to my knowledge has ever estimated how many words a person may talk in a day. It must vary with the language used, with one's age, character, occupation; with the season of the year, and economic conditions. A gossip in a village, or a cleric on his daily rounds, will score a larger output than a prospector or a sheepherder. Harpo Marx, they say, is silent only before the camera, otherwise entirely normal.

Let us assume a person averages one hour of continuous talk a day—which seems conservative. As a lecturer, I can deliver about 6,000 words in an hour, at a tempo somewhat slower than ordinary conversation. Let us assume that at least two billion of us the world around can talk—which includes nearly everyone three years of age and up. Combining the assumptions, the total works out to twelve trillion words a day, or more than four quadrillion words a year. All this is, of course, under pre-machine conditions. To it we must add the amplification of words by the great organs of mass communication—radios, public-address systems, television sets, moving pictures, sound trucks, bus loudspeakers with their captive audiences, and those appalling airplanes which can spray a whole city with commercials. Words heard through mass media vastly increase the total output, and they not only multiply, but accelerate, like compound interest. The Chinese are becoming very adept at broadcasting, as the Russians have long been.

Power words

Most of the words we use are concerned with day-by-day living, but now and again a phrase charged with feeling will churn the verbal ocean. "No taxation without representation!" was such a phrase; "*Liberté, égalité, fraternité*," was another. "*Cartago delenda est!*" "Bonnie Prince Charlie," "John Brown's Body," "Remember the Maine!" "A Place in the Sun!" "The War for Democracy," "Peace on Earth, Goodwill to Men" . . .

Some words are considered so holy they must never be spoken aloud, such as the ancient Hebrew word for God. Some words are so shocking that they must be spoken only in subterranean circles. Some words are so magical that people believe they can cause injury, dementia, even death. Some words can make us sick, and others can make us well.

A Japanese word, *mokusatsu*, may have changed all our lives.[1] It has two meanings: (1) to ignore, (2) to refrain from comment. The release of a press statement using the second meaning in July 1945 might have ended the war then. The Emperor was ready to end it, and had the power to do so. The cabinet was preparing to accede to the Potsdam ultimatum of the Allies—surrender or be crushed—but wanted a little more time

[1] See the account by W. J. Coughlin in *Harper's Magazine*, March 1953.

to discuss the terms. A press release was prepared announcing a policy of *mokusatsu,* with the *no comment* implication. But it got on the foreign wires with the *ignore* implication through a mix-up in translation: "The cabinet *ignores* the demand to surrender." To recall the release would have entailed an unthinkable loss of face. Had the intended meaning been publicized, the cabinet might have backed up the Emperor's decision to surrender. In which event, there might have been no atomic bombs over Hiroshima and Nagasaki, no Russian armies in Manchuria, no Korean war to follow. The lives of tens of thousands of Japanese and American boys might have been saved. One word, misinterpreted.

Language map

A language map of the world today would look very different from a map of nations. All South America except Brazil and the Guianas would be one color—Spanish.[1] The United States and Canada would be one color, except for the province of Quebec. In Europe, little Switzerland would be three colors, Belgium two, and big Germany one. The world map would require a whole spectrum of colors, for the students of linguistics have identified at least 2,500 active and differing speech communities, not counting dialects. There are still a number of communities in New Guinea and other outposts which have not been studied. The linguists complain that their graduates are too few to send out expeditions and collect these rare flowers of speech before they become extinct. There is, as we shall see later, a rigorous scientific method for such collection. Once on a sound track, furthermore, a language can be studied and preserved to perpetuity.

The most widespread languages are: [2]

English, spoken by 250 million, and understood by 250 million more in India and elsewhere—a total of 500 million.

[1] Not counting Indian languages.
[2] Estimates made for the author by Dr. George Trager of the Foreign Service Institute.

Russian, spoken by more than 100 million, understood by 100 million more as a second language. A Russian can partially understand Ukrainian, Polish, Czech, and other Slavic languages. The whole Slavic language group may number 300 million.

North Chinese is third in extent.

Then come *Spanish, German, Japanese, Hindustani, French, Italian.*

The above are the big speech communities, with 50 million and more in each group. For every live tongue in the world today, there is probably at least one dead language—Sanskrit, Greek, Latin, Inca, and untold native tongues. Hebrew, once dead except for ceremonial purposes, is being revived in Israel. It will be interesting to see if the revival can be made permanent in an entirely different cultural background.

Language and culture

A blasphemy in one society, when translated, may be just a harmless phrase in another society. No American family would name a son "Jesus," though Spanish families do it constantly. Blasphemies to a Christian mean nothing to a Buddhist, and vice versa. The language map of the world, though markedly different from a map showing nations, would correspond broadly to what social scientists call "culture." This English word itself is unfortunate because it is so easily confused with "culture" in the sense of the fine arts and the classics. But the concept it represents is one of the most fertile discoveries of science, and explains many things which previously had no answers. The culture concept establishes the vital principle of *relativity* in human affairs.

We cannot talk usefully about a language without talking about culture, for they are inseparable. The most important element in any culture is language, not only for day-by-day communication, but for preserving the community from generation to generation. Individuals die, but the culture which flows through them, and which they help to create and to change, is all but immortal. Without words the flow would cease, the culture wither away.

The food, shelter, and clothing habits of some societies may seem simple and primitive, but there are no primitive languages. The tongue of Australian bushfellows is more complex than English. No child ever learns to talk by himself. His flexible vocal apparatus is inherited, but the enormous complexity of organized speech—whether that of the bushfellow or of Bernard Shaw—must be learned from somebody who has already mastered it. Actually it requires many instructors—mother, playfellows, teacher, a whole active community—properly to induct a youngster into the use of his language. As we shall see, he is born with a powerful drive to exercise his speech apparatus, and soon learns to understand the main structure of his spoken language, whatever its complexity.

Man probably gets his explanation of the universe, his "world view," from the language he learns, and it differs with every language. Indo-European languages favor a two-valued view of things, the either-or logic, whereas the Chinese language is structurally multivalued, allowing for shades of gray. The language map is far more significant than maps showing that historical upstart, the sovereign state. National boundaries are fragile; compare Europe in 1953 and in 1913. But culture and language go back to the dawn of the race, moving in glacier-like periods. The most significant thing about the culture concept is that it gives a truly universal point of view. All present societies around the world come into focus, together with all societies of the past. This provides a steadier frame of reference than any philosophical system yet devised.

The uniqueness of man

It is, of course, possible to communicate without using words. Observe the road symbols along any modern highway, with their messages which may mean life or death to the motorist. Observe the eloquence with which a Frenchman shrugs his shoulders, or an Arabian spreads his hands, or how the face of any human being may light with love or darken with perplexity and fear. (The term "kinesics" has been coined by linguists for such nonverbal communication.)

Animals as well as men convey messages, using sound and gesture, but never meaningful words. Homo sapiens, alone of all earth's creatures, uses words to refine his messages. One can tell a child or a dog to leave the room, and either will understand. But only the child can understand *why* you have issued the order. A parrot can learn the sound of words, but not their meanings, and so never really knows what it is talking about. The parrot can be compared to the sailor who, in port, imitates the sounds of a foreign language—perhaps to find that he has insulted somebody's ancestors in unmentionable ways.

Many creatures beside man live in communities which practice the division of labor and mutual aid—bees, for example. No other creature, however, has such a large brain in proportion to total weight. Did the big brain develop with the ability to talk? Many scientists are convinced that it did. No animal community has developed a true culture, not even the industrious beaver. "The evolution of verbal concepts," says Julian Huxley in his *Evolution in Action,* "opened the door to all further organizations and achievements of man's thought." The Biblical phrase "In the beginning was the word" was in one sense true, for man was not man until he spoke. The cosmos, however, had a different origin.

Homo sapiens, though a relatively large animal, is one of the most defenseless of earth's creatures. His claws, teeth, hoofs, hide are deplorable in contrast with those of others. Why does this relatively helpless specimen survive? Man gets out of tight places by using his head. It is now fairly well established that complex human thought is impossible without words. This is contrary to the common assumption that thought precedes and is independent of its verbalization, but, as we shall see, that assumption is becoming increasingly shaky. The evidence indicates that it is language which gives man his unique place in nature. With his power to manipulate words and so to reason on many levels, he surmounts the need for fangs and armor.

The human nervous system at birth has ample room for the development of speech, and every normal child is impelled to exercise this power. No other creature has the equipment or the drive. As language is mastered, the ability to use abstract thought develops. Valuable conclusions and processes—such as the discovery of fire, the lever, a storable grain—are handed down from generation to generation. Culture grows first by word of mouth, lately by written records, currently also by microfilm and tape recording. The end products of the culture of Western societies are now all around us in Megalopolis, over us in jet airliners, under us in oil wells and bathyspheres. We can travel at twice the speed of sound, communicate at the speed of light, bounce radar beams off the moon. We are controlling plagues, stamping out syphilis, moving in on tuberculosis and polio, eliminating poverty over great areas.

This is all very wonderful, celebrated in many books—including several by your author—but we are finding that it is not nearly good enough. Parallel with these advances has come a perversion of the word. The quarter inch of cortex has created, along with the plays of Shakespeare and the abatement of yellow fever, a jangle of contention and a dreadful zoo of verbal monsters. This has always been true to a degree, but now the mass media are making it far worse.

When we stop to think, it is perfectly apparent that without words organized warfare would be impossible, Communism would have no appeal to anybody, demagogues would lose their audiences, religious strife and ideological quarrels would be unknown. The inquisitions of Torquemada, Goebbels and Stalin would be unthinkable. The misuse of man's chief characteristic has made his life unduly insecure. It has compounded conflict, and been at odds with his deepest instincts and desires, as a creature that must live amicably in a group to rear his children and survive. Much, if not most, of the pain and misery in the world today can be laid to the misinterpretation of signals, rather than to the stern impositions of nature. We pick up the morning paper to read of fifty drowned in a flood in Holland, and a thousand killed in a religious riot in Asia. The first is legally labeled an Act of God, the second is an act of man.

To endure under conditions of this earth, the race must wage many desperate battles against plagues, blights, erosion, floods, population crises, material shortages, and pathologies yet unknown. We shall need all our strength, resolution, and reasoning powers. It is ironic that we should waste so much energy fighting phantoms created by words.

Preview

It is the purpose of this book to interpret significant findings about language and communication, to point out applications of these findings and the need for further scientific study. We shall report how the verbal mechanism works, so far as scientists have dissected the process, and suggest a number of ways in which it might work better. We will first outline the general field of communication, noting how verbal communication, which is to be our chief interest, relates to other forms. We shall then try to describe in nontechnical language some interesting findings of communication engineers, brain physiologists, perception psychologists; findings of the linguists, the freewheeling grammarians, the animal psychologists, the child psychologists, the cultural anthropologists, the physicists in so far as they are concerned with communication; of the mathematicians with their universal language, the various schools of semanticists (including especially an evaluation of Alfred Korzybski), the students of group dynamics and of the techniques of listening. What have these various scientists to tell us about human talk and human thinking? Many new and exciting things.

The case studies, beginning with Chapter 17—in which your author lays out his evaluation tools as he prepares to write an article—might be called applied communication theory. Enough knowledge has already been rounded up to furnish real help to the layman. It is only a fraction, however, of the help that will come when communication research can command as wide support as, say, guided-missile research does at the present time.

Communication by means of language is man's distinctive activity. It is news today because of the recent progress made in its analysis. It is news because technology has installed mass media to blanket the planet with words, thus compounding the perils of propaganda, half-truths, and plain loud lies. We need a new literacy for listeners, to help them distinguish between the real and the phony, to help them identify motives, know when to shut their ears, when to turn the damn thing off.

Today we face a new and colossal necessity, a technological imperative to control technology. Modern man is obsolete, as Norman Cousins said, unless he can stop world wars, and begin to build One World. This does not mean that we have to love everybody, or entertain everybody, or support everybody, only that we have to learn to get along with them well enough to keep the new lethal weapons from going off. No matter how strong this technological imperative to peace may be, it cannot be followed without improving communication.

Twelve kinds of communication failure

What are the major communication failures at the present time? We shall describe them in some detail later on; here a partial list may not be out of order. On the highest level there are two varieties of failure: (1) misinterpretation of signs coming in to a person from his environment, and (2) misunderstandings between individuals and groups. "Reasonable men," says Beardsley Ruml, "always agree if they understand what they are talking about." Descending a rung or two we find these specific failures:

1. *Confusing words with things.* Because a word is there, it is commonly assumed a thing must be there too. The assumption peoples the world with verbal monsters.

2. *Failure to check abstract terms with concrete events.* "Find the referent," the physical object or occurrence to which the term refers.

3. *Confusing facts with inferences with value judgments.* It was the Queen of Hearts who shouted at Alice: "Sentence first—verdict afterwards."

4. *Spurious identification.* This communication failure has been common on the front pages of United States newspapers in the form of guilt-by-verbal-association.

5. *The wholesale application of two-valued logic.* If an event is not black it must be white, with no allowance for shades of gray.

6. *Failure to assemble the main facts before passing judgment.* Prejudice, it has been said, is a great timesaver; it enables us to form opinions without bothering to get the facts.

7. *Extrapolation.* Plotting one or two points, and then riding the curve to cloud cuckooland. Another term for over-generalization.

8. *Gobbledygook.* Prolixity and obscurity; using ten words where one would suffice, or drowning meaning in polysyllables and technical terms. Very common in large offices, and in some academic groves.

9. *Failure to listen,* to hear the speaker out; failure to assume he has something worth saying.

10. *Failure to appreciate the other man's background and point of view.* What are his needs and wants, and how do they affect his talk?

11. *Failure to appraise motives.* Does the speaker mean what he says or something else?

12. *Failure to allow for cultural differences.* Delegates to the United Nations face this problem every day.

As General MacArthur proceeded from one ovation to the next after his recall from the Pacific by President Truman in 1952, a California policeman was interviewed about the great debate on Asian policy which was rocking the country. "Everybody's talking," said the cop, "but nobody knows what he's talking about."

We can do better than this. In the pages to come it is hoped that the reader will find some principles, and many practical applications, showing how we can do a good deal better.

Chapter 2

KINDS OF COMMUNICATION

"Communication" is a popular subject at present in both lay and academic circles. Lectures, panel discussions, college courses, medical clinics, whole magazines are devoted to it. Students of labor relations are much concerned with "two-way communication." The subject is not easy to pin down, however, because of the great variety of activities which can be included. In this chapter we will attempt a rough survey of the whole area, and try to divide the traffic into five main streams. Although new terms are badly needed to sharpen talk about communication, we will not anticipate the students who will some day coin them.

Let us begin our survey with an example from the solar system.

Flash from Mars

The British Interplanetary Society recently invited Lancelot Hogben to explore the question of how to establish communication with another planet. They could not have found a better man, for Dr. Hogben is both a versatile scientist and a serious student of communication.

Suppose, he says, that our astronomers should observe what appear to be signals from one of the planets—Mars, for instance. Suppose further that we had the technical equipment to return signals. This is not beyond the bounds of probability, for already a radar beam has traveled to the moon and back in something under three seconds.

Good. We now come to a question as fascinating as it is crucial. *What shall the first message be?* What is the common ground between ourselves and other intelligent beings—beings who have in all probability a different physical and mental make-up? Hogben attacks the problem boldly. He says that we should begin with some small talk about numbers. The properties of numbers cannot vary from planet to planet. Most numerical systems—Chinese, Roman, Mayan—grew out of simple tally marks. To count cattle or fields or days, people would cut or draw marks on a stone or log, and name them one-two-three-four in the local language. Our extra-terrestrial Neighbors probably went through a similar stage. So our first message, says Hogben, via radar beam or otherwise, might well be an equation in simple numerals, thus:

"I plus II plus III equals IIIIII."

The numbers would be represented by dots as in Morse code, the "plus" by a dash and the "equals" by a longer dash.

When the Neighbors have recorded this message pattern on their local receivers often enough they ought to understand its meaning. Then by taking it apart, they can learn the first few words—"one," "two," "three," "six," "plus," "equals." More complicated equations will teach them more words. Do not assume, however, says Hogben, that the Neighbors have ten fingers and so have developed a decimal system.

If the Neighbors respond with numbers, the next subject for discourse is obviously astronomy. Both the earth and Mars have the same sun, both obey the great laws of the solar system. Observations of the sun from a planet result in a calendar, and our astronomers can calculate the Martian calendar for their recognition. This should produce a lot of interplanetary words. Then we can go on to chemistry, via the spectrum of bright stars common to both planets. When the interplanetary language can cope with anatomy, Hogben says, we shall learn what the Neighbors look like. Fingers and toes may be a surprise, but some kind of big, active brain is well assured.

On the bridge of the Challenger

Coming back to earth, let us take a look at the communication devices to be found on a modern freighter. My wife and I not long ago went south from Montreal to Trinidad on the *Canadian Challenger*, a 12,000-ton motor ship, with a cargo of flour, bacon, lumber, and steel pipes for the islands of the Caribbean. Aboard her, communication systems moved smoothly, not only from words to nonverbal signs, but over a range of techniques dating from the dawn of man to 1952 A.D. The captain shouts at the boatswain and snaps on the depth finder, all within a few seconds.

Around the captain on the bridge are the communicating instruments Lord Nelson used—signal flags, megaphones, charts and logs, gongs, sirens, bells, mouth whistles. And beside them are mechanisms which would utterly baffle the great admiral. Here is the automatic helmsman, or "iron mike," with both electric and hydraulic controls. It takes a course as directed and holds it more accurately than any pair of hands. Here is the sonic depth finder, which bounces a sound wave off the bottom to measure in fathoms the depth of water under the ship. Here is the radar screen, which bounces beams off anything, fore or aft, and can see a rowboat in a fog up to ten miles. Next to it is a smoke detector so delicate that it can smell anybody's pipe in any part of the ship, and alert the bridge. Here is the radio room, with its special receiver for disaster calls across the seas. Beside the iron mike are the bridge telegraph to the engine room, telephones to all key points, controls for searchlights, foghorn, and for a steam whistle to wake the dead.

Yet the captain told me that he avoided running down a fisherman not by radar and searchlights, but by a yell and a pointed finger from the lookout in the bow! In Dominica, moreover, we saw an elaborate system of electric winches being directed by a longshoreman in ragged shorts and nothing else, who whacked a piece of board against a steel railing in ordered sequences. Thus the *Challenger* employs words spoken and written, sound waves, light waves, microwaves, electrical impulses, wigwags, flag talk, "kinesics"—an altogether bewildering variety of communication devices.

The communication line

Getting in touch with Mars, or maneuvering the *Challenger*, illustrates the factors which enter every sort of communication, earthbound as well as interplanetary. The line begins with an information source prepared to send out something. The message must then be put upon a mechanism capable of encoding and sending it. The signal passes over a channel to a receiver mechanism. Here the message is decoded and forwarded to its destination for possible action. While passing from transmitter to receiver, the message may be distorted by outside forces, such as static, fading, "snow" in television, et cetera—all of which interruptions the communication engineers call "noise." "Noise," they say, "is universal and insidious." The engineers diagram it this way: [1]

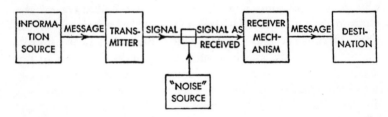

This diagram is basic to all talk about communication. It applies to any communication line, whatever the symbols sent over it—words, letters, dots and dashes, music, pictures, nonsense phrases. When the word "message" is used in the pages to come, and it will be used repeatedly, let the reader recall this diagram.

In communicating with the Martians, the information source would be the astronomers on earth designing the message. The transmitter would be the radar tower or other technical equip-

[1] Diagram taken, with slight modifications, from Shannon and Weaver, *The Mathematical Theory of Communication*. See bibliography, page 301.

ment. The "noise" might be cosmic rays. The receiver mechanism would be the Martians' technical equipment where the earth message was recorded. The destination would be the Martian scientists, figuring out what was meant and how they would reply. Observe how the function of listening is equally important with that of talking.

A man enters a telegraph office in northern Maine and prints on a blank: "STATLER, BOSTON—PLEASE RESERVE OUTSIDE DOUBLE ROOM NEXT THURSDAY," and signs his name. An operator transforms the words into the dots and dashes of the Morse code. They go over the wire to the receiving mechanism in Boston, subject to whatever "noise" may be on the line. There the office transforms the familiar clicks back into words, types them on a blank and sends them via messenger boy to the Statler Hotel for action.

Now let us take a homely message, uncomplicated by radar, telegraph wires, or any technical equipment. A mother calls to her small boy, "Come here!" The mother's brain is the source, the message is two words, the transmitter is the mother's vocal cords, the channel is the air which conducts the sound waves, and the receiving mechanism is the child's ear. The destination is the child's brain, where the message is decoded and evaluated for appropriate action. Appropriate action in the circumstances may be, of course, to move as rapidly as possible in the opposite direction. "Noise" can come from a passing plane, a playmate's shout, a corner of the garage which deflects the signal.

An engineering theory of communication

Telephone and radio engineers continually encounter hard problems in communication. Their task is not primarily to clarify the *meaning* of messages, but to take the message as given—whether a Bach concerto, a plug for Wheaties, or a hotel reservation—and deliver it to destination with high fidelity. For this they need some scientific theory to design the transmitting equipment. Dr. Claude Shannon, an expert in telephonic switching, has provided one very useful theory. He and his co-author Warren Weaver pose various questions, of which two particularly concern us.

A. How accurately can the symbols of communication be transmitted? This is the engineering problem.

B. How precisely do the transmitted symbols convey the desired meaning? This is the semantic problem.

Dr. Shannon's theory deals only with problem A; Weaver brings in problem B. I would not dream of taking you, even if I could, through Shannon's twenty-two theorems. They include the use of Boolean algebra, the Stochastic process, the Markoff chain, probability theory, the ergodic process; and they end in a special form of the concept of entropy. From this blizzard of equations emerges a design for a system which can handle a maximum of messages with a minimum of "noise." The theory is now being applied to the practical operation of television and radio, guided missiles, and computing machines.

How about problem B, the meaning of the message? As a social scientist Weaver tackles this one, following the severe demonstration of the twenty-two theorems. For question B, he says, another box might be inserted after the *receiver* box in the diagram above, to be called the "semantic decoder." Its purpose would be to give the message a second decoding in terms of its meaning to the receiver. Also "noise," which is always mechanical on level A, should be expanded to cover "semantic noise," or distortions of meaning not intended by the sender. (The distortion of the word "*mokusatsu*," we remember, may ultimately have produced the noise of two atomic bombs.) The diagram, after allowing for level B, would look like this:

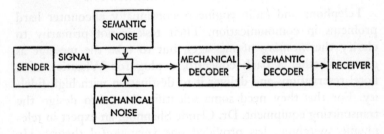

Even the clearest message loses something in its journey, and entropy is the name for the loss. Entropy is the idea that things are running down—like a watch, like energy in a heating system, like the universe—at least in some theories of the cosmos. And now, says Shannon, like messages. There is no question about entropy on level A, and it probably operates on level B as well—in the transfer of meaning. Semantic entropy may take us into questions of the total situation, the mental equipment and condition of the receiver, and so forth—very deep water.

This brief excursion into the work of Shannon and Weaver will assure the reader that minds of the first order are attacking the problems of communication. The physical scientists are joining the social scientists and the semanticists. We shall need them all. "Language," says Weaver, "must be designed (or developed) with a view to the totality that man may wish to say; but not being able to accomplish everything, it should do as well as possible, as often as possible." We shall never be able to communicate perfectly; "noise" will always get in. But we can improve the present performance.

Verbal tent

One must be careful not to think about "communication" as a *thing*, an entity. It is a label to cover a wide variety of tangible things; a verbal tent above a very large and active circus. If we disregard the tent and look carefully at the activities beneath it, we can formulate what might be called an *operational definition* of communication.

Suppose for convenience we divide the universe outside our heads into three parts: (1) the natural environment, (2) animals, and (3) men. Within the frame of inanimate nature, people and animals are on the move, behaving. To some of their behavior we apply the term "communication." It is more convenient than saying each time: "Adams is sending out signals which Brown is trying to decode." Continuing to look steadily outward at things, we can identify the following five varieties of communication:

1. *Messages in nature.* The events which comprise inanimate nature—earth, air, water, mountains, sun, stars—cannot deliberately communicate to people, except in the poetic sense. Nature sends no personal messages to you or to me. But you and I are receivers, and we must be ready to catch every significant signal given off by nature. It is not a good idea, for instance, to stay under a large tree when all incoming signals indicate that it is about to come down. The tree is not talking to you, but you will do well to heed the sound of cracking, the sight of shaking limbs, the frightened cries of birds. Referring to the second diagram above, there is no conscious sender at all; but signals are coming in to you to be semantically decoded for immediate action.

Signals keep coming to animals and insects too, for nature is constantly sending out rays and waves in all directions, to be decoded by whatever organisms they may concern; think of the infrareds and ultraviolets streaming perpetually from the sun. Our bodies send out signals, of which we may be completely unaware, in the form of sound, scent, and heat. The above traffic is one way, unconscious, looking for no reply. Some students would not include it in "communication" at all, but I think it must be mentioned. It fits the diagram.

2. *Animal communication.* Consciously directed messages are first encountered in the insects. A bee will perform a dance in the hive, which tells other bees where to go for nectar—as described in Chapter 6. This traffic, so far as scientists have learned, is all one way. The other bees do not send messages back to the scout: "Did you say northeast by east for those cherry blossoms?" The bees *respond* by taking action, but they do not *reply*. This distinction is important; a response is not necessarily a return message to the sender.

Crows provide an early example of two-way communication. A message is consciously sent to other crows in the group: "*Caw, caw.* Look out!" and a reply comes back: "*Caw, caw, caw.* I'm looking out." The other crows respond also by changing their flight direction.

Higher animals send and receive many messages, as when a tomcat calls and a tabby answers. They also conduct two-way communication with people, as we shall see in Chapter 6, where the author's cats are interviewed. The traffic is almost entirely nonverbal. (That parrot has already been taken care of.)

3. *Man to man.* Conscious, two-way, verbal communication appears only with man. Here we also find plenty of conscious, two-way nonverbal communication—as on the bridge of the *Challenger,* and plenty of one-way traffic, as in warning signals. Billions of messages a day are always in transit between individuals and groups. They are both spoken and written, and are often amplified by mass media. They can be recorded for future readers and listeners in documents and on sound tracks. One of the earliest means of communication between distant points was fire. Homer told of flaming beacons which spread the news of the fall of Troy.

Let us follow an illustrative sequence in man-to-man communication. Adams on the street sees smoke coming from the window of a house across the way. He decodes the signal and evaluates the situation. He shouts "Fire!" to Brown in his doorway. The latter hears, decodes, looks, evaluates, rushes in to his telephone and says: "Fire Department, emergency!"

"Where?"

"On Pine Street."

Brown then shouts to Adams for more information, and both summon neighbors to come on the run and help get out the furniture.

The sequence begins with a strictly impersonal smoke signal from nature, but almost immediately human communication lines begin to open in all directions. Some are verbal, some are not; all follow the Shannon diagram. When the Valley Volunteer Fire Company at last arrives, communication lines become more entangled, if possible, than their hose.

4. *Man to himself.* Inside any individual a communication process is always in action. Signals are coming from every part of the body to the brain, where action is taken to keep the

organism stable, action mostly on the unconscious level. A pain in the stomach, however, may urgently demand a conscious response.

Reflective thinking is quite another kind of internal communication. Here is your author trying to write this paragraph. He is referring to notes on cards written to himself earlier, consulting memories and experiences in his mind, and verbalizing many words and phrases, before he encodes any of them on paper to transmit to the reader.

Planning future action, drawing inferences from observation, analyzing situations and the behavior of other people, rationalizing personal desires with one's conscience or with cultural standards—all are examples of self-communication.

Prayer seems to be in a special class. One sends a verbal message, often very deeply felt, to an unseen receiver. Except for miracles, the circuit is one way.

5. *Men and machines.* Finally, machines are built and triggered by men to send out signals which affect the behavior of other machines, or of men. A thermostat starts a furnace when the temperature drops to 68° F.; an alarm clock rings a bell at 7:15 A.M. These are all one-way messages—unless one "replies" by cursing the alarm clock.

This seems to cover the chief kinds of activities going on under the verbal tent of "communication." As we said earlier, it is time that new terms were invented to tighten the concept. Out of the vast array, we shall concentrate chiefly on the meanings of verbal messages—conscious, two-way traffic. Our attention will be focused on the semantic decoder of the Shannon-Weaver diagram; but a number of collateral activities, such as animal communication, will be touched upon.

Nonverbal messages

The most omnipresent sign without words in America today is the red and green traffic light, whose one-way message is "stop" and "go." Increasingly our highways are using symbols rather than words: + for crossroads, ⊢ for road on right, 2 for curves ahead. The United Nations is now working on a world-wide system of standard road symbols to enable the motorist to understand what's ahead anywhere from Patagonia to Archangel—a true international sign language.

Before the machine age, nonverbal signals included fire beacons, smoke columns, mirror flashes, drums, tree blazes, horns, whistles, uniforms, insignia. Science has now added such useful items as whistling buoys, block signals for railroads, Geiger counters, and ethyl mercaptan—which, injected into the ventilating system of a mine, can warn miners of danger by its penetrating smell.

Is sign language verbal or nonverbal? It can be both.

In the dusk the two mutes walked slowly home together. At home Singer was always talking to Antonapoulos. His hands shaped the words in a swift series of designs. His face was eager and his gray-green eyes sparkled brightly. With his thin, strong hands he told Antonapoulos all that had happened during the day.[1]

Deaf and dumb people spell out words, but when two normal persons meet, with no knowledge of each other's language, their gestures are likely to refer to acts and objects. One of them pretends to drink by making a cup of his hands, and the other hastens to get him water. Or one warns of danger by pointing, frowning, and shaking his head.

The professional linguists are making a study of bodily movements that carry meaning, to which they give the awesome name *kinesics*.[2] Here again is a verbal tent, a smaller one, to cover the variety of movements we make with face, head, hands, feet, to reinforce our words or substitute for them. Watch the hands of the next person you talk to and you will see how important kinesics is to the communication process.

The studies include headshaking for "no" or bad news, laughing, nodding, deadpan expression, raised eyebrows, winks, squints, glares, whistles, pouts, sneers, kisses, shoulder shrugs, arm-waving, pointing, handshaking, beckoning, drumming

[1] Carson McCullers, *The Heart Is a Lonely Hunter*, Houghton Mifflin, 1940.

[2] R. L. Birdwhistell, *Introduction to Kinesics*. See bibliography, page 302.

with fingers, teetering on toes, shuffling feet, crossing legs, clapping hands, and so on. There are about 300 symbols in the Birdwhistell monograph, each representing a bodily movement. An observer who has learned the symbols can record the messages. Cases are given, duly symbolized, of a mother and squirming child in a bus; of a hostess receiving guests who are an hour late for dinner, and many others.

This highly original piece of research emphasizes once more the superiority of speaking over writing in certain important respects. The receiver of a message not only hears the spoken words, with all their wealth of tone and accent, but he *sees* with his eyes an elaboration of meaningful gestures as well.

Every motion, the linguists say, is part of a pattern, and seems to be learned rather than inherited. Some cultures use their hands more than others; American Indians use the dead-pan expression more than Latins, and so on. A New York publisher has issued a book composed principally of photographs of a Frenchman's expressive face. His messages were supposed to be readily decoded without the help of words.

Writing and records

Writing came late in human development, but for all its lack of overtones and kinesics, it has unique and powerful properties. It can preserve messages as no vocal communication can ever do. If laws and codes, for instance, were carried only by the spoken word, they would be distorted so rapidly, and to such a degree, that the administration of justice in a civilized society would be impossible.

Science too would be impossible beyond primitive trial and error. Without written numbers, mathematics would not develop much beyond simple counting. Logic, applied to the manipulation of numbers and algebraic symbols, expands knowledge in explosive ways. It has provided us with the principles by which steam engines, electric motors, automobiles, and airplanes can be built. Without writing, the machine age is inconceivable. Perhaps the most powerful words ever developed on this planet are the symbols $E = MC^2$. (Energy equals mass multiplied by the speed of light, squared.)

Under the big tent of communication, writing and records occupy a tremendous space, both figuratively and physically. They can be referred to at any time—days, years, centuries after they were made. The hieroglyphics of Egypt, the stone tablets of Moses, the lovely stelae of the Maya, all helped to preserve knowledge for future generations. Libraries, museums, books, accounting records, musical scores, documents, paintings, drawings, blueprints, not only accelerate the transmission of culture—in both senses of the term—but help internationalism too. At a guess, 75 per cent of the contents of the great library in Leningrad parallels that of the Congressional library in Washington—a situation to give pause to any book burner. Their main stock belongs to the world, not to any nation. With microfilm, furthermore, a whole new science of record-keeping opens for both words and photographs.

A day's talk

Let us illustrate with some personal and domestic observations. One wakes in the morning to a few moments of verbal reflection, gets up, turns on the eight o'clock news, shaves, admonishes the cat. Throughout the day one is sending or receiving messages, some on the long-distance telephone. One reads a few moments in bed before switching off the light.

If a hundred, or a thousand, social science guinea pigs, in various walks of life, recorded their daily communication behavior, patterns might come to light on which to base a more comprehensive theory of communication than is now available. A very rough review of my daily verbal behavior indicates four main lines of traffic:

1. Exchanging messages with other human beings—verbal, two-way talk. This seems the most vital kind of communication in my day.
2. Receiving verbal messages without replying to the sender. This includes all kinds of reading, radio and television listening, the theater, the movies, et cetera.

3. Sending verbal messages without expecting a reply. Writing books, articles, and some letters; lecturing, broadcasting; some instructions and warnings.

4. Internal reflection; talking to one's self, making plans, imagining things.

The first and third categories include plenty of kinesics—gestures and bodily movements as one talks.

One's communication day might also be classified along the lines which have interested the grammarians: messages carrying information, messages carrying the sender's evaluation of an event, messages carrying instruction and advice.

Scanning my day, it appears that communication trouble for me is at a minimum with homely matters where objects and referents abound. It increases with personal problems of family, finance, goals; with group discussion, instructing children, sizing up people, human relations generally. It reaches its maximum with large, remote matters, subject to ideological intrusion, where referents are few and far between. I have serious difficulty in understanding, talking about, or writing about, such terms as "the eternal," "humanism," "loyalty," "Capitalism," "Communism," "Fascism," "totalitarianism," "Democracy," "freedom." I suspect that a good communication theory would declare many of these terms out of bounds, too vague and dangerous for human use unless most carefully nailed down—"freedom to do what?"

Communication in all its aspects obviously covers an enormous field. It is not an entity but a verbal tent with at least five active rings, full of performers. To recapitulate them:

1. Signs from nature, to be correctly interpreted.
2. Meaningful messages among animals, and to man from the higher animals.
3. Meaningful messages among people.
4. Internal messages, covering a wide range from unconscious reflexes to reflective thinking.
5. Messages from machines to man, as taped by man.

A student of semantics, thinking of all the varieties, would want to say communication$_1$, communication$_2$, communication$_3$ . . . The total field as defined above covers messages one way and two way, live and deferred, unconscious and deliberate, verbal and nonverbal. Verbal messages can be spoken or written, and man alone sends them. (If that parrot is trying to get in again, throw him out! Certainly he can "talk," but talk$_1$ is not talk$_2$.) In all two-way traffic, listening is as important as sending. Your reading this book is as important as my writing it.

Talking can be called primary communication; writing secondary; wigwagging or Morse code tertiary. Talking symbolizes experience: "I caught a big fish." Writing is thus a symbolization of a symbolization. Words make it easy, you see, to get away from direct experience. The communication field is not only wide but deep.

No message arrives in quite as good condition as it starts. "Noise" attacks it, and it must obey the laws of entropy. It is our theme, however, that messages can be better handled and decoded than is now the case. Before opening a line to Mars, there is plenty of work to do at home.

Chapter 3

THE ENCHANTED LOOM

Knowing, apperception, awareness, are functions of the way the human body is organized. It is a miraculous organism, in the sense of trying to duplicate it. Like organized society, it is utterly dependent on its communication system, and indeed, as we shall see, the two networks interlock. The mass media of modern society, for all their scientific ingenuity, are much less remarkable than the communication network which integrates a human being.

The nervous system has powerful transmitting equipment, sensitive receivers, trunk lines connecting all major points, and a central office which sorts and then transmits messages. Yet the system is built in minute spaces, out of what would seem to be unsuitable materials, mostly water. Sir Charles Sherrington, the great specialist on the eye, once called the brain "the enchanted loom."

Precisely how this system works is still a good deal of a mystery, but the neurologists and brain specialists, not to mention the designers of computing machines, are steadily adding to our knowledge. Unfortunately, there are only about a hundred first-class researchers studying brain connections, as against a thousand times as many good chemists.

Signs coming in

Signs and messages are constantly flowing in from the world outside through our senses, of which scientists have identified at least twenty. These include, along with sight, hearing, touch, smell, and taste, a temperature sense, a muscular sense, a distance sense which is especially keen in the blind, a sense of balance—the disturbance of which makes us seasick—and so on.

Despite these sensitive receptors, we miss a great deal of what is happening. I have watched a wren, for instance, singing with all its might. Suddenly, while its small throat and mouth and every feather go on quivering, the sound stops. The song has passed into registers beyond the range of my ears.

Our skin is sensitive to vibrations up to about 1,500 per second, but beyond that we feel only a steady push. The eye misses ultraviolet rays, electric waves, X rays, cosmic rays, and the deadly gamma rays. It sees light waves only in a relatively narrow range. Above a given speed, a three-bladed electric fan appears to be a flat surface.

Like an ornithologist we can train ourselves to see more, or feel or hear more, but always far below the total range of what is there, often below what other animals can perceive. Our senses catch only hints and snatches of what nature has to show, leaving the brain to create a whole picture and attach meaning to these scattered indications. Some events which reach us from the submicroscopic world, such as cosmic rays, are not consciously recognized at all, but the body may have to deal with them. Cosmic rays, by hitting the genes, may cause sudden biological mutations. We are drilled by about 100 cosmic rays every minute of our lives.

The senses usually see enough to adjust the organism to its environment. They perceive what the individual needs to survive—or has needed in the past—and little more. Those high notes are doubtless useful to a wren, but not to me, though I should love to hear them.

Three levels

What the eyes see, the ears hear, and the fingers touch, gives our minds the shape of the ordinary or macroscopic world of the senses. Every person, due to his structure and experience, sees it a little differently. What I can see up there in a tree, for instance, is nothing compared to what a bird lover will observe. Nobody knows what a given animal can see, or probably ever will except in the crudest sense; but we may be sure it is a very different view from ours, and from that of other species.

With the invention of the microscope some four centuries ago, a whole new world was opened to inspection, and knowledge took a great leap forward. The age of scientific medicine began. Plagues and diseases were studied, identified, and fought off with the help of this wonderful new tool. Today the electronic microscope permits us actually to see some of the larger molecules.

Human eyes will probably never see the atomic world which lies below the microscope world, except indirectly, as in an X-ray tube. It is perhaps the most "real" of all. Only mathematical physicists can talk about it intelligently, for the language which can best describe it is that of calculus. Here in the submicroscopic realm, substances as we see and feel them on the ordinary level dissolve into electric charges rushing about at more or less the speed of light, forming the patterns of space-time events.

Eddington compares these levels in a famous passage about his writing table. He has worked on this table for years, he says; it is familiar, dependable, and substantial. Under a powerful microscope it would look very different but the "substance" would still be there. When the observer goes down to the submicroscopic level, however, it becomes a strange structure indeed. It is mostly emptiness with electric charges shooting across its outline. Despite the void his tablet is satisfactorily supported, as the particles at their headlong speeds hit its underside and hold it steady. "If I lean upon this table, I shall not go through; or, to be strictly accurate, the chance of my scientific elbow going through my scientific table is so excessively small that it can be neglected. . . ." [1]

[1] *The Nature of the Physical World*, Macmillan, 1928.

We are aware of reality on three levels: normal, microscopic, and atomic. Any object—a writing table or an apple—
is very different on each. Until recently, only the first level
was accessible, but now science has opened up the other two.
All three are important for our study of communication.

Nerve fibers

The signs come in to eye, ear, skin; what happens then?
All over the body are delicate receptors to decode the signs,
and nerve fibers to conduct the message at some 200 miles per
hour to the brain. In the eyes alone are about one million sensitive cells called cones, each connected with a nerve fiber,
which forwards messages concerning patterns of light and
shade. Patterns received in the ear require fewer and less intricate conductors, and in the nose very much fewer. But the
sense of smell, though relatively feeble in man, is associated
with deep emotions. Some familiar scent can carry one back
to early childhood, in a wave of excitement tinged with
mystery.

The goal of evolution in developing this complex network
is not, of course, to produce poetic images, but to keep the
organism alive; the poetry comes later. Every animal, says
Dr. J. Z. Young, requires information about changes in its
environment.[1] Also its brain needs information about internal
changes—say a cramp in a leg muscle or a shift in blood chemistry. Messages from both outside and inside are carried by
nerve fibers, with the aim of keeping the organism in a steady
state. In the next chapter we shall note the impressive array of
what engineers call "feedbacks," with which the nervous system helps the organism maintain its equilibrium.

Young calls the fibers which carry information to the brain
input nerves, those carrying messages out from the brain to
other parts of the body he calls *output* nerves. They are
grouped in bundles, like wires in a cable, each nerve fiber
carrying one faint impulse, say a simple item of information,

[1] *Doubt and Certainty in Science*. We shall rely a good deal on this
important book in the next few pages.

like temperature. The interconnections, however, are exceedingly complex, with many alternate routes if one is blocked. The fibers are sometimes two feet long and average one one-thousandth of an inch in diameter.

Recent research has demonstrated how a message is carried. The impulse which travels along the nerve fiber resembles the dot of a Morse code—an electrical signal fired along the fiber in a series of bursts. A booster mechanism keeps the signal going. Just how this works is in some dispute, but physiologists agree that the nerve fiber is a chain of relay stations, many stations to the inch, constantly regenerating the signal.

Some fibers are naked, but evolution has introduced an improved model clothed in a sheath, which works about ten times as fast as the old model, with only one-tenth the energy. To achieve the same efficiency in any other way would require fifty times the space in the brain. We might then resemble the Grand Lunar in H. G. Wells's story, whose brain had to be propped up, and constantly cooled, by attendants.

Nerve fibers, like molecules in a gas, operate in large masses, and the effect can only be measured statistically. What the whole crowd will do, not what one fiber will do, is the important consideration. Says Young:

Unless we are careful we shall forget that it is not the single units but their combined effect that is important for conveying the information. We have to find ways of speaking about the action of whole populations of cells, as well as about the individual ones. We are helped by the fact that science has already developed the mathematical language of statistics—and we may be able to advance a long way by applying these statistical methods to the nerve-cells and their traffic of information.

The nervous system has the ability to slow down output messages—which is fortunate for me at this moment. Writing would be impossible if hand and arm muscles contracted all at once. Many thousands of fibers are involved, each in control of only a small amount of muscle. Thus the writing muscles can be brought into play gradually and smoothly, not in one big jerk.

Automatic action can handle a variety of signals. Here is your small son, says Young, under the table as you write. He tickles your leg, but you are concentrating too hard to notice. A reflex makes the leg muscles move your foot a little. He tickles again with no response. About the fourth or fifth time, the nerve impulse crashes into your consciousness and you exclaim "Hey!"—causing Junior to beat a fast retreat. Your internal apparatus has made some complicated connections. So has Junior's.

The enchanted loom

Why does Junior stop tickling? Because he has "learned" that it is risky to make passes at Daddy when he is writing. How did Junior learn, and by what mechanism does he recall it now? One stern word and he retreats to his toy box. Here we come down to bedrock indeed in our quest for meaning. What is happening in Junior's brain, or anyone's brain, when he *learns?* Can we form any picture of the "enchanted loom" in action?

We know the steps involved in learning—drive, cue, response, reward, according to Dollard and Miller.[1] We know also many examples of learning in animals, from Pavlov's drooling dogs to Massermann's drunken cats. But we do not know in what patterns the fibers interweave to correspond with these changes in behavior—only that the patterns must be complex.

There are some ten to fifteen billion nerve cells in the normal human brain. The latest mechanical computer has only 23,000 valves. To build a computer to equal the brain's potential would require many city blocks to house it, and all the water of Niagara to cool it. "Yet all that such a machine can do," says Young, "and much more, goes on gently, gently in every human head, using very little energy and generating hardly any heat."

The brain is the central office of the nervous system, decoding and interpreting the messages from input nerves, send-

[1] *Social Learning and Imitation.*

ing messages to the muscles over output nerves. The mathematical sum of theoretically possible interconnections between fifteen billion units is something to give even Mr. Einstein pause, for it is rather more than all the molecules in the universe!

From billions of possible connections, our central office can select the right combination, often select it instantaneously. Here you are with your foot on the accelerator, approaching a signal light at a dangerous road intersection. If the light is red, the excitation from the retina must be transmitted through the nervous system so that the cells in the motor cortex send impulses down to the leg muscles which make the throttle close. If the light is green, impulses must go down to keep the throttle open. The whole complicated transmission is to be handled, and your safety guaranteed, by neurons which form no conception of "red," "green," "stop light," "traffic cop," "accident," at all. Yet the system works! It works because of past experiences that have opened connections in the nervous system.[1]

Thingumbobs

We now approach a conclusion that is hard to prove experimentally but for which there is strong evidence deductively. In deference to William James, I call it the *thingumbob principle:* Every experience is registered in the brain. How it is registered, and how permanent it is, no one quite knows. That a host of experiences are there to be recalled, is demonstrated every time we act.

James calls our attention to an amoeba in the water swimming. It sees a shape and somehow decodes the message: "Hello! Thingumbob again!" Without memory of previous thingumbobs it might well be done for if the shape is that of an enemy. How about the first one, you may ask. There is always a first experience, which is one important reason why it is so

[1] See also illustration of a railroad engineer in W. R. Ashby, *Design for a Brain.*

necessary to protect the young of all species. Human young are not adequately stocked with thingumbobs until they are twenty years old, if then. A wren is dismissed from the nest after a few weeks.

When the message comes through to the brain of Junior, aged three, there on the floor under his father's desk, he already has enough experience to refer the present message to the past and take suitable action—to wit, stop annoying his father. Otherwise, experience tells him, there will be trouble.

Dr. Young provides a striking demonstration of how the thingumbob principle works, not with a child or an amoeba but with a small octopus. He puts a white metal square and a crab into the creature's tank. The octopus goes briskly after the crab but gets a sharp electric shock, which sends him back to his home corner. The next time the white signal and the crab are presented, the octopus approaches more warily, only to receive another shock. After three experiences he will not leave his corner if he sees the white square. But if he sees a crab *without* the square he will attack and eat it.

Young then takes the octopus out of the tank and performs a surgical operation, removing part of its brain. Now the creature will come dashing out of his corner for a crab, square or no square. His learning mechanism has been disconnected, and he can no longer associate metal squares with electric shocks.

A person born blind sometimes acquires sight by modern surgery. Contrary to expectation, it is not a pleasurable experience. The first sensation is physical pain, accompanied by a spinning mass of lights and colors. It takes months, sometimes years to learn to see, and for a few patients it has hardly seemed worthwhile. "I can do much better with my fingers," said one. For weeks a triangle cannot be distinguished from a square. The eyes have never reported messages to the brain before and so there is no experience of seeing.

How are memories stored?

There are various theories of how thingumbobs are accumulated. Some scientists believe a print is made on brain tissue, like a negative. Others suggest that the patterns of experience are in continuous movement around closed circuits in those astronomical numbers of brain connections.

Ashby, in his book, *Design for a Brain*, suggests that a given item of memory cannot be located always in the same area. If it is to be found at all, we must look for it in various parts of the nervous system that have had time to adjust their performance. It is not a matter of energy, he says, but of order—the order in which the organism made its original adjustments to environment. On this theory our memories are all over the place—hopefully beyond the reach of surgical attention.

Is everything which ever happened to a person recorded somewhere in the nervous system? In 70 years everyone can theoretically receive fifteen trillion separate "bits" [1] of information to store. Dr. Ralph W. Gerard reports a bricklayer who, under hypnosis, described every bump on the top surface of a brick he had laid in a wall twenty years earlier. Can all the "bits" be tapped? Some laboratory scientists, including Young, are inclined to think so; others doubt it. The psychoanalysts have amply demonstrated that many childhood experiences are stored, and may be summoned to consciousness by appropriate techniques. Certainly enough memories are registered to help us act as current messages come in. Sometimes the memories are distorted when we recall them; which is another reason for communication failure.

Physiologists used to identify three well-marked functional regions in the brain: the *medulla* for automatic functions, the *thalamus* for emotional matters, and the *cortex* for conscious movements and for reasoned thinking. Recent research throws considerable doubt on these tidy classifications. Like memories, other brain activities seem to be well scattered. But perhaps a valid distinction can be made between automatic reflexes, emotional activity and that "quarter inch of cortex," which handles delayed responses and verbal thinking, and has been called the chief glory of man.

[1] Bit: an engineering term for the smallest unit in a message.

Young tells us that the motor area directing hand movements in the cortex is larger than the area directing leg movements, while the area in control of the muscles of tongue and lips is greatest of all. He believes that this is direct confirmation "of the thesis that man is primarily a communicating animal."

Experience builds pattern after pattern in the brain. This constitutes a child's real education, in contrast with his formal schooling. Learning to manipulate words, without experiences to refer them to, is rote learning and a blind alley. A new message coming over the nerve fibers is referred to the accumulated patterns, wherever they may be stored. The brain proceeds to predict the situation and to lay out a course of action. Prediction is always based on past experience—which is a reason, I suppose, why we find it so hard to change our habits.

One definition of a painful event, says Young, is an incoming message for which there are no patterns—as with those blind persons who later see. A pleasurable event, on the contrary, is one which fits the patterns. Is this a reason why Mr. Roosevelt's New Deal was not a pleasurable event to settled citizens?

Some conclusions

Do we know enough about the human nervous system and the brain to improve our day-to-day performance? I am confident the answer is yes. The lessons for education are dramatic. "I do not see," says Young, "why it is impossible to teach nearly everyone to follow complicated arguments, and draw correct conclusions—even by the use of elaborate mathematics." Every normal person seems to have the equipment for a very fine performance. What most of us need is broader firsthand experience as a basis for building patterns, and more practice in evaluation.

If the physiologists are right, every one of us creates the patterns in his brain, beginning the day he is born. The world he apprehends at any given time is shaped by those patterns.

He has, moreover, the power deliberately to seek new experience, create new patterns, and even change the shape of his world. The most dramatic proof of this is what happens when the blind learn to see. By keeping at it, they can change a spinning mass of lights and colors into the normal panorama of earth and sky which the rest of us learned unconsciously in early childhood.

Human societies, like the human body, are kept in equilibrium by a system of communication. "The use of words to insure cooperation is the essential biological feature of modern man." Professor Young might well have omitted the word "modern." Those relatively large speech centers were evolved primarily to integrate the individual with his community.

An individual without language could hardly qualify as a human being, so extreme would be his handicap. Similarly an individual without a community around him is in danger of losing his humanity. The culture concept is cardinal in any serious study of communication, for the networks of the body interlock with the networks of society. Biologists, as well as physiologists and psychiatrists, are finding that their work is hampered, their conclusions incomplete, until they bring the surrounding group into the field of study.

The networks of the body interlock with the networks of society; here is, perhaps, the most important finding of our whole inquiry into communication.

Chapter 4

MACHINES THAT THINK

At the Massachusetts Institute of Technology and elsewhere, scientists and engineers are analyzing communication with practical ends in view, such as improving the telephone system. They are also constructing electronic computers, able to solve in a few minutes an equation which might take a man the rest of his life.

One of these monsters was performing over television on election night in 1952, and Americans by the million had a chance to get acquainted with the angular features of "Univac." Early in the evening he was fed cards punched with some preliminary returns, together with comparative figures from the same precincts in 1948. Univac promptly declared an Eisenhower landslide. Alarmed, the attendants hushed him up, announcing a severe nervous breakdown. Univac refused to be hospitalized, and indicated moreover that the odds in favor of his findings were four to one. As all the world knew a few hours later, Univac was correct.

"Maniac," built by John von Neumann, can solve in an hour and a half a problem for which "Eniac," an earlier model, needed twenty-four hours. Furthermore, it has only 3,000 vacuum tubes to Eniac's 18,000. Maniac is now forecasting the weather, using data from 361 grid points in the United States, Canada, and the Atlantic. Upon these data Maniac performs 1,660,500 operations in 48 minutes, to predict atmospheric conditions several miles up, a day ahead. It is hoped that predictions can ultimately be calculated for eight altitude levels, and then, say the scientists, we could really come close to figuring out tomorrow's weather.

Electronic computers can also act as controlling mechanisms. In this role they take data from thermostats and other registering devices, and proceed to operate an entire manufacturing process. The engineers have even threatened to make a model which can play chess. Its game might not be brilliant, they say, but very safe, for it would have all the alternatives figured out before it moved a piece. But if its human opponent cheated, it would go all to pieces in a real nervous breakdown!

Cybernetics

For these mechanical monsters of tubes and wires, and the elaborate mathematical theories behind them, Dr. Norbert Wiener of the Massachusetts Institute of Technology has invented the name *cybernetics*.[1] The word comes from a Greek root meaning pilot or governor, and he defines it as "a study of messages which control action." Cybernetics has to do with the mechanical and electrical equipment for communication between man and machine, and between machine and machine, that fifth class of communication listed in Chapter 2.

In developing this equipment, the engineers are trying to copy some of the functions of the human brain, and thus their effort throws light on how the brain itself operates. The *Scientific American* devotes a whole issue (September 1952) to computers and control mechanisms, with articles at various levels of difficulty, from simple descriptions to advanced mathematics. Says one writer, G. W. King:

The most effective known mechanism for the retention of information is the human brain. Recent physiological experiments suggest that the brain operates not with continuous signals but with sampled digital information, probably on a binary system. Nerves

[1] See his books, *Cybernetics* and *The Human Use of Human Beings.*

seem to transmit information by the presence or absence of a pulse. The brain, with its ability to store vast amounts of information in a tiny space, and to deliver specified items on demand, is the model which automatic control design strives to imitate.

We have already seen how pulses run along the nerve fibers to the brain, with action either "on" or "off," like the current which forms the signals of Morse code. In a computer, electric pulses are made to register on counters or tapes, and in the brain a similar process may take place. This is what Mr. King means when he says the brain may store information on a "binary," on or off, basis.

There are two main types of computers, *analogue* and *digital*. The first responds to physical temperatures, pressures, motions; the second responds to numbers only. The speedometer on your car is a simple analogue, transforming the revolution of the car's wheels into miles per hour. A desk calculator is a primitive digital. You punch numbers into it which it then manipulates. These simple mechanisms have been enormously speeded by vacuum tubes, feedbacks, and magnetic memories.

The digital type is drawing ahead of the analogue, for the latter becomes more complicated with the physical problem and must keep adding wheels, cogs, cranks, connections, and other Rube Goldberg attachments. The navy's "Typhoon," for studying guided missiles, may be the last big analogue.

The digital machine takes regular decimal system numbers punched on a card, and encodes them in arrangements of the two symbols, o and 1, of the binary system, corresponding to the *on* and *off* of an electric current. The current can then flick around the circuits at approximately the speed of light. (Any decimal number can be written in binary terms: 13, for instance, becomes 1101.)

100,000 to 1

Suppose we call at the I.B.M. building in New York and inspect "No. 701," unveiled in the spring of 1953 and twenty-five times faster than the 1948 "Mark" at Harvard.

We enter a room that resembles an ultramodern kitchen, with eleven units in soft gray-blue—they might be cabinets, refrigerators, washing machines. Our guide opens the doors of various units to reveal instrument panels, revolving magnetic drums, batteries of cathode ray tubes, reels of magnetic tape, and the slot into which punched cards are dropped to start things going. One unit, blinking and flashing like a jeweler's counter in the sunlight, turns out to be hundreds of small tubes doing sums—the arithmetic unit. The drum, the magnetic tape, and the big cathode ray tubes are memory units.

No. 701, they tell us, can add or subtract 16,000 times a second, multiply or divide 2,000 times a second. These figures mean little to me until I can relate them to something I know, some thingumbob. How fast do I, as a sometime C.P.A., do simple arithmetic?

I write out two four-digit numbers—say 4752 and 8691. With pencil and stop watch in hand I add the figures—six seconds; subtract and check—eight seconds; multiply them—fifty seconds; divide to three decimal places—eighty seconds. (These times are the average of half a dozen trials with different four-digit numbers.)

Assuming that the computer can multiply numbers like these 2,000 times a second, instead of once in fifty seconds, it is clear that No. 701 is 100,000 times a better man than I am! Still more, he never grows tired. The latest models are being designed to correct possible mistakes.

What actually happens when a problem is tackled—say the 56,000,000 operations required to help a driller find oil, computed from a contour map of the region where he is prospecting? First, the problem has to be stated by a highly trained mathematician. He writes out a series of complicated equations, which are then reduced to simple number sequences and punched on cards. This is "programming," and may take a long time. The cards are then fed into the receiving unit. It hums away, other units begin to hum, until out of the last one comes the answer, neatly punched on wide tape.

To program the path of a guided missile requires 763 instructions, all in number form. Having swallowed them, No. 701 will perform 1,100,000 operations in two minutes. (This calculation I could toss off in a matter of fifteen years.) It can compute the density and velocity of air at selected points on a section of airplane wing, and thus help aircraft engineers design better wings. Eight million operations are completed in seven minutes, a job that would take a desk calculator seven years.

No. 701 and his brothers and cousins have, like the human brain, the power to store memories and to learn from experience. This gives them the right to be called "machines that think." A computer's memories may be stored in cathode ray tubes; no one can yet tell us exactly how human memories are stored.

Electronic mouse

The prize example of a machine that learns from experience is undoubtedly the Bell Laboratory's electronic mouse. His body is an electromagnet two inches long, his feet are three retracted wheels, his whiskers are copper wires. The "cheese" he seeks is an electric terminal. You put him in a maze about three feet by three composed of forty movable aluminum partitions. In one corner is the "cheese," reached by only one possible route. You throw a switch and away goes the mouse. He bangs into a wall, bounces back, tries another direction with energy unimpaired. Bang, bang, bang! but he is continually getting nearer the goal. Finally, after about two minutes of strenuous buffeting, he reaches the "cheese" and pokes his copper whiskers into it; a bell rings.

Pick him up and put him back at the starting point. Away he goes again, but this time he does not hit a single wall. He goes right to the terminal, with hardly a false move, and cuts his time from one hundred and twenty seconds to twelve. If you place him in a part of the maze not visited before, he will bang around again by trial and error until he finds a section already visited, then he goes in straight course to the cheese.

If you shift the walls of the maze to form a different pattern, he will remember any parts which remain unshifted.

Quite a mouse. He operates with the help of a thinking machine under the metal floor of the maze. It is composed of motor-driven electromagnets, and ninety "relays," of which fifty are memory units. A relay performs the task of a vacuum tube in a computer.

The mouse was invented by Dr. Claude Shannon, whom we met in Chapter 2. Dr. Shannon says it can quickly solve "more than a million million mazes, learning each one rapidly, then instantly forgetting it in order to be ready to learn the next one." The significance of the exhibit, he says, lies in the four distinct mental processes which the mouse-machine performs. It can:

1. Solve a problem by trial and error.
2. Remember the solution and apply it at a later date.
3. Add new information to the solution already remembered.
4. Forget one solution and learn a new one when the problem is changed.

The mouse is helping Bell Laboratories improve telephone switching equipment—that type of giant brain which can remember the telephone number you dial into it, and automatically search the circuits until it finds a clear line to the party you want. Before long, thanks in part to the mouse, it will connect you automatically with any telephone in the U.S.

Feedbacks

Experts in cybernetics have a good deal to say about "feedbacks." They put these devices all over their machines to check performance, and they compare them with similar controls throughout the human body. A short, handy definition of a feedback is that it answers the question: "How am I doing?" It is thus a straight communication mechanism.

On the bridge of the *Canadian Challenger* we noted the "iron mike," an automatic device for steering the ship, and an excellent example of a feedback. When the mike has been "taped" on the course, it will recognize any deviation to port or starboard, and send a message to the rudder to correct the error. A vane on a windmill to keep it pointed into the wind was an early type of feedback. The "governor" with its swinging balls on a steam engine is a classic example.

When I visited a cyclotron in a Washington laboratory, I was given a memorable initiation into the feedback principle. My hosts seated me at the control board, switched off the automatic control and told me to grasp the manual controls. Keep the cyclotron on a steady electrical course, they said, as shown by arrows upright on the dial. The arrows began to swing far to the right. I hauled them back and over they went, way to the left! No matter how delicate my touch, I could not hold the arrows where they belonged. Compared to the smooth automatic control built into the cyclotron, my efforts were gross and clumsy. I now know how feedback *feels*.

The physiologists find that our bodies are full of feedbacks to stabilize the organism. A man standing on his two legs is one of the least steady of natural constructions. His weight is seldom adjusted to keep him upright, and he is always about to fall over. What holds him on his course is a set of feedbacks, in the canals of his ear, in the nerve ends of his feet, in the horizon sense of his eye. These send messages to the muscles via the brain to keep him from capsizing. A person with his feedbacks put out of commission by alcohol can give us an alarming example of man's natural anatomical instability. If you throw a cat into the air, gently please, her feedbacks will see to it that she lands on all four feet.

The feedback principle has wide application. Social scientists studying face-to-face groups are adopting the idea. If a conference is working on a problem around a table, the leader may halt discussion from time to time while he summarizes the situation. He tells the group "how they are doing," and whether they are getting off the course. Or group members may be asked to estimate the progress of the meeting, and fill out questionnaires at its close as to how they have done.

"Feedback is the control of a system by reinserting into the system the results of its performance" is a more formal definition. "A portion of the output of a system is fed back to control the input" is another. The student of semantics uses the principle when he rechecks his information before coming to a conclusion. It helps him delay his responses, avoid snap judgments, and think in terms of relationships. In Chapter 16, your author will give a feedback for preceding chapters, and ask in effect: "How are we doing?"

The theory of control systems is now well understood for "Univac," No. 701, and Dr. Shannon's mouse. The concepts, according to an author in the *Scientific American,* "are not without relevance to the grandest of all problems of science and philosophy: the nature of the human mind, and the significance of our forms of perception of what we call reality."

Design for a brain

W. Ross Ashby, the British scientist mentioned earlier, has tried to describe how a man, armed with all we now know about the nervous system, would go about designing a mechanism which imitated the brain. His book, which he calls *Design for a Brain,* is a combination of cybernetics and physiology. The mechanism would not need to be nearly so complicated as the brain, Ashby thinks, but it must accomplish the brain's two great functions: (1) it must learn by experience and store memories; (2) it must produce adaptive behavior—continually refining performance in the interests of survival.

Ashby uses as his type case a kitten approaching a hearth fire. At the first encounter a variety of things can happen, none in the best interests of the kitten. She may walk right into the hot ashes, spit at the blaze, dab with paw, sniff, arch her back, crouch and stalk. Gradually she learns respect for the fire, and how to adjust to it. She finds exactly the right spot on the hearth rug to keep warm. If the fire blazes up she retreats; if it dies down she moves nearer. What is going on in her brain to produce this adaptation to fire? What machine can parallel it?

Dr. Ashby takes us on a rather technical journey through feedbacks, step-functions, part-functions, parameters, and variables, and finally emerges with a mechanism capable of learning by experience. On closer inspection this proves to resemble a digital computer.

The thesis of the book is stated twice, once in standard English, once in mathematics, and is so arranged that the reader can turn from the English to the mathematics, and vice versa. Thus we have the story in *two* languages, expertly cross-referenced—which must be some kind of landmark in semantics. The mathematics acts as a stern judge of the prose, allowing nothing to be said which cannot be restated in the form of a rigorous equation. A better way to get rid of hunches and opinions would be difficult to imagine.

Encounters with the environment mark the nervous system of kitten or man easily, extensively, and permanently, with traces distributed according to the "accidents" of the encounter. As encounters multiply, the traces tend to be so distributed as to prepare for subsequent encounters. The kitten learns not only the best place on the hearth rug, but where to move under different conditions.

Ashby compares the patterns formed by experiences to drops of rain which run, joining and separating, down a window-pane. There is no order in any one raindrop's behavior, but the whole pattern is orderly. A similar shower would produce a similar pattern. Memory traces are scattered throughout the cortex, unified physiologically but not anatomically. Memories, he believes, are not stored in any fixed place.

The feedback principle is cardinal in Ashby's design. Here, he says, is an antiaircraft gun, controlled by radar rays returning both from the target plane at which the gun is aimed, and from its own bursting shells. The feedback minimizes the distance between the plane and the shell burst, causing the gun to aim ever closer to the target. "Such a system, wholly automatic, cannot be distinguished by its behavior from a humanly operated gun, where the gunner uses errors to improve his next shot."

The design for a machine to act like the brain is unthink-able without feedbacks. But with them, like the AA gun, it can theoretically "be both wholly automatic, and yet actively goal-seeking. There is no incompatibility." A machine with feedbacks is usually actively stable (though it could be made actively unstable), and can correct its own errors. "Once it is appreciated that feedback can be used to correct any devia-tion we like, it is easy to understand that there is no limit to the complexity of goal-seeking behavior which may occur in machines, quite devoid of any 'vital' factor."

Will giant brains someday become our masters? They will not. Without a man to program them they are so much junk. A man can shave with an electric razor, drive his car to the office, operate a self-service elevator, and start a dictaphone going, all within a few minutes. An electronic computer can surpass him in speed, accuracy, and persistence, as a derrick can beat him at lifting, but it can never equal him in versatil-ity. The computer can never reach his power of abstract thought, never write a line of poetry, never be curious about the cosmos, never have a new idea.

Computers are giving us some dramatic sidelights on how the human brain stores memories, and how we learn from experience. They are destined to do a lot of supervising in mass production plants such as oil refineries, and in communi-cation industries. They will become more and more clever, rapid and useful in answering more kinds of questions—like predicting the weather. But that is all they can do with ques-tions. They will never be able to ask one.

Chapter 5

A CHAIR IS A CHAIR

Working on another aspect of the "grandest of all problems" are the students of perception theory. What is the relation between that chair out there—that chunk of "reality"—and our perception of it?

Adelbert Ames, the pioneer in this field, began his career as an artist. Perspective fascinated him, and made him curious to know more about how the eye and brain perceived things. He developed an extraordinary talent for designing laboratory equipment to test theories, and the results of his early experiments were so arresting that he neglected his painting to become a specialist in seeing.

He organized the Hanover Institute and set up a laboratory in the basement of a Dartmouth building, although he had no formal connection with the college. A foundation became interested and gave him funds for constructing ever more ingenious tests. Today parts of the equipment have been duplicated at Princeton by Hadley Cantril, and at several other universities.

Social scientists all over the country are arguing about the conclusions to be drawn from the Ames experiments. Some think they mark a revolution in psychology. Others are impressed but not so sure about the revolution. Still others say they knew it all before. Rather than involve ourselves in this debate, let us take a guided tour through the laboratory. I have tried it in both Hanover and Princeton; it takes about half a day.

Laboratory tour

Here is a big room, dimly lighted, and resembling an old-fashioned photographer's studio. All around are strange mechanisms draped in black, like cameras or huge stereopticon instruments, connected with a system of cords and lighting. Our guide leads us from one construct to the next, snaps on a light in their rear parts, and directs us to look through an aperture, sometimes down a dark tunnel which may be ten feet long. He asks what we see down there, and acknowledges our answer with a noncommittal "H'm." Buttons are pushed, fans revolve, handles are pulled, more lights are snapped: "Now what do you see? . . . H'm." There are more than a score of constructs.

The visitor is both bewildered and excited. He looks through a peephole and sees a chair about five feet away. It appears to be a perfectly good chair. A view through a different hole shows that it isn't a chair at all, but loose pieces of wood suspended by wires. Convinced that to sit on such a contraption would produce grave spinal injuries, one returns to the original peephole and sees the chair reappear, as solid as ever! What one part of the brain has grasped intellectually, other parts may refuse to accept. Past experience with chairs is so strong that it overrides purely intellectual demonstrations.

Looking down one of the tunnels, we see two dimly lighted round balls side by side, some eight inches in diameter. At the touch of a button, one of the balls starts moving down the tunnel toward us, while the other remains where it was. There is no doubt in our minds about the forward march of that ball. Examination shows, however, that neither ball has moved; the one which seems to move has been slowly blown up to a larger size by a jet of air. A similar effect of forward movement can be produced by gradually lighting one ball more brightly.

The cockeyed room

And here, ladies and gentlemen, is the famous "cockeyed room," with the perspective all wrong in its construction, but making a quite satisfactory rectangular exhibit to the eye. It has had its picture in many newspapers and in *Life* magazine, and is perhaps the best known of all the Ames constructs. The room is set up life-size, some twelve feet long. Through the front window, the observer sees its floor, ceiling, back windows, and door, all as they should be, and all brightly lighted.

But when the observer tries to walk on that floor he finds it slopes dangerously, and his feet go all wrong. He discovers that the windows and door are a carpenter's nightmare, and the ceiling cants at a crazy angle. It takes a strong stomach to stay in that room without feeling seasick. Our guide gives us a pointer and tells us to touch a corner of the room. We don't come within three feet of it, and we hit things with the stick which visibly are not there!

Let us return to the first point of vision. We watch two people of approximately the same height enter the room; each goes to a back corner and turns to face us. Behold, one has become a giant, the other a dwarf! We can take a picture of them, and still they appear giant and dwarf, as the photograph in the newspapers shows clearly. One person is actually nearer to us, but the angles make them appear equidistant to the eye. If they appeared their actual sizes, the room would become distorted. We cannot have both; and the eye insists on a rectangular room, even at the cost of creating giants and dwarfs! Stability seems to be more important to the organism than denying the existence of monsters.

Such weirdly shaped rooms are seen as "normal" . . . because our past experience has made it a "better bet" to perceive level floors, upright walls, rectangular windows, etc. Such perceptions . . . have provided us with adequate prognoses for successful action. . . . When people are observed in the distorted room, the assumptions we have built up concerning their shapes and sizes come into direct conflict with our assumptions as to the "normal" shape of the room.[1]

Mr. Ames has prepared quite an exhibit, not one to be recommended for vacation hours. What does it all mean? The psychologists are building hypotheses, but the over-all conclusion is not yet clear to the inquiring layman—who has seen himself moving in a railroad station, when actually it was the other train that moved. First of all, the exhibit is a fine demonstration of the *relativity* of perception. Two other preliminary conclusions also emerge, and both support what we have been learning about the nervous system and the brain.

The thingumbob principle is strongly upheld. Says Kilpatrick: "The organism . . . calls upon its previous experience, and assumes that what has been most probable in the past, is most probable in the immediate occasion." In the past, when two objects of equal size were seen side by side, and one grew larger, the probability has been that it was moving toward us. This is what the brain concludes after consulting memories, and what the eye sees in consequence. Have we not learned to judge whether an automobile is coming toward us, or going away from us?

The other principle supported by the Ames exhibit is that we do not see *all* of any space-time event, but only enough to deal with it. Our brains abstract what we need in this particular situation, and let the rest go. We take a chance. In the case of that chair, our brains bet wrong, so to speak, because in our experience a space-time event which has the look of a substantial chair can be sat upon. One wonders what an Eskimo from King William Island who had never seen a chair would make of the exhibit. Perhaps he would see sticks and wires. I wish this could be tested—though it would cost something to fly him down in a plane without seats.

I remember once being perched on an 8,000-foot mountain top above timber line in the Canadian Rockies. We were on skis, with about fifty feet of snow under us. There were no

[1] Mimeographed report by F. P. Kilpatrick, *Demonstrations in Perception*, Princeton, 1952.

trees, no rocks, nothing but the horizon, snow, and sky. I started down the slope and when it seemed to level off I prepared to do a smart turn and stop. Far from stopping, I took a spectacular fall on a 30° grade. My eyes, you see, had no guides in the form of shadows to tell my brain what was level and what was slope. They had nothing to go on but a world of unrelieved white, and no experience to help them in such an unprecedented situation.

Flight of the imagination

While we are on the subject of perception, and recalling that almost any American child is now ready to voyage through interstellar space, perhaps I may be permitted an imaginative excursion myself. It will be more limited, however, than the one on which Junior fares forth every evening on television.

Suppose a germ as lethal to man as the blight was to the chestnut tree sweeps the planet. Not a human being is left alive. *What does the world look like?*

"Just the way it looks now," you reply, "only without people. Lots of room on the highways. Mountains, oceans, trees, animals, the Eiffel Tower, and the Empire State building, all there." In the light of the analysis so far in this book I am afraid you are wrong. Though the world as it looks to you now is not quite what it looks to me, all normal humans agree on the existence of mountains, oceans, trees, animals, and the Eiffel Tower. This is the fundamental datum that we can count on for all our mundane plans.

But if, following the assumed blight, there were no human eyes and brains to see these events, there would be nothing to see in the familiar terms. Seeing, we remember from Chapter 3, was built up pattern by pattern, beginning at birth. Mountains, oceans, trees, as we have been wont to perceive them, must therefore disappear. (People born blind, who later receive their sight, see nothing at first but spinning colors.)

The animals, we assume, live on. They continue to perceive their small portion of the world as heretofore. But as their brains and their experiences are different, they see the world very differently from humans. What a bee sees, furthermore, must vary wildly from what a chimpanzee sees. The Arctic tern, winging from one polar region to the other, probably has the widest range of vision; a barnacle on a rock perhaps the smallest.

Now let us assume that a second virus in another biological calamity wipes out all the animals. How does the world look *now*, with no living creature to see it? In the light of what has gone before, I am afraid that we must insist it looks like nothing at all. It has no look; a visual void—blank, zero.

But before collapsing into the arms of Bishop Berkeley, let us descend in our imagination through the microscopic level down to the submicroscopic, the universe of the atom, as sketched earlier. Here, thank goodness, things are normal. The atoms swirl as before in the vast emptiness of Mr. Eddington's writing table. Whatever the atomic structure of our world was before the plagues, it persists after them. There will be different knots in the plenum, but the plenum, the physicists say, is constantly reknotting itself.

There is, of course, nothing to be seen on the normal or macroscopic level, for there are no eyes or brains remaining on earth to see. No creature remains that has had the experience of seeing. But the atoms, obeying their statistical laws, are still doing business at the old stand. This is as close to "reality" as I am able to get.

All right, metaphysicians, now it's your turn. . . .

Eleven points in perception

Grounding our space ship once more on earth, let us list the steps in perception so far as we have been able to identify them:

1. Take a space-time event, say a chair—which is also a knot in the plenum.
2. It gives out radiation on the submicroscopic level.
3. The rays strike the living organism, human or animal, at some sensitive point, say the eye.

4. Their pattern is decoded and passed over nerve fibers to the brain, perhaps on a binary system.

5. Here it is decoded semantically.

6. And referred to past experiences, maintained somehow in the cortex, probably in a number of places.

7. Whereupon the individual whose brain it is remarks: "It's a chair. I've sat in thousands of them."

8. The chair has a great number of characteristics; any "event" has an astronomical number.

9. But the brain abstracts only those characteristics needed by the organism to deal with the chair now.

10. What we "see" is thus only part of what is there. The "reality" we perceive is abstracted by our senses—as a cartoonist abstracts Winston Churchill's face with two curved lines and a cigar.

11. When we use words as symbols for the abstraction that we "see," they are an abstraction of an abstraction. When we use generalizations like chairs-in-general, or "household furniture," we abstract again. The semantic moral is to be conscious of these abstraction levels, and not to lose sight of the original chair.

"Reality" is not a stone which one can kick with his foot. The stone was Dr. Johnson's answer to Bishop Berkeley, when the Bishop said that everything was in the mind. Reality is a tougher proposition than any stone.

Chapter 6

BEES, MONKEYS, AND CATS

Before going on with human communication, let us explore some findings on animal communication. The higher animals possess nervous systems something like our own, but with fewer connections in the cortex. Even the lowly octopus has association paths which can be severed. Insects have a very different apparatus for receiving and decoding signs, but manage to send some extraordinary messages.

Ballet in the hive

Honey bees, according to a brilliant study by Karl von Frisch, have an elaborate communication system, quite unlike anything man has yet contrived.[1] When a scouting bee comes upon an appetizing bed of blossoms, he returns and gives accurate directions to the hive, though the bed may be as much as four miles away. His comrades then make a "beeline" for the flowers.

What does the scout say to his comrades? One must read Frisch to get the full details of this amazing conversation. In essence, the scout performs a geometrical dance on the vertical plane of the honeycomb, using the sun as a triangulation point. The other bees, watching the performance, are informed of both the direction and the distance of the food supply.

Other recent studies suggest that migrating birds have a built-in apparatus for perceiving longitude and latitude, even

[1] *Bees: Their Vision, Chemical Sense and Language.*

when out of sight of land over the ocean. The bird, however, is telling himself where to go, while the scout bee is telling the hive, and so engaging in true social communication.

Our initial reaction is astonishment, followed by a question: Since a bee has only a few thousand nerve cells in its brain, where man has fifteen billion, is it not probable that the dances upon the honeycomb, and the response by the hive, are instinctive and unlearned? Are the bees doing any thinking in the human sense of the word? May their wonderful performance be as automatic, and as emotional, as swarming out to sting an enemy?

There is no evidence that bees transmit new experiences to the next generation and so have anything to correspond to a culture. Moralists who discover "lessons" to be learned from a bee, especially his thrift, prudence, and working habits, ignore this distinction. Whatever the bee's virtues, he is born with most of them, while we have to learn to be virtuous. We live on the same planet with these creatures, derive from the same remote ancestor in the warm salt of the early seas; but our worlds of experience hardly touch. Bees, ants, and their kind have societies from which we are intellectually excluded, but which obviously require communication as well as specialization. The organizations are miraculous from our point of view, but doubtless prosaic enough from the bee's. Whether they are "better" or "worse" is a meaningless question.

Viki's world

We find less organization, and apparently less communication, in a much higher species. Comparing apes with primitive man, Dr. William Howells asks us to look at the troubles of a chimpanzee in a laboratory.[1] The ape has mastered a problem machine which delivers bananas, but it is a two-monkey job and he needs help to operate it. How is he going to explain the contraption to an uninitiated comrade without words? No talk, no bananas! Sometimes, says T. C. Schneirla of the Mu-

[1] *Mankind So Far*, Doubleday, Doran, 1944.

seum of Natural History, a chimpanzee can get the idea over by sign language; and Yerkes has shown photographs of co-operative pairs helping each other. But Howells' ape went hungry.

Up to the age of three, a young chimpanzee is about as smart as a child of the same age. At the Yerkes Laboratories in Florida, two psychologists, Catherine and Keith Hayes, adopted a female chimpanzee baby, and raised her like a member of the family. They recorded their observations, and later gave the American Philosophical Society a careful account of "Viki's" development.[1]

Viki's interests and abilities developed in roughly the same sequence as a child's, though she tended to play more strenuously in climbing and jumping. She built with blocks, cut with shears, scribbled, and showed about the same skill and enthusiasm in these activities as most three-year-olds. She imitated the family tasks of dusting, washing dishes, sharpening pencils, painting woodwork, pressing photographs in albums. She learned to saw, hammer, and sandpaper furniture.

By manipulating Viki's lips, the Hayeses taught her to vocalize three words—"mama," "papa," "cup"—but they were rough approximations, and the last two were often confused. As an infant she babbled much less than human babies do, and even this disappeared when she was five months old. The Hayeses conclude that the human and chimpanzee species "are much more alike psychologically than has heretofore been supposed. Man's superior ability to use language may be his only important genetic advantage." This advantage, furthermore, is cumulative. Language is a means of sharing knowledge —as the baffled chimpanzee in front of the banana machine eloquently demonstrates. After the third year, human children rapidly outdistance Viki with her three uncertain words.

Chimpanzees by nature, observes Dr. Yerkes, are social animals.[2] They live in nomadic groups of ten or twenty, each

---

[1] Summarized in *Scientific American*, July 1951.
[2] Robert M. Yerkes, *Chimpanzees*, Yale University Press, 1943.

with a male leader, societies much smaller than those of primitive man.

There is no single system of signs—vocal, gestural, or postural—which may properly be called chimpanzee language. Yet combined, the varied signs which are commonly observed serve to keep the animals in effective touch, well informed about one another's presence and attitudes, and also about especially significant features of their environment.

Monkey puzzles

Another scientific couple, at the University of Wisconsin, matched monkeys against children of similar ages (two to five) in a series of puzzles, carrying rewards of peanuts or candy for the correct solution.[1] Neither monkeys nor humans possessed any inborn spontaneous ability; all learned by the slow, laborious, fumble-and-find process. The Bell Laboratory's electronic mouse was much brighter. Each group used trial and error until they had accumulated enough "learning sets"—thingumbob patterns to apply in similar problems—to discard some of the fumbling behavior and push ahead faster. There seemed to be no "instinct" factor at all; insight came with experimentation.

As a group, the children learned one of the problems more rapidly than the monkeys, but made the same type of errors. The smartest monkeys, however, learned faster than the dullest children. On a more complex problem, the situation was reversed: "The monkeys did better than most of the children."

The Harlows, like the Hayeses, conclude that the higher animals possess intricate nervous systems and can solve difficult puzzles, sometimes faster than children of the same age. But language presently gives the children an incomparable advantage. The child goes on in a spiral of accumulating knowledge. Words become stimuli for the particular "learning sets" most appropriate for solving a given problem. Listen to yourself talk, say the psychologists, as you tackle a problem. Viki

[1] Harry and Margaret Harlow, "Learning to Think," *Scientific American*, August 1949.

can make many of the sounds, but she lacks the semantic apparatus to make sounds meaningful in complicated ways.

Communicating with cats

In *The Tyranny of Words*, I checked some observations on the world outside by referring to my yellow tomcat, Hobie Baker. How did Hobie see the world out there? How did he receive meaning, and what was his communicating apparatus? I know a little more about his equipment now than I did then, enough to realize that I can never remotely approximate his perceptions.

Hobie disappeared some years ago on what was probably romantic business, and we never saw him again. After a suitable period of mourning, we acquired two short-haired gray tiger kittens, one with white trim, named "Boots," and one without, whom we call "Shadow." For four years, off and on, my wife and I have been observing how these brothers—altered males—communicate. Our observation falls far short of laboratory science, but we have tried to keep animism out of it. How do these cats send and receive messages, with us and with each other? Here is an annotated list of answers; but first an arresting contrast.

Save for a few trips in a closed car to the vet some seven miles away, the cats have never left home. Their range on foot has never been seen to exceed a mile in any direction. So their entire world comprises some three square miles of garden, swamp, pasture, and woodland, the sky above them, a section of state highway to avoid, and the inside of our house. This is all they know of their planet, their solar system, their universe. It is about all that Viki knows. Yet we humans can sit in this house and see in our imagination all the lands, all the oceans, correctly ordered, out to the uttermost reaches of space, and back through history and geology to the beginning of the world.

Cats to humans

Between them, our cats have seven methods for announcing their desire to go out:

1. Proceed to door and look around hopefully.
2. Place a paw in the crack of the door and scratch gently.
3. Raise head and cry gently.
4. Sit up on haunches in front of door—with or without being asked.
5. Rub chin on abutting furniture.
6. Rub against human leg, then go to door. Repeat.
7. If no action results from the last, Shadow will lie down halfway to the door in an abandoned pose, and purr like a calliope.

Other methods of communicating to humans include:

Digging claws into a person's knee to beg food at table.
Playing the banjo on the screen door as a request to come in.
Bringing rats, mice, moles, et cetera to the house for approval. (In one season they brought in over a hundred moles by actual count.)

Whether cats feel affection for humans I do not know; but they seem to express pleasure when attention is paid them, by purring, licking human hand or foot, pretending to bite, extending and retracting claws in their forepaws, rolling over, rubbing against legs, jumping into the lap, raising tail to vertical as a greeting out of doors.

Humans to cats

Our notes show the following kinds of communication from humans to cats:
We whistle to summon them, clap hands, snap fingers, call them by name.
We talk to them, using such expressions as "No!" "Bad cat," "Fine cat," "Good boy," "Get down," "Sit up," "Want to go out?"—along with a running stream of more sophisticated talk for our own amusement. Their behavior is certainly influenced by these sounds, but it is the *tone* of voice that counts. Here is the proof: Both cats have been taught to sit up by way of saying please. If they wish to go out, for instance, we say "Sit up," and often they do. But if we say "Lie down," with the *same intonation*, they will still sit up.
I am not sure that they recognize their names. What they

do know very well is that they are being addressed, and attention is being paid to them. My wife and I also use a series of gestures and caresses (kinesics). We stroke them, pat them, tickle them under the chin and behind the ears, poke them gently with the foot, roll them over; we also push them away and carry them out the door. The standard way to housebreak a cat is by punishment, or in scientific lingo, by setting up a conditioned reflex, associating pain with the act to be stopped.

After teaching the cats to sit up, I checked the method against the standard sequence of learning theory—*drive, cue, response, reward*—as expounded by Dollard and Miller. The drive is the cat's hunger; the cue is a piece of meat suspended in air; the response is first a wild snatching, later a restrained begging with paws held down; the reward is the meat. It takes about an hour of intensive work, and a few minor wounds, to teach a cat to sit up. Then he seems to have it built in for life.

Cat to cat

This communication line is harder to trace, and suggests that a cat, unlike a chimpanzee, is a relatively unsocial animal with little need of communicating to his fellows. Boots and Shadow —unless they practice telepathy—seem to communicate more with us than with each other.

They often rub noses to find out what the other has caught or eaten—the kiss of suspicion rather than affection. One growls if the other approaches his mouse; they cry out when scratched in a brotherly brawl; they co-operate occasionally by washing one another in places hard to reach. They will sleep together peacefully and eat amicably from the same dish —at least most of the time. And that about exhausts the list, as far as we can trace it. Tomcats and their girl friends have other methods of communication, some of them highly vocal. Mother cats train their kittens. I have never heard one of our cats warn the other by cries—as crows and monkeys do, or summon help from the other against a strange dog.

Over-all reflections on cats

If I show Boots a charcoal sketch I have made of him, he may sniff the paper, but takes no real interest. I doubt if he "sees" it at all. Held up to a mirror, both cats see something, but apparently nothing of significance. Presently they yawn. They like something more dynamic, in three dimensions, preferably with a smell. A dog out the window gets an immediate, tense reaction. They seem to take meaning from life at first-hand, not from its symbols and abstractions.

This coincides with the findings of the psychologists about monkeys. The higher animals have learning curves, feelings, sentiments, which often parallel the human equipment. Our cats show genuine curiosity about their three square miles of world—I have seen them studying an airplane in the sky— and show considerable intelligence in solving practical problems. Boots, for instance, can let himself into the house through the heavy garage door by jumping up on the latch—a service as useful to him as it is useless to us, especially in winter. This he must have learned by observation or experiment. He would like to know more about planes in the sky, fire on the hearth, sun lamps, motorcars, any purring or buzzing gadget. He would like to understand what we say to him, especially if he is hungry; you can see him visibly concentrating. It is sad that Boots, lacking language, can pursue his inquiries only such a little way.

From our four years of observation it seems clear that communication between humans and cats is kinesic rather than verbal. The tone of voice means a good deal, especially a harsh "No!" Human gestures and body movements mean the most of all. We speak a sign language together, a remote and clumsy one on the whole.

From another point of view, however, I can enter into an understanding with any cat anywhere on earth—Mexico, Trinidad, France, Egypt, Bermuda. I shall be recognized immediately as a friend, and can teach him to sit up. What kind of communication is this? It seems to be a special international kind. The cat, having no speech community and no culture, is a world creature, prepared to deal with humans anywhere on universal terms.

Dogs and others

Animal psychologists grade chimpanzees at the head of the class for intelligence, followed by other apes, and then elephants. Below come raccoons, dogs, seals, cats, horses, rats, goats, and so on, in an order suitable to the animal lover's fancy. Some species excel in certain tests, some in others. I happen to like cats but hold no brief for their superior intelligence.

Dogs seem to recognize words better than cats. A dog was described in *Science* who understood the word "table" and would go to one at command to get his food, even outdoors where he had to locate a picnic table. A dog's ears are probably keener than his eyes, and like his sense of smell, superior to the human sense. A dog can hear sounds inaudible to us—perhaps the wren's top notes?—and will answer a special whistle which a man can blow but cannot hear. A "wolf" on a park bench can have a field day with such a whistle if girls are airing their dogs on leashes.

Eugene Reynal reports that his father's foxhounds were given similar, two-syllable names—Danger, Dagger, Draper. Each dog learned to respond to his own name when called from the pack, though summoned in identical tones. Hounds, he thinks, have half a dozen identifiable cries when hunting or in kennels, to which they mutually respond—possibly reply in the two-way sense. Reynal says, too, that his troupial definitely responds to its image in a mirror, taking it for another bird to be fought or flirted with.

The great gulf

A photographer for the American Medical Association succeeded in 1952 in getting a shot of the world outside through the eye of a dead sheep. He hopes to repeat the experiment with an eye kept artificially alive. But why should he bother?

We have gone far enough in our quest to be sure that both sheep and man see more with the brain than with the eye.

Grace de Laguna, writing in *Human Biology*, develops the idea. An animal's inability to speak, she says, is a significant indication of what it *experiences*. "If an animal cannot express its thought in language, that is because it has no thoughts to express; for thoughts which are not formulated are something less than thought." A cat or a dog is unable to describe what he sees, in part because what he sees is inexpressible in human words. So if an experimenter had the power to look out of a dog's eyes, he could never describe what was there, "for the words of human speech apply to a world of things and qualities, acts and relations, which do not exist for the dog."

We have long been aware of the fallacies of animism, imparting human qualities to animals. Here is additional proof; animals could see the way humans see, or vice versa, only if we exchanged *brains*. The eye is only one part of the process of seeing.

Lacking speech, animals see the events on the material level directly and as-a-whole; they rarely appear to classify, though the Harlows' chimps could do so. Man, as he masters words, chops the world up into classes and qualities. Power to classify, to transmit and record, brings tremendous results in culture and science; but this unique advantage is partly offset by a serious liability. We chronically forget that nature is a seamless web, and that the tidy classifications may be only in our heads. Where does "mind," for instance, cease, and "body" begin? The chopping up process, though analytically useful, is purely for convenience. If we are not careful, we begin to believe that the verbal classes are substantial entities out there beyond our skins.

Viki, Boots, and their friends make no such mistake. They deal with reality at firsthand, unclouded with verbal mists. For the long pull it is not impossible that an ape or a cat or a bee may have a better survival value.

Chapter 7

THE DRIVE TO TALK

Viki, the chimpanzee, babbled like a human baby soon after she was born, but at five months she stopped. Babies go right on exercising the whole vocal system until that momentous day when the gurgles, squawks, and cries crystallize into a recognizable word. It may come as early as ten months in the case of a few precocious infants—destined possibly to become United States Senators. It may be as long as thirty months in the case of youngsters who are more reserved.

Suppose we call the baby "Jerry." He arrives with a birth cry—not to communicate but to clear his lungs—and enters what William James has called a big, blooming, buzzing confusion. He brings a number of reflexes, and no thingumbobs at all. Nothing frightens him except certain loud sounds and losing his balance. He is calm in the presence of snakes, lions, and devil masks because he has had no experience with which to compare such monsters. He does not even see them until he has learned to use his eyes, a matter of some months.

Jerry, like Viki, begins to babble and utter random cries soon after birth. Presently they become meaningful. He wants to be fed, or changed. When the cry is directed to people rather than to the universe in general, communication may be said to begin—conscious, purposeful sound-making. It will not take long for Jerry to sense that he can influence his environment by crying, and the family must learn to distinguish the urge-to-power signal from the distress signal. This is long before any words appear. As early as four or five months Jerry enjoys making a noise and likes to have people talk or sing to him.

Jerry lies on his back and coos, exercising his mouth, lips, tongue, and vocal cords. He makes sucking and grunting noises, says "a-a-ah!" and other long vowel sounds. After months of this, the day comes when the open vowel babblings turn into "ma-ma-ma-ma," or "da-da-da-da." To produce this first articulate word takes not only Jerry's vocal apparatus; it takes his whole body, including his feet. Sometimes he seems to kick the sounds out—as anybody knows who tries to hold him on this momentous occasion.

Jerry may use rhythm as he speaks, and he needs plenty of room for gestures. Kinesics and words are one highly charged pattern. As children grow older they will use their bodies relatively less, but plenty of adults might be struck dumb if you tied their arms. When I first began to do public speaking, I had to pace up and down the platform to get the words out. I have a friend who goes into a kind of jig when he is seized with an idea.

Situation-as-a-whole

Jerry's first word, says Professor LaBrant of New York University, is probably neither noun nor verb, but a giant molecule of language.[1] "Mama" does not refer at first to that person there, she suggests, but to a generalized feeling which might be translated: "I don't feel just the way I want to feel, and I would like to have whoever it is come in and pick me up and fix me . . . and do it the way I am used to having it done." If the mother comes and does just that, splendid. But if she comes and sets up a different situation, Jerry will go right on howling. "If the mother does the wrong thing she will discover that *she* is not at all the 'mama' he means."

The word "mama" is thus for a brief time a symbol for a total situation. Similarly the early use of such a word as "go"

[1] *A Genetic Approach to Language.*

is more than a simple verb. If Jerry has always "gone" in his baby buggy, "go" means a complex of acts, including perhaps putting on his coat and hat. If you try to make him "go" some other way than the accustomed one you may be sorry. "The child is not born with a subject-predicate statement," says LaBrant. He seems to be born more like Viki or Boots, ready to respond to situation-as-a-whole.

J. C. Fenton notes that a child learning to talk tries to express as much as possible by a single word. The word "up" may mean, at various times, "Please take me on your lap—give me the book that is on the table—that tree is tall—the moon is in the sky." [1]

The above applies to children of all cultures. They babble, they lie on their backs and practice, they produce "a-a-ah" and other long vowel sounds, with "mama"—or something close to it—often as their first word. The sound means "mother" in many languages. They all learn to talk with their whole bodies; all use early words to evoke a total situation, with the classification of specific things coming later.

Stockpiling words

Jerry's words pile up as the months go by. Even when he is learning their meanings he keeps on experimenting with their sounds. Rhymes, say Gesell and Ilg, please him as early as eighteen months.[2] By two years his whole speaking equipment—mouth, lips, tongue, larynx, and thorax—is undergoing rapid organization. Jargon is giving way to sentences; soliloquy is taking the place of babbling. Jerry seems to be compelled "to exercise his vocal abilities, to repeat words, to name things, to suit words to action and action to words." The drive to talk is on him.

At four he develops a sense of humor. It comes with his enlarging vocabulary, and includes nonsense rhymes, exaggerations, and stories he invents, often with silly language. About

---

[1] *A Practical Psychology of Babyhood.* Quoted by Werner Wolff.
[2] *Infant and Child in the Culture of Today.*

this period, too, Jerry inaugurates his Great Quiz Program. The Quiz Kids answer questions, but Jerry asks them; asks about eight million of them. One way to keep from going quite mad in the blizzard of questions is to remember that this is the way, and the only way, that Jerry can learn to deal with his world. He must have names for the things around him, and explanations about their use. He is taking the step that Boots, the cat, could never take. He needs sympathetic attention, too, and some of the questions that seem unnecessary may come from a sense of loneliness and insecurity.

Young children . . . should have the greatest support from the parents during earliest weeks, months and years. . . . The most important objective of training is teaching the child to speak and think, for only with the aid of his language can he learn to wait, hope, reason and plan. . . .[1]

All children must go through this infuriating stage of accumulating words by asking questions, or be handicapped for life. "The input cannot be left to chance," says Young. "It must be sorted, ordered and named, and somehow made consonant with our plan of life."

By the time he is four, a child may utter 10,000 to 12,000 words a day. By six he understands a huge number of words, and has a speaking vocabulary of at least 2,500 different words. He uses every part of speech and every form of sentence. When he enters school he normally will speak rather well, for "he has had millions of specific bits of practice in his pre-school years. . . ."[2] A child learns early that to mispronounce a word is humiliating in company; other youngsters will tease him for it.

LaBrant is inclined to raise the above figures, following recent word counts. She cites a case of a child of five using 35,000 running words a day, and says that actual counts show a vocabulary of at least 5,000 different words at age six for most children. The number will depend on the family back-

[1] Dollard and Miller, *Personality and Psychotherapy.*
[2] David H. Russell, *Children Learn to Read.*

ground. A professor's boy usually knows more words than a truck-driver's—though he is not necessarily any more intelligent. LaBrant gives an illuminating case of a child learning a new word:

> Tommy's mother dressed him one morning in a new outfit with a big pearl button in front. "Stand still while I button this," she said. All morning Tommy played with the word: "buppon," "buppon." That night on his grandfather's lap he played with the buttons on his grandfather's coat. "Buppon?" "Yes, button." He explored the buttons on his grandfather's shirt. "Buppon?" "Yes, button." Finally he toyed with the scarf pin. "Buppon?" "Well," said his grandfather, "it's like a button. I call it a pin. . . ."

LaBrant commends grandfather for saying he *calls* it a pin, rather than it *is* a pin. The word is not the thing. The word "pin" cannot prick your finger. "We call it a pin, French people call it '*épingle*,'" is good semantic training.

The pattern is set

Every child between two and five is learning the phonetic pattern of his mother tongue. The pattern for English has been formulated by the linguists with an algebraic nicety, as we shall see in a later chapter. Indeed the linguists can give us the basic structural formula which children must learn in any one of scores of languages. By the time Jerry is six, they say, the sequence of sounds is ingrained and automatic. Even the nonsense language he makes up will conform, "venturing not a jot beyond."

When he studies French at school, Jerry will try to construct the syllables according to the ingrained English formula—which sounds come after which, and the pattern of vowels and consonants. He will learn French more readily if the teacher tells him about the patterns which each language has, putting him on guard. In English, French, or any European language, for example, we never begin a word with a *ng* sound; though we end one with it, as in "hung" or "cling." In the pattern which an Eskimo child learns, however, many words start with the *ng* sound.

The pattern of each language is rigid, and no sounds that deviate from it can be pronounced without great difficulty. Such words as "mome raths," "glub," "squonk," all fit the English formula, although they have as yet been given no meaning. Every English word must contain a vowel, which is not true of all languages. In English a word may begin with a vowel, which in some languages is impossible.

An infant can learn any language with equal facility—English, Eskimo, Chinese, or the formidable language of the Vancouver Island Indians which contains such a one-word blockbuster as: "namamamamahln'iqk'okmaqama," meaning: "They each did so because of their characteristic of resembling white people." Looking at this astonishing symbol, we are prepared to believe the linguists when they say no language is primitive; all have complex patterns.

Word trouble for Jerry

The word is not the thing. Said grandfather: "We call this a pin, but that we call a button." If all of us who teach young children to talk would take the time to make this simple explanation, the world might be spared a great deal of trouble. Once the word is identified with the thing, trouble begins— word magic, rank superstitions, guilt-by-association, belief in the physical reality of abstract terms like "Fascism"—all become possible. A mist comes between the child and his environment which distorts his judgment.

Here are one or two sad examples of this confusion among young children. Asked to define various terms the children reply:

The *sun* is so called because it behaves as if it were the sun.
The *stars* are so called because they are that shape.
The *table* is so called because it is used for writing.
Pigs are so called because they are such dirty animals.

One of the earliest lessons to impress on Jerry is that words are arbitrary noises. Somebody made them up; he might make one up some day himself. Any sound might be used for any meaning, provided it fits the phonetic pattern. There are a few exceptions in English, in such words as "buzz," "boom," "crack," where the term imitates the sound. It is curious that our most frequent verbal sound effect, especially for children, "shush," had great difficulty in attaining the dignity of a word and making the dictionary. By and large, any noise we make with our mouths can theoretically symbolize any event, provided the people of the speech community agree that it shall. No vote, of course, is ever taken, for the agreement is one of that vast number of agreements in the culture which are made and followed unconsciously—a fact worthy of considerable reflection.

A good way to illustrate the above is for the mother or teacher to assemble the words for "dog" in half a dozen languages, and have Jerry note the differences. If he were a little French boy he would call his pet *"chien"*; a little Russian, *"sobaka"*; a little German, *"Hund"*; a little Hopi Indian, *"Pohko,"* and so on. Words in all languages are usually pure creations, having no meaning in themselves.

The incredible leap from the spoken word to the letters on the page may be taken in two installments. Here is the sequence as the child psychologists demonstrate it.[1] An infant toddles up to another, pokes him, cries out with delight, "Baby!" A month later you show him a photograph of a baby, and after managing to focus his eyes and recognize the image, he says "Baby" and pokes the picture. To his disappointment it does not feel like a baby. Much later his mother shows him the second symbol, the word under the picture. "See, it *says* 'baby' too." This is so remote and confusing that he turns away and rejects it.

Meanwhile the child often tries to comprehend what his mother is doing when she reads. He will look at her face and then at the book she holds. Something goes into her eyes, and out of her mouth comes a story—a message chain to baffle the communication engineers. Roma Gans and her collaborators,

[1] Gans, Stendler, and Almy, *Teaching Young Children.*

describing this event, make a bold suggestion: read the comics to your child, where the pictures help the words! Reading can then be developed as fun, not a cause for anxiety. But of course, pick your comics.

Another early trouble for Jerry is the "one-proper-meaning" superstition. Schoolteachers are often the victims of this verbal malaise and pass it on to helpless children. There are very few words which carry only one meaning. Some English words have more than a hundred meanings, depending on the context. Webster's International Dictionary has 109 entries for "run." This is one of the points that makes English such a live and flexible instrument of communication. And what are the schoolmarms going to do with those cases where a simple change in accent *reverses* the meaning? "Yes, you did!" can mean you did, or you didn't, depending on where one puts the accent.

A few battleships, a few diamonds, a few kings, may mean three or four. But a few peas, a few raindrops, a few tea leaves may mean hundreds, thousands. The meaning of any given word by itself is usually far less important than the context or situation in which it occurs. This is readily proved by sentences where the key word is missing. The reader has not the slightest difficulty in grasping the meaning and supplying the missing word. Thus:

The car ran off the ———— into the ditch.
The ———— made a perfect three-point landing.
That awful ———— of the Joneses' barked all night.

The youngster would not be crippled by the one-proper-meaning superstition unless he was locked up in a schoolroom and overawed by fixed rules. He would continue experimenting, and by trial and error would outrun the superstition. School may discourage him from learning new words by insisting on proper meanings. In Chapter 25 we will take the roof off a schoolhouse and try to see what is happening to young verbalizers capable of 10,000 to 35,000 running words a day.

All human talk, aside from numbers, formulas, and a little prose in scientific papers, is by nature loose, inexact, flexible. Meaning tends to be a problem in probability rather than perfect exactitude; which is the more reason for pushing the probability ratio as high as we can, and helping our children to do so.

Chapter 8

THE COMMUNITY AROUND US

Contrasting young Jerry with chimpanzees, cats, and other higher animals, we see that it is not only language which marks him off, but the community around him. He is enveloped in an organization which feeds him, guards him, educates and disciplines him, for about a quarter of his whole life. After he becomes an adult member of society, he still cannot survive without its continual ministrations.

We have been thinking of language primarily as a skill belonging to each individual, but language is also the cement which binds the community together. It acts to express the group's solidarity, to instruct the slowly maturing young, to help us overcome the difficulties of the environment. Jerry is as unthinkable without his community as the community is unthinkable without him, and neither can function without language.

What is culture?

"A social organism," said William James, "is what it is because each member proceeds to his own duty with a trust that the other members will simultaneously do theirs. A government, an army, a ship . . . all exist on this condition, without which not only is nothing achieved, but nothing is even attempted."

James stated the obvious, in advance of the modern anthropologists. Yet how many stop to realize the importance of the community around us and the vital relationship we bear to it? A public opinion survey, conducted in both America and Germany, asked: "Do you believe that other people can be trusted?" Sixty per cent of Americans said "yes," and only 6 per cent of Germans. This small proportion helps us to understand the insecurity of the German people following the war. But the two Americans out of every five who do not trust other people reflect our own ignorance of what the community means.

We *must* have confidence in the members of our society who run the trains, land the planes, set our broken bones, get telephone calls through, honor our checks, operate elevators, deliver letters, keep the electric power coming, put out the fires, pump the water, educate our children—to say nothing of those who shave us. Neither can a primitive society survive without close, unremitting co-operation among its members. Margaret Mead did find a tribe in New Guinea, the Mundugumor, where people had actually ceased to trust each other. What with infanticide, continual hand-to-hand fights, and head-hunting raids, this society was in grave danger of becoming extinct. The British government had to step in to save it.

Social scientists divide culture into three parts:

1. *Habits*, customs, rules for behavior, which Jerry begins to learn almost as soon as he is born. Not a single item of the enormous list is inherited; all must be taught him by the community—what to eat, what to wear, when to bathe, how to behave on all occasions, as well as how to talk.

2. *Belief systems*, which give the child his standards of right and wrong. What to think about God—or the gods—about the world, society, the crown, the flag, property, sex. Here Jerry absorbs the symbols of his society.

3. *Artifacts*, all the man-made utensils, weapons, constructions, machines, which the society has developed or borrowed, and many of which every child must be taught to use. The Sears Roebuck

mail-order catalogue gives a suggestion of the artifacts now to be reckoned with in American society.

The laws of the culture concept are something like Boyle's law of gases—statistical in their application. We may never know what an individual will do in a given situation, any more than we know what a single molecule of gas will do. But we can find the pattern which the whole group will follow. A freak may enter a church and begin to whistle, but Western culture automatically stops most of us from whistling in church. If an observer knows the patterns of the culture, he can predict behavior with high probability—which is the test of any science.

The three departments of culture listed above are clear enough in our heads, but in actual living they often merge one into the next. To illustrate them, let us compare how the day begins for an American businessman, and for an Eskimo *pater familias* on the Arctic Ocean.

Floral Heights

Sinclair Lewis awakens George F. Babbitt, real-estate dealer, on an autumn morning in his suburban home outside the up-and-coming city of Zenith, U.S.A. "His face was babyish in slumber, despite his wrinkles and the red spectacle-dents on the slopes of his nose. He was not fat but he was exceedingly well fed; his cheeks were pads and the unroughened hand on the khaki-colored blanket was slightly puffy." Babbitt stirs as the milk truck bangs, the furnace man slams the basement door, the whistling newsboy throws the rolled up morning paper with a thud against the front door. He dozes, in and out of sleep, until the new alarm clock with all the latest attachments—cathedral chime, intermittent ring, phosphorescent dial —rouses him for good and all. "Babbitt was proud of being awakened by such a rich device. Socially it was almost as creditable as buying expensive cord tires."

He thrusts his feet into his slippers and makes his tousled way from the sleeping porch to the bathroom. All houses in

the subdivision of Floral Heights have sleeping porches.[1] The
bathroom is even more beautiful in Babbitt's eyes than the
alarm clock—"an altogether royal bathroom of porcelain and
glazed tile and metal sleek as silver. . . . The tub was long
enough for a Prussian Guard, and above the set bowl was a
sensational exhibit of toothbrush holder, shaving brush holder,
soap dish, sponge dish, and medicine cabinet." He brushes his
teeth ceremoniously, shaves, bathes, parts his thinning hair, and
wonders for the hundredth time what to do with the discarded
razor blade.

Then comes the routine of getting dressed. The coat of the
brown suit does not need pressing, but the trousers do. This
presents a serious problem, to which his wife contributes: "Oh,
Georgie, why couldn't you wear the brown coat with the
blue trousers?"

"Good lord! Did you ever in all my life know me to wear
a coat of one suit and the pants of another? What do you think
I am? A busted bookkeeper?"

The proper necktie for the day is another problem, together
with the ceremonial of changing all the artifacts contained in
his pockets—the fountain pen, silver pencil, watch chain,
penknife, cigar-cutter, seven keys (the use of two of which
he has forgotten), the loose leaf notebook, elk's tooth, wallet—
and the Boosters' Club button for the lapel of his coat. The last
displays two words, "Boosters—Pep!" and it makes Babbitt
feel loyal and important, associating him with Good Fellows
who are well up in business circles.

Suitably dressed at last, he goes downstairs and joins his wife
and three children around the breakfast table. A dish of prunes,
coffee with cream and sugar, toast, cereal, eggs, jam, constitute
the standard menu in Floral Heights in the 1920's. Babbitt has
played poker until late last night and his mood is not too
amiable. He engages the family in a series of arguments, some
reasonably bitter, about the correct name for a "dinner jacket";
about the futility of social work and the danger that those who

[1] This cultural compulsion has since eased. Babbitt would have a
ranch-type house today with a picture window but no sleeping porch.

engage in it may turn into socialist agitators; about the superiority of business to all other professions—the last sermon being addressed particularly to his son Ted, a senior in high school.

Disquieted and on the defensive, Babbitt gulps his second cup of coffee and retreats to the garage. It is built of corrugated iron and he intends to replace it with a frame structure the minute he can afford it. "No class," he thinks.

"Among the tremendous crises of each day, none was more dramatic than starting the engine. It was slow on cold mornings; there was the long, anxious whirr of the starter. . . ." But it starts, and he is happy again. As he drives to the office, the tall towers of the new skyscrapers of Zenith loom white and ethereal in the morning light. He warms to his city and his place in it. He parks his car and pushes the elevator button. The business day begins.

King William Island

Two thousand miles north of Zenith, another male, of Babbitt's build and age, with more hair on his head and a Mongolian slant to his eyes, also awakens on a fall day. His name is Utak, a seal hunter of the Netsilik tribe of Eskimos. He is giving up the bow and arrow of his ancestors for the rifle of the white man, but most of his culture is still native.[1]

First, he hawks and spits for several minutes. Then he crawls part way out of his deerskin sleeping bag, grumbling at his wife and baby, who are still in it. He takes up a circular knife and cuts off a great piece of frozen fish from a nearby pile. This he proceeds to eat after delivering another lecture to the family. As his stomach fills his mood improves and he begins to tell about a dream he had in the night. After each bite of fish, he sucks his fingers noisily before going on with the story.

Puffing and blowing and still largely in the sleeping bag, Utak reaches around, lights the Primus stove (another borrowed artifact), and brews some tea. He gulps down two or

[1] Gontran de Poncins, *Kabloona*, Reynal and Hitchcock, 1941.

three mugs, says *"Una-i-kto"* ("It is cold"), and eats the tea leaves left in the mug. Having breakfasted and aroused the family, he gets into his clothes of animal skins (he sleeps naked), tugs on his caribou boots, and wraps himself in his great fur parka. He takes his fishing tackle, his spear and a snow knife, and creeps to the door of the igloo. Here he removes the huge snow block and sets out for his morning's work of fishing through the ice.

If he is lucky enough to spear a seal, "all the hunters kneel round the seal to perform the rite of thanks. . . ." There will be a hush as he picks up his knife to make a small incision. He puts in his hand and draws out the red liver, steaming in the cold air. A seal provides the whole family with food for a long time.

Utak built his igloo spiral fashion out of blocks of hard snow—a permanent winter home on King William Island. On hunting trips he will build a small snow house for the night only. In the igloo live various relatives, as well as his wife and children. It contains, among other artifacts: a seal oil lamp, a drying rack for clothes above the lamp, a sleeping bench of packed snow one foot high, soapstone pipes, skin scrapers, a louse catcher with handle of deer bone, deer skins, a bowl carved from the skull of a muskox, assorted sizes of stone bowls, and a heap of frozen seals. There is no bathroom, no sleeping porch, and no razor blade problem.

Two cultures

It has been said that "those who know no culture other than their own cannot know their own." Our first impression is one of acute contrast between Utak and Babbitt; but as we go deeper, we find that the similarities are just as interesting and important. I once compiled a list of more than thirty major cultural traits found in all known human societies—the characteristics which make all mankind one.[1]

---

[1] *The Proper Study of Mankind.*

We note, for instance, how both fathers begin the day by admonishing their families. We note how customs, beliefs, and artifacts are intermingled in both establishments. Babbitt had strong beliefs about not wearing a brown coat with blue trousers to the office. Ten years later, in the 1930's, he would not have felt so strongly.

Babbitt is a Christian, at least in theory. Utak worships no supreme being, but is keenly aware of supernatural forces. When a seal is caught, he and his neighbors are careful to thank "the Spirit of the Waters, she who shepherds the seal in the recesses of the sea." Utak believes that a shaman is probably to blame for bad weather, and that famine may come as the result of breaking a tabu. (Babbitt's coat and pants tabu is not so serious.) If the person who has broken the tabu will confess his sin, Utak believes, the famine may be broken too.

Babbitt is conditioned to a society where competition on all levels beyond the family is strenuous. Utak wages such an unrelenting contest with the cold of the Arctic that he and the fellow members of his society must face it together; they cannot afford the luxury of competition. They regard personal gear as private property, but often share food and shelter. They have no government as such, no writing and no body of law. Public opinion is the only policeman, but it is immeasurably strong. There are only two punishments: community disapproval, and death. The latter penalty is rare, decided only after long consideration by the unanimous verdict of the whole community.

All Eskimo tribes share a single language, though they may live thousands of miles apart. It is a complex language, rich in expressions about hunting and animals. There are many words for different kinds of snow—a point which all skiers can appreciate. Where Babbitt has an adding machine in the office, Utak counts with the help of his fingers and toes— twenty being "a man brought to the end." Utak, however, has no money to count.

Both men are vital individuals, with many unique characteristics. But each is laced into his community, obeying implicitly the commands of the culture. If they had somehow been transferred at birth, Babbitt would have been eating raw fish in an igloo at dawn, while Utak would have been performing bathroom ceremonials in Floral Heights—for each the most natural thing in the world.

Rings of culture

Before civilizations arose, with far-flung transportation systems, a society tended to be small and compact, like Utak's. There was always, however, some communication, with diffusion of ideas, weapons, foodstuffs, between societies. Thus when Indian corn was developed in Central America many thousands of years ago, it gradually spread to communities all over North and South America. It saved the lives of the little company of Pilgrims that first winter in Plymouth, Massachusetts.

Civilization is normally based on a grain which can be stored—corn, wheat, rice. It usually requires, too, a beast of burden and a handy method for weaving textiles. As these greater societies developed, a person within the boundaries of one of them might acquire several rings of cultures coming from a number of earlier societies which had merged. To illustrate: my own way of life today, as an American of English descent, is clearly the resultant of at least five culture rings, as follows:

1. *Civilization* as such, from which I receive city living habits, architecture, mathematics, writing, going to school, eating cereals, using money, paying taxes. (Utak had none of this.)

2. *Western civilization*, from which come the Christian religion, science and advanced technology, Arabic numerals, the sovereign state, music in the diatonic scale, the institution of the free market, military conscription, and so on.

3. *Anglo-Saxon culture*, from that part of the West where English is the mother tongue. Here I receive my particular

language, which, as we shall see, tends to shape my view of the world. Here too are such useful legacies as political democracy and the Bill of Rights. Here is the idea of romantic love as the proper basis for marriage, prudery about sex, the convention, if one is a male, of restraining his emotions.

4. *American culture.* In this ring, like George Babbitt, I piously follow the great motorcar complex with its hundreds of new habits and beliefs. Like Babbitt, I subscribe to competition in sports, money-getting, acquiring prestige. Other American traits are the ability to laugh at oneself, exaggeration in storytelling, jazz music, the cult of cleanliness—much stimulated by the manufacturers of plumbing and soap—the idea that education is the answer to all human problems, and a strong sense of manifest destiny. We have taken over also a number of Indian words—half our states have Indian names, like Connecticut—and a few Indian artifacts, like corn, snowshoes, and canoes.

5. *New England culture* is much attenuated now, as compared with a century ago. Still it gives a nasal twang to my speech, a taste for clam chowder made with milk, a tendency to count my pennies, and respect for the sturdy virtues of early rising, hard work, and a full woodpile. New Englanders do not call a new acquaintance by his first name as promptly as Californians do. The proper way to address a person is very important in any culture.

In addition to these five rings, every American belongs to one or more sub-cultures, depending upon his occupation, income, and antecedents. A doctor's patterns are different from those of a taxi-driver or a boiler-maker. I belong to the middle income group, and have learned the special patterns of three professions—accountant, writer, lecturer. The last comprises some very curious folkways indeed, especially the ceremonials of dining with the committee.

The tens of thousands of automatic patterns and rules embraced in these rings and sub-rings are all learned; no one of them is inherited. Born of the same parents, but shipwrecked

as an infant on a Pacific island and reared by kindly Poly-
nesians, I should have acquired a very different set of customs,
beliefs, and artifacts, together with an utterly different language. Furthermore, I should *look* like a Polynesian; my talk,
my gestures, my dress, would more than offset the inherited
features of my frame and face. I should have my present intelligence, or lack of it, far less general knowledge, and a totally
different "world view."

Culture and history

This whole idea broadens our base of communication not
only through space around the world, but also through time.
Every one of us is both a creature of his culture and a carrier
of it, in that he passes it along. A few are also creators of
culture if they contribute large changes—Confucius, Jesus,
Mohammed, Galileo, Watt, Lincoln, Einstein. But also many
little people are responsible for many little changes. Everyone counts, on this scale; nobody is unimportant.

The concept sharply corrects traditional ideas about history.
"The spectacular rise and fall of certain civilizations," says
Ralph Linton, "should not blind us to the fact that cultures
have never fallen." To destroy a culture, the whole society
must be obliterated, together with its language. The Maya
civilization fell before the Spaniards, but the Indians still speak
the Maya tongue in Yucatan and Guatemala, and still follow
the maize ceremonies.

History as written often disregards culture, to dramatize
those unstable characters far out toward the end of the frequency distribution curve—kings, seers, generals, demagogues.
While the popular view is that the leader makes the times,
anthropologists can show the opposite to be more often true.
Can one imagine Hitler, for instance, coming to power if the
times had not been out of joint in Germany? The German
people had lost a war, lost territory, suffered a ruinous inflation, and in their frustration and bitterness were ready for
somebody like Hitler, who promised them release.

Formal history, with its accent on the heroes and the glandular cases of mankind, stands the social pyramid on its apex. The culture concept puts it back upon its base. It may be less dramatic, but it gives us the closest fit to the truth about man and his society that the scientific method has yet produced. Furthermore, the culture concept enables us to look over the walls of our own culture and see the other peoples of the world behind their walls. We realize that Babbitt appears as outlandish to Utak as Utak seems to Babbitt, and that each has the better of it in some things, and the worse of it in others.

The culture concept makes me, at least, a little more optimistic about some of our pressing problems. Compounded of the judgment of millions of individuals, culture is the final arbiter of the way of life of a given society. It always has swung in the direction of survival if there was time for the judgment to operate. Gangsters, juvenile delinquency, death on the highways, city blight, soil erosion, all the evils which agitate us now—and with reason—will ultimately be taken care of. It may require a long time, but the remedy must come if society is to survive.

Frequency distribution curve

The frequency distribution curve, mentioned earlier, helps to explain the behavior of any population. Like the culture concept, it is a useful corrective to loose generalizations about *all* children, *all* parents, *all* Americans, *all* Frenchmen. The curve is shaped like an inverted U, and scientists have found that it applies to most characteristics of living things. It is a semantic tool with a fine cutting edge.

Suppose 200 gulls, sitting on a rock in the bay, take to the air as you sail near. If you watch them carefully you will not say: "What a flock of timid birds." One timid fellow, you note, goes up first, then another, then three or four, then the mass of them. But a dozen are left, and one big buff-colored veteran refuses to budge until your boat is practically on top of him. If you plot the number of gulls leaving, second by second, on cross-section paper, you will have the standard frequency distribution curve, something like this:

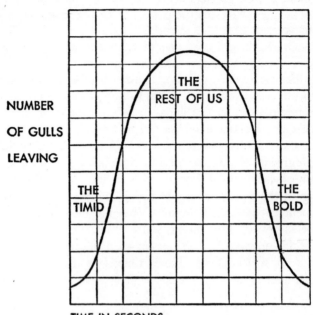

NUMBER

OF GULLS

LEAVING

THE REST OF US

THE TIMID

THE BOLD

TIME IN SECONDS

On the far left are the timid, on the far right the bold, in the middle the mass, the rest of us. So it is with unruly and saintly children, with geniuses and dullards, with the strong and the weak, with beautiful women and plain. So it is with the measurable characteristics of all mankind. The frequency distribution curve supports the culture concept in explaining the behavior of groups, and strongly supports semantics by breaking up large, loose, generalizations. Not all gulls are timid; not all Americans are money mad; not all Swedes are blond. Plot the curve.

Culture and evolution

The cultural process begins slowly but accelerates as inventions fan out. Julian Huxley in his *Evolution in Action* sets forth the breathtaking idea that culture may provide a substitute for evolution in the case of man! Certainly it is providing an alternative mechanism for change in addition to changes in the genes. "This is man's method for utilizing cumulative experience, which gives him new power of control over nature, and new and more rapid methods of adjusting to changing circumstances."

Instead of growing fur we use up more energy from coal and oil in the form of central heating. Instead of building resistance to the tropic sun, we invent pith helmets and air conditioning. To get to the top of Mt. Everest, we strap on an oxygen tank. Thus we modify environment, leaving biology unchanged. Evolution works in the opposite way, modifying the organism to fit the environment.

From whatever direction we view it, the culture concept is cardinal to an understanding of ourselves and our world. Language is an inseparable part of it, and to the important story the linguists have to tell we will now turn.

Chapter 9

LINGUISTICS

"Noises made with the face" began several hundred thousand years ago, but "scratches made with the fist" are much more recent. A small, highly trained band of scientists—only a few hundred of them in North America—are studying these noises and scratches by the methods of technical linguistic research. Live speech is their primary interest; written words, they say, are a "symbolization of a symbolization," without the intonations, gestures, and accents which make spoken words so distinctively human.

Linguists believe that the classical grammarians put the cart before the horse when they began to analyze writing rather than speech. Let us write out a Class B joke—there it is, worth only a brief smile. But an accomplished entertainer, say Groucho Marx, can take those exact words, and by gesture, facial expression, accent, a pause at the right moment, produce roars of laughter from an audience. He adds a new dimension of meaning impossible to convey in the written word.

Your true linguist is saddened when he contemplates the wild flowers of speech which are destined to die out before one of the fraternity can get a tape recorder on them. The fraternity have most Indo-European and Amerindian languages under control; but hundreds of native languages have never been properly recorded, and some are becoming extinct. There are not enough trained scientists, let alone funds, to collect them.

In addition to being a Ph.D. with a working knowledge of

French, German, Latin, Greek, and at least one language outside the Indo-European family, the professional linguist must
be able to run a field study in an unrecorded tongue. Like an
anthropologist, he may pack up his helmet and mosquito net-
ting and go out to the Pacific islands or to Africa for a long,
uncomfortable residence in a native village while he observes
and records local customs. Instead of studying the total culture,
however, as the anthropologist generally does, he specializes
in the local language. Nobody in a native village of this sort
knows how to write, and so the linguist can botanize happily
on speech.

The first thing to do in the field, George Trager tells us, is
a job in human relations. Unless the head man is behind you
unreservedly, you may as well repack your equipment. The
next task is to locate a native speaker with no inhibitions and
plenty of time on his hands. If you have a common language
to speak together—Spanish, say, or Malay Pidgin—so much the
better. If you have a tape or disk recorder in your luggage,
so much the better. When you get to the stage of meaning,
you start, like Lancelot Hogben, with *numbers*. "How do you
say 'one, two, three' in this village?"

Patterns of sound

Linguists, like communication engineers, do not give their
first attention to meaning. Like engineers checking the fidelity
of the message at each step from sender to receiver, linguists
put down the sounds they hear, regardless of the sense. They
have developed an elaborate code to record these sounds. Presently certain sounds repeat themselves and a pattern begins
to form.

Every language has its unique noises and patterns. There are
certain sounds a speaker of English must make, and others
which he must not. Speakers of a different language may have
a pattern which permits sounds impossible in English. An
advertising man, for instance, after a week of dreaming, can
christen a new breakfast food "Thrub," but he cannot call it
"Dlub"; not in English he can't. If he tried to call it "Nfpk"

he would be fired. A linguist can learn to say "dlinpfk" as readily as "glimpsed"—which latter would floor many a native islander. We have already noted how English permits no words to begin with *ng*, while Eskimo is full of them.

In spoken English the linguists have identified a total of forty-five building blocks, as follows:

Vowels	9
Semi-vowels (Y, H, W)	3
Consonants	21
Degrees of stress	4
Levels of pitch	4
Transitions, spacing, etc.	4
Total	45

Stress, pitch, and transition sounds modify speech but not writing, except as punctuation marks supply a rough substitute. The entertainer with his Class B joke illustrates their use. To refer to these modifying elements in speech, the linguists have invented the term "superfixes"; and a little later we will give some examples. In analyzing sounds the linguists borrow from the physiologists, to study the action of the mouth, tongue, and vocal cords. They do not say much about the brain—having perhaps troubles enough.

Every language has its own rules for ordering and arranging its building blocks into structures of words, sentences, and ultimate meanings, including cosmic ideas. A linguist searching for patterns among the blocks will produce a code, or an algebra, which looks like this: [1]

$$/^2l\grave{o}h\eta+^3\,\acute{a}yl\ni nd^2|\ ^2iz\ (+)\ni+l\hat{o}h\eta+^3\grave{a}yl\ni nd^1\sharp/$$

This is the phonemic transcription of the sentence, "Long Island is a long island." If two graduate students are sent on a field trip to the same native village, one after the other, they will return with almost identical records, so exact has the science of linguistics now become.

[1] George L. Trager and Henry Lee Smith, Jr., *An Outline of English Structure.*

When students try to analyze an unknown tongue, one of their first difficulties is in separating units. Where does one word end and the next begin? We experience this difficulty in listening to rapid speech in a foreign language, young children in listening to their mother tongue. "In field observation," say Smith and Trager, "one sometimes misses a great many data and one has all the language thrown at one, as it were, on all levels at once."

A language, no matter how appallingly chaotic to the ear of one not used to it, is always highly systematized, and so more easily analyzed than other systems of behavior in the culture. Its data are extremely formal. Primitive cultures are found, in the sense of a scarcity of artifacts (no alarm clocks), and low living standards; but, as noted earlier, linguists have never found a language that could be called primitive. Utak's Eskimo was just as sophisticated as Babbitt's English. All tongues are complex, their complexity apparently corresponding to the human brain in a one-to-one relation. Stories about tribes with only grunts and squeals are biological fakes. The language of every speech community is suited to the interests of that culture. English is better for taking care of automobiles, but Dinka, a Sudanese tongue, is better for taking care of cows. In Arabic there are more than 6,000 different words for camel, its parts and equipment. Eskimo boasts several hundred inflected forms for a single noun. Says Benjamin Lee Whorf:

> The crudest savage may unconsciously manipulate with effortless ease a linguistic system so intricate, manifoldly systematized, and intellectually difficult, that it requires the life-time study of our greatest scholars to describe its workings.

Phonemes and beyond

Dr. Henry Lee Smith, Jr., now of the Foreign Service Institute, is a linguist known to all America. He was the "speech detective" on the radio, who used to tell where you were reared after he heard you speak. He has such an acute ear that he can often identify the particular section of the city you come from. For more than twelve years he and Dr. George Trager have been listening to English and recording it by techniques constantly improved and refined. Instead of going to New Guinea, these scientists have been gathering the wild blossoms of American speech—and some of them can be pretty wild.

In *An Outline of English Structure*, Trager and Smith work out the linguistic patterns from the sounds, and build up perhaps the most intensive scientific analysis yet made of any language. It is modestly presented and highly technical, but its steps are reasonably clear even to the layman. First, the single sound unit called "phoneme"; next, the group of phonemes—which may be a word, or part of a word—called "morpheme"; then the arrangement of morphemes into "syntax"; and finally a discussion of cultural aspects and meanings of the patterned sounds, called "metalinguistics." The conscientious linguist, you see, puts meaning off as long as possible.

My wife and I sat in front of a blackboard in Washington while Dr. Smith demonstrated the way speech is analyzed, and how the patterns develop. He showed us what profound changes in meaning can come from the faintest change of intonation. The strange symbols of the linguists' code flew over the blackboard, usually somewhat faster than we could follow. But the general approach was clear, and gave us an exciting glimpse of what this new science is already able to do, and how important it is for any study of communication.

How a language grows

Language grows organically in the culture; new terms are invented as needs arise. For millenniums nobody examines speech or suggests improvements; it develops as naturally as cells in the body. One theory is that a single society of primates at some remote period began to talk, became Homo sapiens, and spread around the world. Different societies developed different languages from this primal base, but in due course lost all interconnections. After about 5,000 years, similarities between languages having a common origin are too slight to find readily, says Dr. Trager.

The definition of a *word* still troubles linguists. A word is not necessarily a single idea; it may contain several ideas. Sapir quotes a word from Nootka, an Amerindian language, which denotes: "I have been accustomed to eat twenty apples while engaged in doing [so and so]." Words are units, however, in most languages, and native speakers will normally have little difficulty in dictating a text to a scientist in the field, word by word.

Language, like culture, is forever changing, but changes have some regularities. In studying trends, says the philologist Joshua Whatmough, the mathematical methods of the communication engineers can be helpful.[1] Language tends toward equilibrium, and becomes more and more "shuffled." Linguists apply the regularities for predicting and determining trends. Their findings have practical value. The only hope of untangling the prehistory of Melanesia, for instance, is through comparative linguistics. Social classes are clearly distinguished. Dr. Smith believes that W. Lloyd Warner, the anthropologist who studied the class structure of the town of Newburyport, could have saved time and increased accuracy by using accents and word choices as his measuring rod. Instead Warner arranged his classes inductively, from "lower lower" to "upper upper," after a long series of interviews. He found that people were constantly moving up and down the ladder; Americans do not stay put. In moving up, one shifts his phonemes a bit, and other speech habits.

Linguistics blends field and laboratory science with literary scholarship. It employs the scientific method with rigor in analyzing speech, allowing no value judgments nor arbitrary labels of "correct" and "incorrect." Linguists ask: What are the sounds? How are they accented, pitched, divided? What is done with the arch of the tongue? They are not interested in how things *ought* to be said, but how, in fact, people are saying them out there in the street.

[1] "Natural Selection in Language," *Scientific American*, April 1952.

Talking vs. *writing*

"Written language," said Sapir, "is transferred speech." The linguists give writing a secondary place as an agent of communication, and strongly object to teaching it in advance of speech to foreign language students. Although their preference pains me as a writer, I am forced to admit they have strong arguments, especially that speech is so very much older, and carries a richness and subtlety of meaning often denied to writing.

When I talk to you, even over a telephone wire, it is direct communication, dependent upon a space-time connection. Writing, on the other hand, is indirect, and the time of sending and the time of receiving may be far apart. We still read Homer.

Spoken words are qualified by gestures, facial expressions, stress, and pitch. Written words can be punctuated and italicized, but the effect, as we noted in the Class B joke, is minor compared with speech. Trager and Smith provide many striking examples, of which the following is typical: Take the words LIGHT HOUSE KEEPER. Written thus, they fail to explain which of three events may be referred to. But when spoken, the several meanings are quite clear, thus:

1. For a man who keeps a lighthouse, accent *light*.
2. For a woman who runs her house on a kitchenette basis, accent *house*.
3. For a blonde housewife, accent *light*, and space it off.

Unless recorded in shorthand, or on tape, disk, or wire, the spoken word is impermanent. A few minutes later, as any lawyer can tell you, neither speaker nor hearer can be counted on to remember exactly what has been said. Here we encounter perhaps the major asset of writing: *the statement stays put on the page.* An hour later, a year later, a thousand years later, it remains exactly as written. The inscribed record preserves the accumulations of both culture and science, and develops and refines them. Where is the secret of Damascus steel or of

Sandwich glass? They were handed down by word of mouth and are now lost forever. Where is the secret of cold rolled steel or shatter-proof glass? In the Patent Office, if not in any technical library.

Another asset is the relative precision of skillful writing. Even a careful speaker of standard English does not always say exactly what he means; he may rely on the hearer to grasp his meaning from vague words supplemented with gestures. But in writing one has time to think, compare, and choose. The stenographic transcript of the best unwritten speech (as I well know, for I have had to correct them), must be pruned of superfluous "ands," "wells," "nows," and loose dependent clauses.

Spoken words need no alphabet and rarely need to be spelled. Happy nature folk do not torture themselves with "spelling bees." Written words must be spelled; and in many languages, especially in English, the spelling is neither phonetic nor consistent. Even Spanish is not completely phonetic. This is why most linguists advocate spelling reform, but, aware of the culture concept, they know that it must come gradually.

Spoken words show personal variations and dialects, and can display salty individuality. Written words either ignore these differences or distort them. They cannot be spelled as delivered, except in phonemic symbols. Mark Twain did his best with Jim's dialect in *Huckleberry Finn,* but the result was still distorted.

Every normal child, as we have seen, uses his mother tongue fluently at an early age. Yet millions of normal ten- and twelve-year-olds are classified as "non-readers." They find it difficult to transfer sounds into symbols. More understanding teachers would doubtless help, but the fact remains that Homo sapiens is a talking animal, whose brain centers for writing and reading have only recently been opened up.

New light on grammar

Linguists are wary of the classical grammarians for the same reason. When, after a thousand centuries of live talk, students began to be curious about how it worked, they started their structural investigations at the wrong end, with writing. Thus the grammarians never appreciated the full power, flexibility, and subtlety of language. Their ideal was to halt and petrify words; to study statics rather than dynamics. They tried to establish "one proper meaning" for terms whose meaning varied with context and with time. The great Dr. Johnson tried to freeze English as of the middle of the eighteenth century, thereby misunderstanding a vital function of language—namely, to grow and change with the culture. Fortunately the classical grammarians could not control the popular tongue. They put up a bamboo fence to stop a steel tank. Their inflexible notions about "correctness" were often intolerable to fast-talking school children.

Linguists are rapidly displacing the old-fashioned grammarians. Here, for instance, is Charles C. Fries, of the University of Michigan, with modern ideas about grammar.[1] He began his study by listening to live speech. He collected recordings of talk, direct and over the telephone, from three hundred different speakers, all in "standard English," but all live and colloquial. The conversations added up to some 250,000 running words, and from this raw material he built his grammar. He does not go back to phonemes but attempts an analysis on the syntax level, through signal words and word order. He says:

As native speakers of English we have learned to use certain formal clues by which we identify the various kinds of units in our structures. The process is wholly unconscious unless some failure attracts attention—just as unconscious as our response to sight clues with the muscular adjustments of balancing when we walk.

A child, observes Fries, learns the structure, or grammar, of his language unconsciously; until he knows it, he can neither receive nor send messages. Take such a story-book phrase as "the hunters killed the wolf." Jerry at three will know perfectly well that it was the hunters, not the wolf, who

[1] *The Structure of English.*

survived. He cannot know this without a firm grasp on the grammar, structure, order of his language.

Parents, trying to help their children learn to communicate, often make it harder. Baby-talk, for instance, forces the youngster to work for trash. Talking in long, complicated sentences delays his understanding. The real way to help Jerry is to use simple words and sentences, but never to talk down. Pronouns come hard; use names in the third person. "Jerry, come to mother" is a good deal better than "Wasn't it a dreat bid boy that can walk right over to Muddikins on his itty bitty footsies."

L. M. Myers of Arizona State College takes out after the classical grammarians from a somewhat different angle.[1] They were soaked in Latin, he says, until it ran out of their ears. They tried to explain English on the principles of Latin inflections, which English, as spoken, mostly lacks. Linguists and anthropologists, he says, have disproved the naïve theory of *one universal grammar* underlying all languages. The reasons for supposing that English must have the same inflected cases as Latin, or even that it must have inflected cases at all, are nonexistent. Latin words tend to be in fixed categories, *i.e.*, parts of speech; while the majority of English words shift from one category to another, and the number which shift is growing.

When the grammarians imposed rigid Latin rules on flexible English, they tried to codify something which was not there—or was only occasionally there. So English grammar as it has been taught in the schools, says Myers, is full of spooks— the subjunctive mood, gender, logical or otherwise, and a quite imaginary difference between gerund and present participle. When this ghostly discourse is eliminated from classrooms, students get a better understanding of the English language. Nor will they be haunted for the rest of their lives by vague fears of being "incorrect."

"Our traditional grammar works just so long as we use

---

[1] General Semantics Bulletin #8, Spring 1952.

doctored sentences," said a publisher to a convention of teachers. "It fails when we apply it to sentences that people actually speak and write." [1] There is reason to think that children who come to see the importance of meaning and communication can learn structural rules more readily. "What does language do?" can be followed presently by "How does it do it?" But first, a fresh analysis of spoken language should replace the debatable rules which cumber the old grammars.

Grammar as I learned it in school rolled off me without leaving a perceptible trace, except that uneasy feeling about "correctness." The only conscious grammatical efforts I now make are (1) not to split infinitives—and why shouldn't I?— (2) not to displace "whom" by "who"—but again why not? "Shalls" and "wills" can go climb trees. I take my grammar from the deep, unconscious wells of the culture, and so far it has served me to say what I want to say with reasonable economy. I agree with Allen Upward that it is to those wells the writer should repair, rather than to his grammar books.

Out of bounds

These considerations indicate what James Joyce had to contend with when, in his monumental experiment, *Finnegan's Wake*, he flouted not only the grammarians, but the principles of linguistics. Had he understood the culture concept he would never have attempted it; he would have realized that he was out of bounds. Here is a sample of his laboratory work:

The fall (ba ba ba da l g h a r a g h t a k a m m i n a rr o n n k o n n b r o n n t o n n e r r o n n t u n n t h u n n t r o v a r r h o u n a w n s k a w n t o o h o o h o o r d en e n t h u r n u k!) of a once wall strait old p a r r is retaled in bed and later on life down through all Christian minstrelcy.

Even an Eskimo would have trouble with that falling wall as a verbal sound effect. All of us have the power to change our culture, including our language, by a very small amount.

[1] Lee Deighton, "The Survival of the English Teacher," *ETC*, Winter 1953.

Joyce tried to make a huge change, forcing communication into a channel where, by its nature, it could not go. This sad case of an authentic genius out of bounds should be a warning to other avant-garde writers, and should reinforce what the science of linguistics has to teach us about communication. Every child in every culture must pack into his brain an astronomical number of arbitrary sounds, with patterns for their arrangement into meaningful speech. Once the structures are set, they can be changed only slowly—which is one good reason why it is as senseless as it is unkind for any in-group member to ridicule the accent of a foreigner.

Once the structures are set, we are bound together with links stronger than steel. Everybody in a speech community accepts the common words as completely as he accepts earth and sky. Nobody says: "I'm tired of the word 'culture,' I shall call it 'bluttle' from now on." (He would probably be committed.) When there is no word for a new event one is presently invented—"television" is an example. Slang creeps in, and, when really useful, stays—"O.K." is an example. But for the great body of our mother tongue we agree to keep it as we learned it, lest we suffer the fate of Babel. Of all the unconscious agreements which hold society together, this is the strongest.

Now let us see how the language we learn shapes our world view.

Chapter 10

WORDS AND THE WORLD VIEW

Linguistics as a study of patterned sounds has been called the most exact of all the social sciences. One can predict with it, and prediction is the ultimate test of any science. From this rigorous base, some linguists, especially the late Benjamin Lee Whorf, graduated into a larger inquiry: How does a given language mold the thought of the man whose mother tongue it is, and his view of nature and the world? In this inquiry the vistas are even more exciting, though prediction is probably lower.

Whorf, had he lived, might have become another Franz Boas or William James, so brilliant were his powers of projecting scientific data into fruitful generalizations. He died in 1941 at the age of forty-four. A graduate of M.I.T., he became an executive of the Hartford Fire Insurance Company, and took up linguistics as a hobby. Presently it became his consuming interest. His skill in deciphering Mexican inscriptions brought him to the attention of the scientific world and the close friendship of Edward Sapir. In 1930 the Social Science Research Council gave him a grant to go to Yucatan. Maya and Aztec languages led him to the live speech of American Indians, and he spent two years on Hopi alone.

Whorf's only book is a Hopi dictionary, an unpublished manuscript, now in the possession of Clyde Kluckhohn. He published some thirty articles in the learned journals,[1] and

[1] See bibliography for titles of outstanding articles.

might well have gone on to give the world one of the great classics of social science.

The forms of a man's thoughts, he said, are controlled by patterns learned early, of which the man is mostly unconscious. Thinking is a language process, whether in English, Russian, or Hopi. Every language is a complex system, with three main functions.

(1) To communicate with other persons.
(2) To communicate with oneself, or, as we say, think.
(3) To mold one's whole outlook on life.

As he uses words, "a person notices or neglects types of relationships and phenomena, he channels his reasoning, and builds the house of his consciousness." This conclusion, says Whorf, has been largely neglected by the philosophers, but stands on unimpeachable evidence.

Thinking follows the tracks laid down in one's own language; these tracks will converge on certain phases of "reality," and completely bypass phases which may be explored in other languages. In English, for instance, we say, "look at that wave." But a wave in nature never occurs as a single phenomenon. In the Hopi language they say, "look at that slosh." The Hopi word, whose nearest equivalent in English is "slosh," gives a closer fit to the actual physics of wave motion, connoting movement in a mass. (This is only one of several tough matters in physics where Hopi does better than English.)

Perhaps the majority of linguists today, though they are not prepared to follow Whorf all the way, do recognize the vital part which language plays in thought and culture. The study of *metalinguistics*, as they call it, is thus described by Trager and Smith: "Not only does it deal with *what* people talk about and *why*, but also considers *how* they use the linguistic system, and how they react to its use. This leads further to the consideration of how the linguistic system affects the behavior, both conscious and unconscious, and the world-view, of the speaker. . . ." Contrasted with microlinguistics, which takes a long time to reach a unit as large as the sentence, the meta- or super-linguistics considers the "organization of sentences into discourse, and the relation of the discourse to the rest of the culture."

Unconscious assumptions

Most of us were brought up to believe that talking is merely a tool which something deeper called "thinking" puts to work. Thinking, we have assumed, depends on laws of reason and logic common to all mankind. These laws are said to be implicit in the mental machinery of humans, whether they speak English or Choctaw. Languages, it follows, are simply parallel methods for expressing this universal logic. On this assumption it also follows that any logical idea can be translated unbroken, or even unbent, into any language. A few minutes in the glass palace of the United Nations in New York will quickly disabuse one of this quaint notion. Even such a common concept as "democracy" may not survive translation.

Another set of assumptions underlying Western culture, says Whorf, imposes upon the universe two grand cosmic forms: *space* and *time*. *Space* in our thinking is static, three-dimensional, and infinite; beyond the last area is always another area. *Time* is kinetic and one-dimensional, flowing perpetually and smoothly from the past to the present and into the future. It took the genius of Einstein to correct these cosmic assumptions, and most of us are still firmly wedded to them.

The assumptions underlying the culture of the Hopi also impose two grand cosmic forms upon the universe: the *objective* and the *subjective;* the manifest and the unmanifest. The first is everything accessible to the human senses, without distinction between past and present. The second is "the realm of expectancy, of desire and purpose, of vitalizing life, of efficient causes, of thought thinking itself out . . . into manifestation." It exists in the hearts and minds of animals, plants, mountains, as well as men. This subjective realm is intensely real to a Hopi, "quivering with life, power and potency."

All languages contain terms of cosmic grandeur. English

includes "reality," "matter," "substance," "cause," "energy," as well as "space" and "time." Hopi includes the cosmic term *tunátya*, meaning a special and exalted kind of "hope." It is a verb, not a noun—the action of hoping, the stirring toward hope—and is bound up with communal ceremonies, like prayers for the harvest, and for the forming of rain clouds.

The ancient Greeks believed, among other things, in a universal rule of reason. This came easily because their language structure, like all Indo-European tongues, followed what is called the "subject-predicate" form. If there is a verb there must be a noun to make it work; it could not exist in its own right as pure action. The ancient Greeks, as well as all Western peoples today, say "the light flashed." Something has to be there to make the flash; "light" is the subject; "flash" is the predicate. The whole trend of modern physics, however, with its emphasis on the *field*, is away from subject-predicate propositions. A Hopi Indian, accordingly, is the better physicist when he says "*Reh-pi*"—"flash!"—one word for the whole performance, no subject, no predicate, and no time element. (Children tend to do this too.) In Western languages we are constantly reading into nature ghostly entities which flash and perform other miracles. Do we supply them because our verbs require substantives in front of them?

Again, the Hopi language does not raise the question whether things in a distant village exist at the same present moment as things in one's own village. Thus it avoids the idea of *simultaneity*, which has plagued Western scientists for generations, and was only banished by relativity. The thoughts of a Hopi about events always include *both* space and time, for neither is found alone in his world view. Thus his language gets along adequately without tenses for its verbs, and permits him to think habitually in terms of space-time. For a Westerner really to understand relativity, he must abandon his spoken tongue altogether and take to the special language of calculus. But a Hopi, Whorf implies, has a sort of calculus built into him.

Linguistic relativity

Whorf emphasizes that Hopi is only one language of one small tribe, and that there are thousands of other tongues, each imposing a unique view of nature and the cosmos upon those who speak it. Here is still another kind of relativity, a very important kind. No human is free to describe nature with strict objectivity; for he is a prisoner of his language. A trained linguist can do better because he, at least, is aware of the bondage, and can look at nature through a variety of frames. A physicist can do better by using the language of mathematics. Semanticists are now painfully learning how to do better. It is not easy for anybody. Says Whorf:

> We are thus introduced to a new principle of relativity, which holds that all observers are not led by the same physical evidence to the same picture of the universe, unless their linguistic backgrounds are similar, or can in some way be calibrated.

Indo-European languages can be calibrated with each other: English, Italian, Spanish, French, Russian, German, Latin, Greek, and the rest, back to Indo-Hittite, all use the subject-predicate form. All speakers of these languages are capable of observing the world in a roughly similar way, at least on the high levels of "time," "space," and "matter." Hopi cannot be calibrated with them; neither can Chinese, nor thousands of other languages, living and dead.

Chinese and Western languages

Speakers of Chinese dissect nature and the universe very differently from Western speakers, with a profound effect upon their systems of belief. A Chinese writer, Chang Tung-sun, vigorously supports the relativity thesis in a monograph comparing his culture with that of the West.[1]

Kant imagined that he was dealing in universal categories in *The Critique of Pure Reason*, but actually, says Chang, he was only discussing standard forms of Western thought, a

[1] *ETC*, Spring 1952.

very limited approach. Kant's logic was of the subject-predicate variety, which is not normal in Chinese. An intelligent Chinese gentleman does not know what Kant is talking about—unless he learns some Western tongue in which to read Kant's words. (To some readers this will raise another interesting question: Did Kant himself know what he was talking about?)

Our Western verb "to be," observes Chang, used with an adjective predicate, implies the existence of the adjective as an independent quality. When we say "this is yellow and hard," we tend to assume the existence of two qualities, "yellowness" and "hardness," which suggest to a Chinese something Chang calls a "cosmic substance." "The substance is characterized by its attributes, and the attributes are attributed to the substance," says Chang, in considerable astonishment at such a circular performance. The verb "to be" creates great congeries of identities, and blossoms in Aristotle's laws of logic, of which the first is the law of identity, "A is A." Later we will observe some of the trouble this law has caused.

No such law is possible in the Chinese language, where logic follows a quite different path. In Chinese, one does not attribute existence to "yellowness" and "hardness," or to polar words like "longness" and "shortness." Rather one says: "the long and the short are mutually related"; "the difficult and easy are mutually complementary"; "the front and the rear are mutually accompanying."

In the West we say, "This is the front of the car, and that is the rear, and let's have no more nonsense about it!" But in the Chinese view, Westerners are guilty of considerable nonsense in creating "frontness" and "rearness" as entities. Even a Westerner can see that if a car is torn in two in a crash, the part with the radiator grille becomes the "front," and the part toward the now severed windshield becomes the "rear"—*of that segment.* We can see, if we work hard enough, that there are no such entities as "frontness" or "rearness," "difficulty" or "easiness," "length" or "shortness," by themselves out there. The Chinese language has this useful correction built in; we Westerners have to sweat it out with the help of linguistics, semantics, and mathematics.

Linguists have also emphasized that Chinese is a "multi-valued" language, not primarily two-valued like English and Western languages generally. We say that things must be "good" or "bad," "right" or "wrong," "clean" or "dirty," "capitalistic" or "socialistic," "black" or "white"—ignoring shades of gray. When an economist talks about a middle road between "Socialism" and "Capitalism," both camps vie in their ferocity to tear him apart. (I have been that unhappy economist.)

Speakers of Chinese set up no such grim dichotomies; they see most situations in shades of gray, and have no difficulty in grasping the significance of a variety of middle roads. As a result, Chinese thought has been traditionally tolerant, not given to the fanatical ideologies of the West. Racial, religious, and doctrinal conflicts have been hard to maintain in China, because a Chinese speaker does not possess an unshakable confidence that he is totally right and that you are totally wrong. Observe that this is not a moral judgment, but structural in the language.

Marxism in China?

This happy lack of bi-polar thinking raises a most interesting question. Communism, as formulated by Marx and developed by Lenin, is rigidly bi-polar. The heroic worker stands against the wicked capitalist and one or the other must go down. There is no place for shades of gray or for innocent bystanders in this two-valued struggle. Those who are not with us are against us! Look at almost any bulletin of the National Association of Manufacturers, or at any issue of the *Daily Worker*. Which side are you on?

Russian is an Indo-European language, and the two-sided choice is readily accepted by its speakers. The choice was accepted, too, by top leaders of the Chinese Communists today, for they went to Moscow to be indoctrinated, and to learn the Russian language. But 400 million Chinese have not been to Moscow or learned Russian, or any other Indo-European language, and there is small prospect of their doing so.

How, then, can the Chinese people become good ideological Communists, if it is impossible for them to take seriously the central idea of Marxism? Professor Nathaniel Peffer, of Columbia University, a specialist on the Far East, observes that the Chinese culture has endured many conquerors but has always managed to absorb them. Then he asks a related question: Will not the little group of "Reds" in control of the Chinese state be absorbed too? At first these leaders were accepted, he says, as part of the process of the great Chinese revolution which began in 1911. After its completion, the world may find that it was a *Chinese* revolution, not a communist one. In any event the language barrier to Marxism is formidable.

More sidelights on English

The Wintu Indians of North America are even more shy of the law of identity (A is A) than the Chinese, says D. D. Lee, writing in the *International Journal of American Linguistics*.[1] We say, "this *is* bread," but in Wintu they say, "we call this bread." They avoid the "is of identity," and so are less likely to confuse words with things. When a Wintu speaks of an event not within his own experience, he never affirms it but only suggests, "perhaps it is so." When Lee asked her informant the word for "body," she was given a term signifying "the whole person." Thus the Wintus seem to have antedated the psychosomatic school.

The Coeur d'Alene Indians of Idaho have long antedated other modern scientists. They do not speak in terms of simple cause-and-effect relations as we do, but rather in terms of *process*, as Western scientists are now painfully learning to do. Their language requires speakers to discriminate between three causal processes, denoted by three verb forms: growth, addition, secondary addition. "If, given a more sophisticated culture," says Whorf, "their thinkers erected these now unconscious discriminations into a theory of triadic causality, fitted

[1] 1944. Quoted by L. Doob.

to scientific observations, they might thereby produce a valuable intellectual tool for science." Our specialists can do this by taking thought, fortified with mathematics, but the Coeur d'Alenes seem to do it automatically.

In Nootka, a language of Vancouver Island Indians, a number of English nouns turn into verbs. A speaker does not say "a house," but "a house occurs." The suffixes indicate the duration of the house-event: "a long-lasting house," "a temporary house," "a future house," "a house that used to be," "what started out to be a house."

Eskimo, as we have noted, breaks down our single term "snow" into many words for different kinds of snow. Aztec, however, goes in the opposite direction; here we find one word, though with different terminations, for "snow," "ice," and "cold"! In Hopi, "wave," "flame," "meteor," and "lightning" are all verbs, suiting their dynamic quality. Looking into the August sky, a Hopi says: *"Reh-pi."* "It meteors!"

It is easier to recite the story of William Tell in the Algonquin language than in English, because it has enough possessive pronouns to make a distinction between "his," as applied to Tell, and as applied to his son. As a writer I must continually watch my step with English pronouns, lest they trip me up.

Linguistic relativity makes it clear that Newton took his concepts of Absolute Space and Absolute Time, not so much out of profound cogitation, as out of the language he spoke. They had been lying there for thousands of years. Both "time" and "space" affect the behavior of everyone in Western culture.

"Time," especially, causes us to be oriented toward calendars, dates, "the course of history," timetables, clocks, time wages, races against time, accounting, compound interest, actuarial statistics, annals, diaries, the age of the rocks, of the earth, of the solar system, of the universe. The concept of time impels us to look ahead in planning programs, schedules, appropriations, balanced budgets. Our love affair with time causes other cultures, whose languages permit a less hurried outlook, to regard us as somewhat mad.

Summary of linguistics

The linguists are making us realize that language is not a tool with which to uncover a deeper vein of reason, universal to all thinkers, but a shaper of thought itself. Shaping the thought, it helps to shape the culture, as in the Western cult of time. They are making us realize that we get our view of the world outside our heads probably as much from the words inside as from independent observation. When we try to become independent observers, furthermore, these words, unless we take special precautions, may distort the vision. There is no reason to suppose that English, French, Spanish, or any other Western language, with its two-valued logic, its subject-predicate form, and its law of identity, is the ultimate in a communication system.

A study of other cultures and their languages brings humility, together with a deeper understanding of human behavior. It brings a new concept of human brotherhood. Though the language systems differ widely, yet in their order, harmony, and subtle power of apprehending reality, they show that all men are equal. This equality, Whorf observes, is invariant and independent of race, civilization, ethical development, degree of sophistication, science, art. Such a conclusion may shock those who hold that progress is linear, with Western man on its topmost rung; but it is the conclusion to which the study of linguistics strongly points.

Scientists have continually collided with the unconscious assumptions imbedded in language. If their work was to continue in an orderly way, they had to improve communication. So they have invented new languages, such as tensor calculus and multivalued logic; they have erected new concepts such as the operational definition; they have sharpened ordinary language to the most exact and economical statement possible. The results of this housecleaning have been spectacular. We will examine some of them in the next chapter.

Chapter 11

THE LANGUAGE OF SCIENCE

A man, like a cat, is curious about his environment and keeps investigating it. During most of his stay on this planet, man's investigations have been random, but in the past three hundred years they have become increasingly systematic. "Science" is a label for our attempts to find out how the universe works by means of careful observation rather than armchair speculation. The attempts range all the way from the very great events of the stellar depths to the very small events of the insides of atoms—"great" and "small" being always relative to a man.

Thorstein Veblen once described science as "idle curiosity," and that is certainly one motive. Another is to meet a specific human need, as in seeking the causes of polio, tuberculosis, cancer. In great industrial laboratories and in universities, large investigations once set up may be carried along on a kind of scientific momentum.

Common-sense world

Benjamin Lee Whorf gives us a vivid contrast:

Consider how the universe appears to any man, however wise . . . who has never heard one word of what science has discovered. To him the earth is flat; the sun is a shining object of small size that pops up daily above an eastern rim, moves through the upper air, and sinks below the western edge; obviously it spends the night somewhere underground. The sky is an inverted bowl

made of some blue material . . . the "solar system" has no meaning . . . bodies do not fall because of any "law of gravitation,"
but rather because there is nothing to hold them up. . . . For him
the blood does not circulate, nor the heart pump blood; he thinks
it is a place where love, kindness and thoughts are kept. Cooling
is not a removal of heat but an addition of "cold"; leaves are
green . . . from a "greenness" in them. . . .[1]

A well-worn phrase which I learned in boyhood and which
was then held to be the acme of common sense was: "You can
no more do it than you can fly!" Another definition of science
might be: "Knowledge which makes common sense obsolete."
Whorf's picture suggests the enormous stock of common sense
which nature peoples still cherish, and which the march of
science has forced Western peoples to abandon. This march
is a part and product of Western culture, and science, through
its dynamic force, is sweeping the world. As it sweeps, its
terminology is gradually modified, becoming more intercultural and less dependent on the Western world view.

We have seen how one's mother tongue may shape his world
view. The view of every culture is different, and all views are
distorted in various particulars. If an understanding of nature
is to go forward, some method must be found of correcting
these distortions, a method which will make the view invariant
for observers in all cultures. This suggests another way to describe "reality": an event which remains invariant from different viewpoints, or, as a scientist prefers to say, "invariant
under a given transformation of axes." The co-ordinate axes,
which scientists need to help them pin down and understand
events, are clarified both by diagrams and by mathematics.
Scientists and mathematicians are like acrobats in a circus; one
is always giving the other a helping hand. When scientists find
themselves blocked in a major investigation, they may have to
invent a new mathematical language, to express what they find.
Thus Newton took time off to develop integral calculus,
whereby the laws of gravitation could be clarified; and Einstein
used fresh mathematics with which to talk about relativity.

[1] "Language, Mind, and Reality," *ETC*, Spring 1952.

Every great new development in science involves a crisis in communication. How are scientists to tell themselves and their fellow scientists—let alone the layman—what the experiments show? The scientific method demands, furthermore, that whatever B finds can be so clearly communicated to A, that A can repeat the experiment and either reach the same conclusion, or report that B seems to be in error. The description is thus as important as the experiment, for if the latter cannot be communicated it might as well never have been made.

Three kinds of talk

Discussion about the nature of the universe has gone through three distinct stages in Western culture during the last 500 years. First came pre-scientific observations, heavily tinged with the word magic of the Middle Ages; then mechanistic or Newtonian talk, following Galileo; then Einsteinian or relativistic talk, after 1900 A.D.

In the late Middle Ages, observers divided nature into rigid categories, using the "is of identity" (A is A) as borrowed from Aristotle, and many animistic comparisons. Things acted the way they did, thinkers said in effect, because there was a little man inside them. Astrology and alchemy (forerunners of astronomy and chemistry) and magic numbers (especially the number 7) had great prestige, and were seriously discussed by the leading scholars of the time.

Medical men classified the human body according to four elements—earth, fire, air, and water. Each was supposed to affect a person's health, giving him qualities of coldness, warmth, dryness, and wetness. Disease, said the learned men, was due to a failure of proper balance among these essences. Black bile, residing in the spleen, was the equivalent of "earth"; blood was the equivalent of "air"; yellow bile, in the liver, was the equivalent of "fire"; phlegm, secreted by the brain, was the equivalent of "water." When out of sorts, I think I would rather trust myself to Whorf's Indians—who at least located kindness in the heart.

Philosophers of the period asked: What is the nature or

essence of this particular thing? They believed all animals and plants fell into fixed, unchanging categories, and once an event was classified, its essence was known. Scientific curiosity, to say nothing of the advance of medicine, was shackled by rigid verbal forms.

Clockwork universe

Galileo inaugurated the mechanistic period when he dropped his shot from the Leaning Tower in an early controlled experiment. He was curious to know whether heavy bodies fell faster than light bodies, as earlier savants had claimed. He found, to the astonishment of the world, that all bodies fall at the same rate (or would in a vacuum). Later observations by Galileo and others overturned the whole Ptolemaic system, which had placed the earth in the center of the universe. Galileo was tried for heresy and silenced, and Bruno burned at the stake. Scientists began to question essences and qualities and to report observations in terms of "matter," "force," "acceleration." Telescopes and microscopes were improved; results were measured and reduced to numbers; laboratories and observatories were built. By 1650, when the Royal Society was founded, curiosity about inanimate nature was operating freely and vigorously.

Descartes outlined a mathematical interpretation of nature: "Give me extension and motion and I will construct the universe," he said, and Newton proceeded to do so. For the first time men had discovered a systematic method of discovery. "The most astonishing victory of science," says Herbert Muller, "was not over religion, but over universal tradition, custom and common sense." [1] Scientists, as well as laymen, still believed, however, in an orderly universe where everything was explainable. "Nature does nothing in vain," said Newton.

Members of the Royal Society and other scientists thought in terms of Absolute Time, Absolute Space, Absolute Force,

[1] *The Uses of the Past,* Oxford, 1952.

Causation, Matter, and were convinced of the sublimity of Natural Law. These were tangible realities to them, not just convenient concepts. In Book I of Newton's *Principia* we read: "Absolute, True and Mathematical Time, of itself, and from its own nature, flows equably without regard to anything external, and by another name is called Duration."

The medieval world of essences had been replaced with an immense clockwork universe, says Muller, a static cosmos, rounded and finished, and capable of being completely known. Newton and the mechanists broke out of the Middle Ages to make great advances in human knowledge; their talk improved, but was still limited by their world view and the language that expressed it.

The relativity revolution

Einstein published his first treatise on relativity in 1905, and his theories were confirmed by a series of crucial experiments over the next twenty years. Relativity was not, however, readily accepted by Western thinkers. To most people today, as Muller points out, science still means the mechanistic philosophy of the eighteenth century. "This is what they attack or defend." One reason is that modern scientists are talking in languages which the rest of us do not understand.

Scientists today have changed not only their experimental techniques and equipment but their *basic assumptions*. They have at last made an end run around both Aristotle and Newton. Absolutes and entities have all but disappeared, together with the idea of a static universe capable of being completely known. They no longer say: "this is so," but rather: "there is a high probability that this is so"; or, "we provisionally accept this as being so until further investigation modifies it."

Some philosophers today have mistaken the new talk for a retreat to the Middle Ages, and lay down a syllogism to this effect: "Everything is electricity—electricity is unknown—therefore everything is unknown. Science has banished materialism, and metaphysics is again omnipotent." Such a conclusion is mostly ignorance, combined with wishful thinking. Scientists, by getting rid of Absolutes, stand on the firmest ground in their history. The new concepts have produced not only relativity, but quantum theory, electronics, colloid chemistry, genetics, Gestalt psychology, cultural anthropology, to name a few. The new sciences have come not only through the discovery of new facts, but from *new ways of talking about facts.*

Relativity and communication

Although I am not competent to discuss the physics of relativity except on a pretty high level of generality, the reader will perhaps allow me to say something about its tremendous impact on communication. The idea of relativity has invaded all the sciences, including those dealing with human relations, and stimulated an unprecedented mental keenness. To see nature and human nature primarily in terms of process and relations rather than rigid substances, releases a flood of fertilizing ideas.

Einstein succeeded in separating the observer from the observed, and thus derived a picture of the world relatively independent of the human senses.[1] To communicate what he had done, he employed the calculus of tensors which, in the words of E. T. Bell, "threshes out the laws of nature, separating the observer's eccentricities from what is independent of him, with the superb efficiency of a modern harvester."

To measure anything accurately, a man must take a meter stick, a clock, or other instruments, and make readings. Every reading depends on the finite velocity of light from instrument to eye, and on the finite velocity along nerve fibers from eye to brain. Although the finite velocity of light was indicated in 1676, the passage from object to brain was assumed to be instantaneous. Newton did not take the interval into consideration; Einstein did, and the whole splendid edifice of New-

[1] Here I will follow *The Tyranny of Words*, where I outlined the subject as well as I knew how at the time, and see no reason to change it much.

tonian physics had to be revised! Note carefully that Einstein did not destroy Newton's conclusions, he only limited them to terrestrial magnitudes, where they work well enough for practical purposes. In long stellar distances, however, and at great speeds, they become unreliable.

Einstein found no entities to correspond to the terms "length," "mass," "energy," "causality," "simultaneity," as set forth in Newtonian physics. This was a devastating shock to the scientific world, for physicists had long suspended their investigations into pure theory, considering that Newton had said the last word about these matters. Everything was snug and tidy to perpetuity.

Observe what happens next, for it is most important. When Einstein challenged the knowledge of the past, even the immortal Newton, why did scientists tolerate such brashness? *Because he was working in the area of fact, not opinion.* He frankly presented the principles of relativity as a theory derived mathematically, and proposed various tests whereby it would stand or fall. The tests included the motion of the perihelion of Mercury, the bending of light rays as they passed the sun, the displacement of certain lines in the spectrum. The motion of the perihelion has been verified with high precision, and the other two with close approximation. Scanning the proof, scientists, by the nature of their calling, had to agree that he was right. Their discipline made them bow to something many of them hated to believe.

The *fact* has always been for the physicist the one ultimate thing from which there is no appeal, and in the face of which the only possible attitude is a humility almost religious.[1]

The scientist, above all other callings, has both the training and the obligation to say, "I was wrong."

To illustrate the importance of *relations,* there is a very simple experiment which anyone can perform. Set out three pails, A, B, and C, and using a thermometer and the hot and

---

[1] P. W. Bridgman, *The Logic of Modern Physics.*

cold water faucets—and maybe an ice cube or two—give them
the following temperatures:

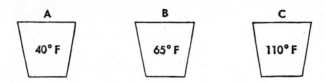

Now dip your right hand in C and hold it for a moment.
Take it out and put it in B. How does B feel? Cold! Put your
left hand in A, transfer it to B. How does the water in B feel
now? Hot!

If you reflect on this experiment, feeling it in your fingers,
you see that "coldness" and "hotness" are reactions inside your
skin and not fixed properties out there in nature at all. The
same pail of water can feel either "hot" or "cold," depending
on where your hand has last been; the *relation* is what counts.

Henri Poincaré has remarked on the baleful effect on
physics of the word "heat." The language structure has caused
us to think of "heat," or "*chaleur,*" as a substance, and scientists
spent centuries looking for something in nature to correspond
to the word. But "heat" is only a symbol for a relation.

Here is a bar of steel; a thermometer shows its temperature
to be 60°. Somebody inquires the temperature of an electron
in the bar. I answer smartly, "Sixty degrees." You answer, "I
do not know." But our talk does not fit the submicroscopic
level. Temperature depends on molecular vibration; and to
have anything to correspond to it, one must have at least two
molecules. An electron is part of an atom, which is part of a
molecule, so there is nothing to be called temperature in its
make-up.

Operational definition

Dr. Bridgman, a Nobel prize winner, gives the clearest account I have seen of the new talk in science, in his book just
referred to. The attitude of the physicist henceforward, he
says, must be rigorously objective, recognizing no "eternal

principles." We must not be knocked galley-west again by a new discovery such as relativity. We must give up expecting nature to be embraced in any one formula. It may turn out that this is possible, but our thinking should not demand it. Concepts must be so ordered that present experience does not bind the future.

After Newton, the door was firmly shut, and when Einstein broke it down the faculty practically froze. We must keep the door open, says Bridgman, and get used to fresh air. Newton's laws were a great advance over Aristotle's; Einstein found a closer fit to nature than did Newton; tomorrow, or in a hundred years, another genius may find a still closer fit.[1] But nobody will ever find a perfect fit. The clockwork universe is beyond repair.

Before Einstein, physical concepts as we have seen were usually defined in terms of *properties*. Now they are defined in terms of *operations*. To define "length," says Bridgman, we take some meter sticks or other instruments, and with our hands perform certain operations. "The concept of length is fixed when the operations by which length is measured are fixed." We do not go to the dictionary to define length, but to the laboratory. *It is impossible to exaggerate the importance of this idea for students of communication.*

We take the meter stick and measure the sides of a house lot. This gives us one concept of "length." Next, we stand in front of the lot and measure a trolley car moving down the street. The car, unlike the lot, is not at rest and the operation has to change to allow for velocity. "Length" becomes a function of velocity, "time" gets into it, and we shall need a stop watch.

Next we want to measure the "length," or distance, between Jupiter and the sun, at a certain moment. We discard meter sticks and stop watches and move on to telescopes, for length

[1] Einstein in 1953 proposed a "unified field equation," to embrace both relativity and quantum theory, and asked for verification. Most scientists seemed to doubt that practical experiments could be set up to verify it.

is now optical. "To say that a star is 105 light-years distant is actually and conceptually a different kind of thing than to say that a telegraph pole is 100 feet away." Turning from stars to molecules, we discard telescopes and make use of electronic microscopes, with quite different operations. At very short "lengths," the concept merges into the field equations of electricity.

Thus "length" is not something which an object possesses, as a man possesses a shirt; it is a word in our heads. Its meaning is determined by what we do, rather than by what we say, and meaning shifts with the doing. To use the single word "length" for house lots, moving trolley cars, stars, and molecules, may be convenient—but is always risky. Some Great Thinker may try to turn it into stone at any moment, declaring that "length is length, now and forever." Instead, semanticists say length$_1$, length$_2$, length$_3$.

The operational approach makes knowledge about nature no longer absolute, but relative. The operation is performed relative to some standard, say the meter stick; and concepts emerge which are definite and verifiable. Scientific concepts, says Bridgman, must be constructable out of the materials of human experience. When they move beyond the reach of operations, they become speculations which cannot be verified. Knowledge advances when we find out how events are related, and in what order—another way of saying that knowledge is structural.

Absolute "length" is a meaningless concept; but the lengths of house lots and solar distances can be measured and put to use. No operations can be performed which will isolate absolute "time" or absolute "space." If we think of time as something in and of itself, says Bridgman, we find nothing in nature to correspond. Scientists observe "local times" on the earth, and "extended times" in the stellar depths. A light-year is a standard measurement in extended time, but it means *space* traversed in a year's time. We must not talk about the *age* of a beam of light, though the idea of "age" is useful in local "times" here on earth. We must not allow ourselves to think of events taking place in Arcturus *now.* "It is difficult to inhibit this habit of thought, but we must learn to do it." (Your author finds it very difficult but not impossible.)

In relativity, time changes with velocity, a notion which destroys the idea of time as a smooth, eternal flow. If you could travel comfortably at the speed of light (186,000 miles per second), you could theoretically live forever. Or if you could arrange to travel a bit faster, you could join the heroine of the old college limerick:

> There was a young lady named Bright
> Whose movements were faster than light;
>> She went out one day
>> In a relative way
> And returned on the previous night.

Delicate operations can be performed to show that a "minute" for you walking in your garden is not quite the same as a "minute" for a jet pilot in the air above. It may be objected that this is all very confusing. On the contrary, it was the old language which confused and blocked the scientists. When Einstein showed a way around it, knowledge leaped forward!

Meaningless questions

The operational definition dissolves many a Great Question which has puzzled philosophers and savants down the ages:

May space be bounded?
May time have a beginning and end?
Are there parts of nature forever beyond our detection?
What is the ultimate nature of matter?

Seizing a meter stick can we perform an operation to clarify the question? If the answer is no, if it is beyond the operational approach, the Great Question becomes a Meaningless Question. We can then relax, for the query is only a verbalization. It may deserve a college bull session, perhaps, but not serious consideration. Some day an operation may be found— though probably not for the four questions posed above. Until that happens, we can argue about it if we want, but we need not expect to find an answer.

Meaningless questions are even more prevalent in social science than in physics, and operational definitions will dissolve them with equal dispatch. Kurt Lewin never hesitated to advise a student: "Only ask the question in your research that you can answer with the techniques you can use. If you can't learn to ignore questions that you are not prepared to answer definitely, you will never answer any." [1]

To the Great Question which stumped medieval savants, concerning the number of angels who could dance on the head of a pin, Wendell Johnson replies: "Bring me a pin, and some angels, and we'll soon find out!" Here is an assortment of meaningless questions in social science and allied subjects:

Is environment more important than heredity?
What is economic value?
Is modern art really art?
Is my trouble physical or mental?
Why was I born?
Is Unitarianism really Christianity?

If you can locate an operation to answer any of these, I wish you would let me know. Meanwhile it is unnecessary to get excited about them—or hundreds like them.

The scientific method

A short and generous definition of the scientific method might be: "Any activity that produces dependable, invariant knowledge, which all competent observers can agree has a high probability of being correct." Usually the method involves three steps: (1) observation, (2) a hypothesis or theory to explain the observation, and (3) verification. The Greeks were strong on the first two and weak on the third. Scientists since Galileo have insisted on number three.

Scientific method demands language clear enough to enable B to repeat A's experiments, and report to the world whether

[1] *Field Theory in Social Science.*

the verification is adequate. Scientific ethics permits no secret formulas and no national monopolies, which is why our atomic scientists have been so disturbed about "secrecy." The insistence of the Soviet government on "Marxian physics" and "Stalinist biology" is regarded by scientists as puerile nonsense; science is not amenable to ideological interpretation.

Meditating on these matters, and watching one's day-to-day activities, it becomes obvious that everybody uses the scientific approach unconsciously in many small personal problems. The approach is exceedingly simple, but it is scientific in the sense that a theory about a problem is verified by an experiment, sometimes a controlled experiment. Here is a rough sample:

I take a broom to brush the lines on my tennis court, following a regular pattern of walking up, down, and across. It takes about ten minutes. One day, before brushing, I stopped and studied the court. Was I taking too many steps? Suppose I changed the pattern and walked so and then so, wouldn't it save time? First observation, you see, then a hypothesis or theory. I grasp the broom and follow the hypothesis. It does indeed seem a shorter route, but is it really? Verification is easy if I pace the distance by the old method, and then by the new. I find to my considerable astonishment that the new route is about eighteen feet longer. My theory, on verification, explodes!

If a woman in her kitchen cooks, let us say, a mess of peas in two different ways, and has the family compare the result, she is performing a simple controlled experiment. A carpenter or a plumber is constantly using the scientific method on this elementary level. If laymen could realize that they too are embryo scientists, the gulf between scientist and layman might not seem so wide.

Summary of scientific talk

I have not tried in this chapter to exhibit my grasp of science. I become easily baffled in high-powered mathematics and modern physics. I am enormously interested, however, in how scientists develop new ways to talk and think. Forget the physics recited here but do not forget the way a modern physicist gets around the limitations of his mother tongue. Let us recapitulate some of his methods:

1. New mathematical languages.

2. Multivalued rather than two-valued (either-or) thinking. In 1930, Lucasiewics and Tarski invented a workable and consistent many-valued logic to replace the formal logic of Aristotle, which had crippled Western thinking for two millenniums. Long before 1930, however, scientists had been escaping from two-valued logic. The rest of us, especially politicians, still cherish it.

3. *Operational definitions*, which flush out absolutes, verbal entities, and meaningless questions. Instead of going to the dictionary, scientists go for meter sticks and clocks or Geiger counters. The procedure can also be used to clarify social and political problems. Try to perform an operational definition of "big business" or "free enterprise."

4. The principle of *relativity*, and the freedom gained by thinking in terms of relations rather than rigid substances.

5. The idea of change as a *process*, rather than as simple linear cause-and-effect. In a process, a given effect is the product of many causes, and is in turn a cause for further effects and so on, in a developing spiral. Everything in nature moves constantly in a process of change, slow or fast as the case may be. For a ripe apple in the sun the process is rapid; for the terrifying cliffs of Everest, slow; for the solar system it is—we hope—subglacial. No event is exactly the same *now* as it was a moment ago. Says Julian Huxley in *Evolution in Action:* "From the condensation of nebulae to the development of the infant in the womb, from the formation of the earth as a planet to the making of a political decision, all are processes in time; and they are all interrelated as partial processes within the single universal process of reality."

6. Scientific prediction is taking the form of *probabilities*, rather than complete certainties. Eddington, we recall, was not 100 per cent sure that his scientific elbow would not go through the spaces between the atoms of his scientific table,

though the probability, he admitted, was small. Thinking in terms of probabilities disarms the dogmatist, and encourages a decent humility in the face of nature. Probabilities in physics are higher than in psychology, but any result consistently better than 50 per cent indicates science rather than chance.

7. *Statistical thinking* is part of probability theory. "The world," says George Boas, "is made up of individual events, no two of which are exactly alike, but any selected class of which acts with statistical regularity." [1] The behavior of a single molecule in a gas is unpredictable, but the behavior of all the molecules in a given container can be calculated. We have already noted in Chapter 4 how Ashby applied statistical thinking to his design for a brain.

These seven ways of talking about nature are not all the new concepts of the revolution in science, but they are among the more important. Most of them have been developed since 1900. The sheer power of the new thinking needs no argument, as it changes the face of the world.

Some of the changes are destructive. We may wish that they had not occurred, but the current debate whether science is "good" or "bad" is another meaningless question. We recall the words of Wendell Johnson: "It is not by applying the *method* of science that we have wrought destruction. We have done it by applying the *results* of science in the very areas of our experience where we have failed to apply the method."

If science attempts to find out how the universe works, semantics attempts to give ordinary talk some of the benefits of the new talk in science. It is the core of Korzybski's work. How far has this attempt succeeded?

[1] *Our New Ways of Thinking.*

Chapter 12

EMINENT SEMANTICISTS

Alfred Korzybski, who died in 1950, was the originator of what he called "General Semantics," a discipline which took the study of language and meaning into some pretty deep mathematical and neurological waters. It is still early to tell whether his contribution was as epoch-making as some starry-eyed followers believe, but it was unquestionably an important addition to the whole subject of communication. In the next chapter we shall look rather closely at his special contribution, and meanwhile observe him here as an individual.

I shall never cease to be grateful for the wholesome shock my nervous system received when I first read Korzybski's magnum opus, *Science and Sanity*. It forced me to realize some of the unconscious assumptions imbedded in the language which I as a writer had been calmly accepting. Nature, he said, does not work the way our language works; and he proceeded to give some suggestions for a closer relationship.

As I knew him in his later years—he was 70 when he died—he had the general aspect of an amiable Buddha, bald as a newel post, with kindly, intelligent eyes behind vast, round spectacles, and with a rich Polish accent. He wore as a kind of uniform a khaki shirt, open at the throat, which sometimes kept him out of hotel dining rooms. He was rude, formidable, over-verbalized and strangely appealing—for all I know, an authentic genius. Poland has produced more than her share of mathematical philosophers.

Piecing together parts of his background, we note that he was a count from a proud and ancient family, with an estate in the country and large properties in Warsaw. Trained as a chemical engineer at the Warsaw Polytechnic Institute, he read widely in law, mathematics, and philosophy. He was also, we are told, handsome and a bit wild, the traditional young noble-man. In World War I he served on the Grand Duke's staff, was three times wounded, and then came to America as an artillery expert for the Czarist Russian Army. He added Eng-lish to his five Continental languages; and while he never got his phonemes straight, he acquired great fluency and came to prefer it. He wrote his books and articles in English and thought in this language. In 1919 he married a talented Ameri-can painter.

He published two books and a score of papers, all hard to read. It took me two years of reasonably steady application to bulldoze my way through *Science and Sanity*, and I do not think this sluggish pace was altogether my fault. By a curious paradox, Korzybski, who had dedicated his life to clearing communication lines, had the utmost difficulty in clearing his own—at least in English prose. When he conducted an oral seminar, with a full display of kinesics and his extraordinary accent, the line was far more open. I can see him now, reach-ing stout, muscular arms into the air and wiggling two fingers of each hand to make the "quote" sign, somewhat the way Churchill made the "V" sign. In semantics the quote sign around a word usually means: "Beware, it's loaded!"

"Time-binding"

Korzybski's chief claim to fame will rest, I think, on *Science and Sanity*, difficult as it is. His earlier book, *The Manhood of Humanity*, is shorter and easier to read.[1] Its thesis is that man is distinguished from the rest of earth's creatures by his language and the ability to pass down what he learns from one generation to the next. Even the most intelligent elephant has to begin over with each generation. "The proper life of man

[1] See bibliography.

as man, is not life-in-space like that of the animals, but life-in-time. . . . Bound-up time is literally the core and substance of civilization."

This passing-down process, to which Korzybski gives the curious name "time-binding," we described earlier when discussing the culture concept, noting that the invention of writing greatly speeded it. Scientists generally confirm the thesis. Both the anthropologists and such sociologists as W. F. Ogburn anticipated Korzybski. He believed, however, that the theory was new. Once the idea was mastered, he thought, the race would achieve "manhood," become fully mature, and shake off its infantilisms, verbal and otherwise.

All through history man has been groping to find his place . . . to discover his role in the "nature of things." To this end he must first discover himself and his "essential nature" . . . then perhaps our civilizations will pass by peaceful evolution from their childhood to the manhood of humanity.

Cultural change, unfortunately, can go downhill as well as up, but the opportunity is undeniably there to find our manhood, as knowledge about nature and human nature accumulates. This aspiration Korzybski shares, however, with many earlier writers and idealists—the early Utopians, for instance, and H. G. Wells. I myself used to cherish a private dream which I called "the man on the cliff." He was boldly outlined against the sky—the man we all might be if we put accumulated knowledge really to work.

Following *The Manhood of Humanity*, Korzybski spent ten years of intensive work writing *Science and Sanity*. It was published in 1933 at the bottom of the depression—hardly an auspicious year to bring out a book, especially a costly one. In it Korzybski explored relativity, quantum theory, colloid chemistry, biology, neurology, psychology, psychiatry, mathematical logic, and what was then available by other students of communication and semantics. Later, he urged his classes to read Whorf on linguistics. The question he set himself to answer was how the structure of language could be brought closer to the structure of the space-time world. He cited the new talk of physicists, following the Einstein revolution. If scientists could teach themselves to communicate more clearly, why should not the rest of us do likewise?

Definitions

Before summarizing what Korzybski discovered, let us glance at some of his forerunners in the field of semantics. The word first appeared in dictionaries about fifty years ago, defined as "studies having to do with signification or meaning." The International Society for General Semantics has issued two short, comprehensive definitions, as follows:

Semantics . . . The systematic study of meaning.
General Semantics . . . The study and improvement of human evaluative processes with special emphasis on the relation to signs and symbols, including language.

Note the accent on "evaluation" in defining General Semantics, and the absence of the word "is" in defining both. Whenever we become conscious about the meaning of a context—"What is the Senator trying to say?" . . . "How can I tell her more clearly?" . . . "What kind of double talk is that?" —we are practicing elementary semantics.

The goals of General Semantics are three:

1. To help the individual evaluate his world. As our environment grows more and more complex, greater precision is needed to interpret it.

2. To improve communication between A and B, also within and between groups of all sizes.

3. To aid in clearing up mental illness. In Chapter 24, we will describe the brilliant work of Dr. Douglas Kelley with battle shock cases during the last war.

Dictionary definitions are useful, but the semanticists make no obeisances to verbal absolutes. David Guralnik, who supervised a recent drastic revision of Webster, reported that his friends were shocked at his temerity.[1] He was shattering their faith in the infallibility of "the dictionary," and probably, by

[1] Paper read before Rowfant Club, reprinted by World Publishing Company, 1953.

extension, of the Scriptures and other sacred writs. Dictionaries, like certain brands of cigarettes, he said, are supposed to
be untouched by human hands. Another serious difficulty was
what he called the "semantic merry-go-round that leads the
reader a wild chase from one entry to another only to bring
him back in a mad finish to his starting point." *"Gangrene:*
mortification of a part of the body. . . . *Mortification:* gangrene." He had to be careful, too, of his etymologies, avoiding
anything that might suggest Mark Twain's famous derivation
of *Middletown* from *Moses*—you drop the "oses" and add the
"iddletown."

From Aristotle to Bertrand Russell

Resolved to refute the logic of Aristotle, Korzybski goes so
far as to call General Semantics "a non-Aristotelian system,"
and invents the symbol, Ā, to abbreviate "non-Aristotelian."
We must give Aristotle his due, however; for along with his
creative curiosity about nature, he was also genuinely curious
about the power of words. Linguistics, cultural anthropology,
and relativity being two thousand years away, he sometimes
mistook the peculiar structure of his own Greek for the universal laws of thought, a most natural error.

Aristotle's formal logic—which we shall look at in the next
chapter—was a great achievement for the time, but today it is
hardly more useful than the medicine of Galen. Galen has
passed respectably into the history of medicine; but Aristotle's
logic continues to distort our use of reason. It is still taught in
the universities, still in active use by philosophers, lawyers,
theologians, and essayists. A standard political speech would
be impossible without the aid of its simple two-valued syl-
logisms.

One of the first students to question the Aristotelian logic
was Bishop William of Occam, who insisted that "entities are
not to be multiplied beyond what is necessary." This principle
was nicknamed in academic circles "Occam's razor," because
it sheared off lush verbalisms. The Bishop was troubled by
the clouds of entities, essences, classes, and Absolutes released
by the Aristotelian laws. The Bacons, both Roger and Francis,

were likewise skeptical. It was Galileo, of course, who broke clean away from Aristotle by substituting experiment and observation for *a priori* reasoning. Instead of deriving the number of teeth in a horse's mouth by logic, it is better to go out in the barn and count them.

A fascinating book might be written on the history of the revolt against language. The age of scientific inquiry, following Galileo, saw an increasing number of first-rate minds questioning the validity of verbal processes. In the last hundred years the critics include Jeremy Bentham, William James, Alexander Bryan Johnson, George Herbert Mead, John Dewey, Ludwig Wittgenstein, Bertrand Russell, F. C. S. Schiller, Rudolf Carnap, E. T. Bell.

Allen Upward, a British philologist, pursued the word "idealism" all over Western cultures in an attempt to get at its meaning.[1] His initial bouts with the dictionary were unsatisfactory, thus:

Mind, defined as thoughts, sentiments, et cetera.
Thought, defined as operations of the mind, ideas, images formed in the mind.

Combining the two, Upward gets a kind of recurring decimal: Mind equals thought equals images formed in the images formed in the images . . . the same tautology we observed with gangrene-mortification.

H. G. Wells was a searching questioner of verbal processes. In 1891, just turned thirty, he wrote a monograph called "Scepticism of the Instrument," in which he quoted a geologist on rock classifications: "They pass into one another by insensible gradations"—a phrase not lightly to be dismissed. This is true, said Wells, of most things in nature. "Every species is vague, every term goes cloudy at its edges, and so in my way of thinking, relentless logic is only another phrase for a stupidity—for a sort of intellectual pigheadedness."

Bronislaw Malinowski, the anthropologist, reported that it was impossible for him to learn a native language unless he spent considerable time in hunting, fishing, and living the lives

[1] *The New Word.*

of the people who spoke it. This sequence illustrates again the intimate connection between language and culture. People talk what they do; that is how talking began.

Lady Viola Welby published *What is Meaning?* in 1903, shortly before Einstein announced his first great work on relativity. A serious student of language and communication, she was perhaps the founder of modern semantics. A few years later Bertrand Russell and A. N. Whitehead, in their profound work, *Principia Mathematica*, were forced to deal with language and verbal logic, as well as mathematical symbols. They evolved what they called the Theory of Types, to offset "illegitimate totalities" concealed in language. Here is an example:

```
+-----------------------+
|                       |
|   ALL STATEMENTS      |
|                       |
|   IN THIS SQUARE      |
|                       |
|   ARE FALSE           |
|                       |
+-----------------------+
```

If we suppose the proposition inside the square to be true, we must conclude it is false. But if we begin by supposing it false, we have to end by finding it true. The "illegitimate totality" in this logical run-around is the little word "all." The "all" must be limited so that a statement about that totality must itself fall outside the totality. *Principia Mathematica* is an excellent example of scientists in the throes of trying to remove shackles imposed by their mother tongue.

The meaning of meaning

A very important landmark in semantic history was the publication in 1921 of *The Meaning of Meaning* by C. K. Ogden and I. A. Richards. The approach was more literary than mathematical, but the conclusions paralleled those of Bridgman, Korzybski, Whorf. It is always exciting when tunnelers from different sides of a mountain manage to meet in the center.

Ogden and Richards present us with the famous triangle where the *event*, or object in nature, is called the "referent"; the brain is the area of "reference"; and the word is the "symbol." The sign comes to us from an object, say a dog; we proceed counterclockwise and refer to memory traces in the brain; presently, we utter the word "dog."

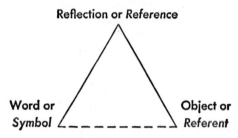

The lesson of the triangle is to keep the object in mind as one talks, to *find the referent* of one's discourse. Too much human talk, as Occam noted, razor in hand, is in abstract terms, where the mind manipulates the words, but loses sight of the space-time events to which the words refer. On this high level logic can be vigorously employed, but it is the logic of Zeno proving that the tortoise can outrun Achilles, the logic of the number of angels that can dance on a pin, the logic of the inside of the square, cited by Russell.

Let us imagine a high-level discussion between A and B about dogs. "All dogs are trustworthy," says A, with a dog lover's rapt expression. "Try trusting one of them with a five-dollar steak," says B, with a dog hater's glare. The difference can develop into a stupendous row on this "all dogs" level. But if A and B can come down to an inspection of some actual dogs, they will find, of course, that $Rover_1$ is so savage he must be constantly chained up; that $Rover_2$ is so gentle he is welcome at a cat show; and that $Rover_3$ to $Rover_n$ are at various stations of trustworthiness between these limits. The variations could be plotted to form the standard frequency distribution curve. By finding the referent down below, A and B avoid a meaningless battle up above. Agreement can be reached in ordinary affairs, as well as in science, when both A and B can point to the same dog, pat his head and say, "You see what I mean?" Up on the high level, anything can happen. "The ablest logicians," say Ogden and Richards, "are precisely those who are led to evolve the most fantastic systems by the aid of their verbal technique. . . ."

Find the referent

"All dogs" cause trouble enough, but where are the referents for those higher and vaguer terms which form the common coin of discussion in political and economic affairs? Newspapers today in America carry many words like these below. What do they mean? What can A and B both point to so they may come to some agreement?

American Way	Leftist, Rightist
Appeasement	Loyalty, Security
Balanced Budget	Monopoly
Big Business	New Deal
Bureaucracy	Politicians
Communism	Socialized Medicine
Creeping Socialism	Spending
Democracy	Statism
Fascism	Subversives
Free Enterprise	Totalitarianism
Free World	Wall Street
Government Interference	Welfare State
Labor Agitators	

Two or more Americans can start an argument on any of these terms which may rage for hours without a referent in sight, beyond "Uh, I knew a man whose brother had it straight that—" Yet below and behind these words are events and issues of the first importance which Americans must face.

Every item in the above list belongs in Korzybski's upraised fingers: "Quote—unquote. Beware, it's loaded!" They are in marked contrast to such low-order terms as 100° F., my cat Boots, pure oxygen, the key of C♯ minor, 40 mph. When I was writing *The Tyranny of Words*, everybody was talking, if not shouting loudly, about "Fascism." I asked a hundred persons from various walks of life to tell me what they meant by Fascism. They shared a common dislike for the term, but no two agreed what it meant. There were fifteen distinguishable concepts in the answers submitted. This gave an idea of the chaos involved in high-order terms.

Today Fascism is out of style, and everybody is talking about "Communism." Reporters from the *Capital Times* in Madison, Wisconsin (1953), asked almost 200 persons on the street to answer the question: "What is a Communist?" Here are some of the replies:

Farmer: "They are no good to my notion. I can't figure out what they are."

Stenographer: "If a person didn't have a religion I would be tempted to believe he was a Communist."

Housewife: "I really don't know what a Communist is. I think they should throw them out of the White House."

High-school student: "A Communist is a person who wants war."

Office worker: "Anyone that stands for things that democracy does not."

Not only was there no agreement, but 123 out of 197 persons interviewed frankly admitted *they did not know what a Communist is*. All this came at a time when Congressional investigations were flooding the newspapers with the "Communist Menace" inside America. The danger of drowning we know about; but where shall the wayfaring citizen point to the specific danger of Communism within our borders, in the light of this exhibit? [1]

We will analyze a number of these terms in the pages to follow. Here we repeat the admonition: "Beware, they're loaded!" Find the referent; keep your eye on that dog.

The semantics of poetry

In addition to *The Meaning of Meaning*, with its insistence on the referent, Ogden and Richards have each done sound work in communication; Ogden in Basic English, his partner

[1] In Chapter 21 the author will try to define: *Who is a Communist?*

as a writer and lecturer on poetry and criticism. Richards, who has taught at Harvard since 1939, constantly emphasizes the importance of communication and the difficulty of conveying complex meanings. Poetry, of course, tries to convey the most complex meanings expressible in language, and when it succeeds can wield great power.

A measure of its failures appears in Richards' famous study, *Practical Criticism*. He tells how he presented a variety of poems, unsigned, to a large and able class for evaluation. Not only did these readers disagree, sometimes diametrically, about every poem, but they often failed to comprehend either its sense or its intention. (None of the poems was especially obscure. What these readers would make of samples of "modern" poetry is past imagining!)

The poet's intention, says Richards, is the first thing for the reader to consider. What is he trying to say? Richards lists ten difficulties the reader meets; for instance, the tendency to "stock responses . . . whenever a poem seems to, or does, involve views and emotions already fully prepared in the reader's mind, so that . . . the button is pressed." Another difficulty Richards calls "doctrinal adhesions," meaning ideological preconceptions in the reader. The whole study illustrates in a startling way what can happen to messages when they reach the semantic decoder.

Common experience is needed to understand any message. "In difficult cases the vehicle of communication must inevitably be complex. . . . What would be highly ambiguous by itself becomes definite in a suitable context. . . . Even in such shallow communication as . . . merely making out the letters in a handwriting this principle is all-important. . . .

"Difficulty of communication . . . should not be confused with the difficulty of the matter communicated. . . . Some very difficult calculations, for example, can be communicated with ease." [1] "The view that meanings belong to words in their own right," says Richards scornfully, "is a branch of sorcery, a relic of the magical theory of names." [2] He pretty well de-

---

[1] *Principles of Literary Criticism.*
[2] *Philosophy of Rhetoric.*

molishes the one-proper-meaning superstition when he says:
"What a word means is the missing parts of the contexts from
which it draws its delegated efficiency."

Richards and Ogden in their side of the mountain emphasized language and the arts. Korzybski in his emphasized the
language of science. The tunnelers met and let in light from
both directions. They meet for us who read them, though I
believe the two schools were not in the closest harmony.

The last twenty years

Science and Sanity made readers slowly, partly because reading rates were slow. Gradually, however, a large circle of interest was built up. My book, *The Tyranny of Words*, published in 1938, was the first attempt to interpret both semantics
and Korzybski's General Semantics for the layman. Other interpretations soon appeared. The total influence of *Science
and Sanity* must now be very considerable, both in America
and abroad. The rancor of some of its critics would indicate
this, if nothing else.

S. I. Hayakawa's *Language in Action,* a Book-of-the-Month,
appeared in 1941, a clear and readable exposition of semantics.
Irving J. Lee of Northwestern University, Wendell Johnson
of Iowa State, Anatol Rapoport of the University of Chicago,
among others, have contributed important books to the gathering literature.[1]

Two organizations were founded, the Institute of General
Semantics, now under the direction of M. Kendig, through
which Korzybski conducted his famous seminars; and the International Society for General Semantics, which, among other
activities, publishes the quarterly journal *ETC,* well edited
by Hayakawa. Many local groups have been formed. By 1953
courses were being given in more than one hundred American
universities, especially favored by speech departments, while
a number of elementary schools were experimenting with
semantic methods to make children better masters of their
language.

[1] See bibliography for these and other titles.

Chapter 13

KORZYBSKI'S CONTRIBUTION

Korzybski often used the simile of the map. A map of the territory, he says, useful as it may be to travelers, is not the territory. Similarly, language is not the world around us, but rather an indispensable guide to that world. The map, however, is worthless if it shows the traveler a structure different from the terrain he sets out upon. Structure in this context means order and relations, what comes after what. If the order of cities on our map does not agree with the order on the territory, we may find ourselves driving to Montreal when we hoped to go to Chicago—in which case it would be better to steer by the sun.

However detailed the map may be, it can never tell *all* about the territory. Similarly, language cannot tell "all" about an event; some characteristics will always be omitted. At the end of every verbal definition, if it is pushed far enough, there are undefined terms; we reach the silent level where we can point, but we cannot say. If there is nothing to point to, the communication line may break. This is one reason why the modern physicists were driven to devise operational definitions.

Apple₁ and Apple₂

Korzybski places an apple on the table and asks us to describe it. We can say it is round, red, appetizing, with a short stem, and one worm hole. But carefully as we may observe it, in the laboratory or out, we can never tell *all* the characteristics of the apple, especially as we approach the submicroscopic level. What all the billions of atoms are up to nobody knows except in the most general, statistical way.

Korzybski sets another apple beside the first, of similar shape and color. Is it identical? We are inclined to think so, but looking more closely we see that the stem is shorter, the red color is less vivid, and there are two worm holes instead of one. Apple$_2$ is not apple$_1$. By the same token, amoeba$_2$ is not amoeba$_1$; Adam$_2$ is not Adam$_1$. Nothing in nature is ever identical with anything else if the observations are carried far enough. Beware of false identifications, says Korzybski; you will only confuse yourself and your hearers. Beware of thinking of "Baptists," "Americans," "businessmen," "workers," as identical. Whatever characteristics they may have in common, they have others which are different. Frank Costello and President Eisenhower are both "Americans."

But certainly an object is identical with itself. Or is it? Let us leave the apple on the table for a month. Is it the "same" apple; is apple$_{Oct. 1}$ the same as apple$_{Nov. 1}$? Obviously not; the clear skin has turned brown and wrinkled, and the firm flesh, soft and rotten. Apple$_1$ accordingly is a *process*, changing its characteristics imperceptibly in a minute, slightly in a day, drastically in a month. Nothing in nature is quite what it was a moment ago. Even the Matterhorn wears slowly away, as rock avalanches come down the *couloirs*. Diamonds last longer than apples, but not forever. Some of the new isotopes have a half life of only a few seconds. Be careful of thinking of apples, diamonds, people, or nations as unchanging events. Remember to correct the verbal map which implies that they do not change. Said Korzybski:

The only possible link between the *objective* world and the verbal world is *structural*. If the two structures are similar, then the empirical world becomes intelligible to us—we "understand," can adjust ourselves. . . . If the two structures are not similar . . . we do not "know," we do not "understand," the given problems are "unintelligible" to us . . . we do not know how to adjust ourselves.

Korzybski, as we have said, was profoundly influenced by the new language of science. Thermodynamics, he observed, could not have been built on such loose terms as "hot" and "cold"; a language showing minute quantitative changes and relations had to be developed. Also science could not have advanced without Arabic numerals and their invaluable zero. "Every child is now more skillful in arithmetic than great experts before the decimal system."

Our languages, continues Korzybski, are full of primitive metaphysical concepts, and the effect is like emery dust in a delicate machine. Whorf, we remember, came to a similar conclusion. General Semantics seeks to substitute a good lubricant for the emery. "We usually have sense enough to fit our shoes to our feet, but not sense enough to revise older methods of orientation to fit the facts."

Stop, look, and listen

How shall we go about revising older methods? Korzybski suggests five little warning signals in our talking and writing:

(1) the symbol *etc.* to remind us of characteristics left out;
(2) *index numbers* to break up false identifications;
(3) *dates* to remind us that objects are in process, in a state of constant change;
(4) *hyphens* to show that events are connected and nature is all of a piece;
(5) *quotes* to remind us that the term we are using is high up the abstraction ladder, and so, "Beware, it's loaded!"

When I first collected and listed these warning signals from the pages of *Science and Sanity*, I thought them rather elementary. Yet I have been using them constantly in my thinking for fifteen years. They work, and their very simplicity makes them the easier to employ.

Etc.

By writing, or by thinking, *etc.* after a statement, we remind ourselves that characteristics have been left out; we have not told *all*. The semantic quarterly is called *ETC*, and thereby warns the reader that it is not the sum total of wisdom.

William James once put it this way: "The word 'and' trails along after every sentence." Forgetting this, we become candidates for the know-it-all fraternity. *Etc.* helps us to keep alert in complicated territory, to delay the dogmatic cocksure response.

Advertisers may tell us about a beautiful streamlined television set with polished walnut cabinet which is being practically given away. The natural reaction of an experienced shopper is: "What are they *not* telling us?" He is using the equivalent of *etc.* on the advertising copy, wondering about the characteristics left out.

In employing this warning signal, however, a warning is in order. Never expect to round up *all* the missing characteristics, for, as we have seen, they are unlimited. Look for enough major characteristics to make a reasonable decision. You will need only a few for a commercial television set, more for a conclusion about U.S. policy in China.

Index numbers

We have been using these little signals in past chapters, and they serve to remind us of the diversity of nature, and of the diversities among human beings: $Adam_1$ is not $Adam_2$. They are useful to break up stereotypes, fixed ideas, and ideological convictions about "Catholics," "Yankees," "women," "Jews," "Negroes," "Japs," "Wall Streeters." How often do we say, "Politicians are no good, look at Pendergast," then in the next breath praise the integrity of Senator Douglas? $Politician_1$ is not $politician_2$.

Index numbers keep us out of the pitfalls of formal logic. Here are Aristotle's three famous laws:

1. *The law of identity.* A is A.
2. *The law of the excluded middle.* Everything is either A or not-A.
3. *The law of contradiction.* Nothing is both A and not-A.

The letter A is the letter A, all right, and the word "Apple" is the word "Apple," with five letters and phonemes all correct. The law of identity works satisfactorily with words in our heads, but for events outside our heads, such as Korzybski's apple, it does not work without extensive qualification. $Apple_1$ is *not* $Apple_2$. An object is not even identical with itself over a period of time. The fresh sweet apple rots away.

Aristotle's second and third laws are full of mantraps. Take, for instance, the distinction between plants and animals—A and not-A. There is a little organism called *euglena*, which becomes green in abundant sunlight and behaves like a "plant," but when the sunlight disappears, it digests carbohydrates like an "animal." Euglena is thus either a "plant" or an "animal," depending on the time of day. Or, perhaps better, it is neither plant nor animal, it falls outside the categories. Medical history shows authentic cases of men being converted into women surgically, and vice versa. In 1953 the newspapers made much of an attractive young woman who was recently a man. The person has been both a "man" and a "woman," thus denying the law of contradiction.

Formal logic starts with language and tries to force nature into its verbal categories. The scientist starts with a wordless observation of nature, and then tells what he observes, constructing new categories as needed. Index numbers help us begin the analysis at the right end.

Dates

Korzybski's time signal is especially useful for events in process, where the change is clearly recognizable. Seeing the date, one stops and reflects that the situation *now* is not what it was a hundred years ago, or a year ago, or ten minutes ago. $Britain_{1066}$ is not $Britain_{1920}$, and $Britain_{1939}$ is not $Britain_{1953}$. $America_{1783}$ is not $America_{1953}$, and to speak of "The American Way" as something fixed and unchangeable is to speak nonsense.

Appending a date helps to break up slogan thinking: "That's the way it's always been and always will be"; "Once a Com-

munist, always a Communist"; "The leopard cannot change
its spots" . . . It offers a personal reminder that one is himself
a process, and if he feels badly now he may not feel badly tomorrow. It helps deliver one from fixed ideas, and replaces
static concepts with dynamic ones.

Hyphens

Nature is all of a piece, but language divides it. This is, on
the whole, a necessary procedure, enabling us to grasp one
thing at a time. We must be careful not to mistake the verbal
categories, however, for the real thing. Korzybski suggests
that hyphens on the page, or in the mind, help us to remember. Instead of "body and mind" it is closer to reality to write
body-mind; to write *space-time, psycho-logics.*

Quotes

The book you are reading is full of examples of this warning
signal of Korzybski's. I try to put quotation marks around
abstract terms which are easy to misunderstand. The quotes
bid the reader slow down, remember that the term means different things to different people, look carefully to the context. Words like "free enterprise," "statism," "appeasement,"
vary for every user, depending on his past experience. We
gave a current list of them on page 133.

Words like "water," "trees," "houses," "motorcars," are
closer to referents, and quotes are seldom needed—except as I
set them off in this sentence. For terms like "the flowers in
that vase," "my 1954 Chevrolet," the communication line is
about as clear as it can get; the referent is being pointed to.

Why use abstractions at all, when they can be so dangerous
to understanding? Why not always point to what you are
talking about? Well, why use water at all when you can
drown in it? Without abstractions we could not think in a
human way. The problem is to be aware of them, to remember
what level the discourse is on, and the quote signs help that
awareness.

Abstraction ladder

We have spoken repeatedly of levels of abstraction, or abstraction ladders. Here is one ladder, starting with the space-time event.

> That apple there on the table
> Apples-in-general
> Apples as part of the term "fruit"
> Foodstuffs
> Living standards
> Economic goods
> Economic systems

When discussing economic systems, it is a good idea to see that apple from time to time, and other tangible products at the bottom of the ladder. Some economists apparently do not eat.

Here is another ladder, beginning at the top and working downward:

Mountains. What can be said about mountains which applies in all cases? Almost nothing. They are areas raised above other areas on land, under the sea, on the moon. The term is purely relative at this stage; something higher than something, farther from the center.

Snow-capped mountains. Here on a lower rung we can say a little more. The elevations must be considerable, except in polar regions—at least 15,000 feet in the tropics. The snow forms glaciers which wind down the sides. They are cloud factories, producing severe storms, and they require special techniques for climbing.

The Swiss Alps. These are snow-capped mountains about which one can say a good deal. The location can be described, also geology, glacier systems, average elevation, climatic conditions, first ascents, and so on.

The Matterhorn. Here we can be even more specific. It is a snow-capped mountain 14,780 feet above the sea, shaped like a sharp wedge, constantly subject to avalanches of rock and ice. It has four faces, four ridges, three glaciers; was first climbed by the Whymper party in 1865, when four out of seven were killed—and so on. We have dropped down to a specific space-time event.

To the question whether it is "safe" to climb the Matterhorn, Leslie Stephen, one of the greatest of the Alpinists, gave two answers of large semantic importance in 1871, long before the word appeared in the dictionary.

Statement 1. "There is no mountain in the Alps which cannot be climbed by a party of practised mountaineers with guides, in fine weather and under favorable conditions of the snow, with perfect safety."

Statement 2. "There is no mountain in the Alps which may not become excessively dangerous if the climbers are inexperienced, the guides incompetent, the weather bad and the snow unfavorable. . . . There are circumstances under which the Righi is far more dangerous than the Matterhorn under others. Any mountain may pass from the top to the bottom of the scale of danger . . . in a day or sometimes in an hour."

Stephen gives us an unforgettable example of the dangers of generalization. The "Matterhorn" in the morning is not the "Matterhorn" in the afternoon. A is not A. Matterhorn$_1$ is an easy day for a woman climber; Matterhorn$_2$ is certain death for the best climber who ever lived.

"Lazy boy"

Korzybski shows how language manufactures substantives out of adjectives, often with unfortunate results. Here is a boy who persists in getting up late in the morning. Soon his parents are calling him "a naturally lazy boy," a boy characterized by a thing called "laziness." "Laziness" is akin to "badness" in the American culture, and warrants drastic correction. The parents try hard words, then cuffs and whippings. The boy becomes deranged and unmanageable. Fortunately, a doctor is called in and finds, after an examination, that the patient's glands are seriously out of order. He proceeds to correct the

condition, and the boy gets up on time. By identifying their
son with "laziness," a substantive, the parents might well have
ruined him for life.

People are labeled "troublemaker," "Red," "good guy,"
"bad girl," and action is taken on that one characteristic, rather
than on the many characteristics which every individual possesses. You pass in society not for the person you are, but as
a labeled dummy. U.S. congressional committees have been
pasting the label "Communist Sympathizer" on many loyal
Americans, to the extreme damage of both the citizen and
the community. Korzybski would have us tear off the labels
and look at the real person.

Twenty-one statements in General Semantics

To the second edition of *Science and Sanity*, Korzybski contributed an introduction which summarized the main principles
of General Semantics. I have cast his list into the following
twenty-one propositions or statements, trying to make a fair
and objective digest. The reader is urged to consult the volume
for himself, in case I have erred.

In any scientific endeavor, we borrow foundations from
those who have gone before—a part of the process of "time-
binding." All the propositions put forth by Korzybski are built
on groundwork laid by earlier scientists. Nobody makes un-
supported inventions nowadays. The first twelve statements
seem to me to rely heavily on the work of preceding scientists,
while the last nine are more Korzybski's own. Certainly he
stated them uniquely. The five warning signals were of course
his own, and I have added them, along with some personal
comments, to some of the statements.

1. *No two events in nature are identical.* This proposition
is accepted by modern scientists. It runs counter to the "is of
identity" in Indo-European languages and to the "A is A"
of formal logic. (As a warning signal, we use *index numbers.*)

2. *Nature works in dynamic processes.* Accepted by modern scientists and by some schools of philosophy. It disagrees

with the linear, cause-and-effect structure of our language. (Warning signals: *dates* and *hyphens*.)

3. *Events flow into one another in nature by "insensible gradations."* Nature is all of a piece, though our language tends to separate it into classes. (Korzybski suggests the use of *hyphens* to join events—such as body-mind.)

4. *Nature is best understood in terms of structure, order, relationships.* Einstein helped to establish this through the principles of relativity. Indo-European languages, with substantives, entities, absolutes, are at odds with the proposition.

5. *Events in nature are four-dimensional.* Modern physicists, as well as the Hopi Indians, think in terms of space-time. Some other languages are structured for three dimensions, and those who speak them have difficulties with the concept of time.

6. *Events have unlimited characteristics.* Our languages leave many of them out and thus may often distort a judgment. (Korzybski suggests *"etc."* as a warning signal.)

7. *There is no simultaneity in nature.* Western languages assume it as a matter of course; modern physicists do not.

8. *There are no abstract qualities outside our heads.* But language may create verbal spooks which seem to be moving out there. Philosophers back to Bishop Occam have been aware of this difficulty. (*Quotes* give a warning.)

9. *Natural "laws" are at best only high probabilities.* Most scientists are now committed to probability theory. The structure of English, among other languages, favors absolute laws and eternal principles.

10. *Multivalued logic is cardinal in understanding and explaining nature.* Indo-European languages tend to force us into two-valued thinking, fortified by formal logic. (Korzybski suggests the use of *indexes* and *etc.* as warning signals.)

11. *A word is not a thing but an artificial symbol.* This has long been known, but the language structure still objectifies words and encourages word magic. (*Quotes* help to offset this danger.)

12. *A fact is not an inference: an inference is not a value judgment.* The distinction is well known to the law, but not to

the laity, and vast semantic confusion results. The distinction may be illustrated by three statements:

(1) This train is going at 20 miles an hour. A *fact.*
(2) At this rate we'll be an hour late. An *inference.*
(3) This lousy railroad is never on time! A *value judgment.*[1]

Asked to define an event, most of us jump to the level of value judgment. A proper identification begins at the other end, with the facts.

Now let us list the nine statements which seem more uniquely Korzybski's.

13. *A map is not the territory.* Our words are not nature, but their structure should correspond to the structure of nature if we are to understand our world.

14. *The language of mathematics contains structures which correspond to the structure of nature.* Korzybski expected a crop of young geniuses in physics as a result of the new talk— and sure enough, they appeared.

15. *"Reality" is apperceived on three levels: macroscopic, microscopic, submicroscopic.* This point is not unique with Korzybski, but his emphasis is unique.

16. *The systems of Aristotle, Euclid, and Newton are now special cases, and outmoded as general systems.* Korzybski does not hold that these three great men were wrong, only that their "laws" cover less territory than was formerly supposed.

17. *Extensional, or objective, thinking is clearer and more accurate than intensional, or thinking inside one's skull.* This is another way of saying "find the referent"—a phrase which Korzybski did not like to use.

18. *At the end of all verbal behavior are undefined terms.* This is the point where the senses must pick up the signs from

[1] If we carry this series one step farther, we have what Dr. Melvin Thorner calls a "purposeful communiqué"; for instance: "Passengers should avoid the unreliable railroad."

nature. Korzybski has emphasized this "unspoken level" more forcefully than any other student.

19. *Language is self-reflexive.* It is possible to make statements about a statement about a statement indefinitely. (No apologies to Gertrude Stein.)

20. *Man, alone among earth's creatures, "binds time";* that is, profits by the experience of past generations. This was well known and obvious long before Korzybski, but uniquely phrased by him. (Not included in his list directly.)

21. *The nervous system can be consciously reoriented to improve evaluation.* Science can restore sanity. Korzybski deeply believed this, titled his book as a result of it, but his proof is not conclusive. If the proposition turns out to be true it may add considerably to his stature. Delayed response, the use of the warning signals, awareness of abstractions, and the rest, do improve evaluation without question. But does the use of General Semantics *retrain the whole nervous system,* so that improved evaluation becomes as automatic as the knee jerk? Psychiatrists are skeptical. Korzybski has been called a "thwarted psychiatrist," perhaps with justice.

A critical evaluation

It seems plain that while General Semantics has made important contributions to the study of communication it has not seized the leadership. Compared with cultural anthropology, with linguistics, cybernetics, the work of Shannon, it is more a point of view than a rigorous scientific discipline.

Korzybski "brought together a useful way of thinking and talking about human thinking and talking," says Irving J. Lee. At his death in 1950, "he had devised and explained the principles; he had not established a training-testing program with equal thoroughness." He inaugurated no clinic for practicing his methods, no controlled experiments to validate them. There are few reliable case studies of effects on individual persons or groups, in the sense that clinical psychologists make case studies.

Korzybski was something of a prima donna, and he had a

few unfortunate prejudices. He was overcritical of the work of others in his field. I felt the sting of this criticism from time to time, though I had done my best to make his work more widely known. At one point the whole movement seemed to be heading toward a cult, with disciples who knew the lingo, but little else. This danger I believe has been safely passed.

Sometimes it seemed as if the originator of General Semantics were trying to set up a one-man philosophy in the great tradition, which would supersede the system of Aristotle, Aquinas, or Hegel. Yet the scientific method, upon which he constantly relied, is incompatible with one-man philosophies. Korzybski could not have it both ways. If he had been more of a scientist he would have written a shorter and better structured book and given himself more time to inaugurate the research which Professor Lee calls for. He would thus have allayed a good deal of frustration in persons like myself who were trying to understand him.

Despite the frustration, some of us kept at it, and rich was our reward. Doors which had been closed began to open; the world took on a new dimension. Among the semanticists who have been carrying on since his death are objective scholars, shy of cults and revelations. They will succeed, I believe, in steering General Semantics into the moving front of the social sciences, where it belongs. Korzybski included in his approach both the natural sciences, represented by physics, and the social sciences, represented by psychology. One of his favorite phrases was "organism-as-a-whole." He did not station himself behind any of the verbal partitions.

Twenty years of General Semantics have demonstrated that one's evaluation of men and events can be sharpened by its use, that certain mental blocks can be remedied, that one's speaking and writing can be clarified.

Students of General Semantics report a better ability to listen, a reduction in the terrors of stage fright, help in cases of stuttering. General Semantics can aid in teaching children, and in bringing "backward" scholars up to mark. It has led to a healthy re-examination of verbal proof and exerted some influence on the law. It promotes techniques of agreement, and encourages a new appraisal of philosophies formulated before Einstein. Perhaps best of all, General Semantics helps the student know what he does not know.

This is no small contribution for one person to make. We owe Korzybski a good deal, not only for what he discovered or highlighted, but for the furor created by his personality. He lit fires, started controversies, caused people to look to their terms, and so gave a much-needed impetus to the whole subject of communication.

"What is the difference, Count Korzybski, between man and other living creatures?" he was sometimes asked. His eyes would gleam behind the great round spectacles and his deep voice with its rolling accent would reply: "A quar-rter-r- of an inch of cor-rtex."

Chapter 14

DYNAMICS OF GROUPS

The networks of the body interlock with the networks of society. Indeed it is possible to define a person as a set of social relationships—or as Harry Overstreet has phrased it, "personality is an interpersonal process." Your "character" is largely defined by your responses to other people.

In this chapter we will discuss some of the new studies of communication in face-to-face groups. We will begin with an account of a local meeting in my home town where the communication network became very badly snarled, and end with a neighborhood meeting in Chicago where the lines were kept clear, with spectacular results. Both illustrate the necessity of continued research in group communication, that strange phenomenon where the whole is more than the sum of its parts.

Public hearing

Some forty neighbors have gathered in the Town Hall for a public hearing called by the Zoning Board of Appeals. An out-of-town purchaser has asked permission to buy an old inn, and operate it as a convalescent hospital. The five board members are on the platform and before them sit the rector, the doctor, the first selectman, the school nurse, housewives, commuters, farmers. Nearly everybody knows everybody. Nearly everybody, too, hopes to hear a proposal he will accept. It is desirable to have the building occupied again and the popular climate is propitious.

The chairman opens the meeting and introduces the prospective purchaser and his lawyer, who come to the platform. The latter, a short, well-dressed man with a bulging brief case, seems extremely sure of himself. He addresses the chair as he would a judge, the neighbors as he would a jury—a jury with a pretty low I.Q. He assures us patronizingly that his client's proposal for a hospital is perfectly legal; fire escapes and emergency exits will be built as provided by law—everything as provided by law. What he proposes to do inside this legal frame is hardly mentioned.

The chairman calls for questions, and now the popular climate has changed. Faces have altered from interested attention to suspicion. A dozen townspeople are on their feet: "What experience have you had in running this kind of a hospital?" . . . "What doctors have you consulted?" . . . "How many patients will you take?" . . . "Is it a home for alcoholics?" . . . "For incurables?" . . . "For mental cases?" . . . "Who is really behind this proposition?" . . .

The lawyer's face reddens with annoyance. Everything is perfectly legal, he says, so why ask such questions? More citizens are on their feet, and their voices are now actively hostile. Somebody intimates that the whole thing is a racket; somebody else that the petitioners intend to unload the property at a large profit to a rest camp for Communists. One of our town leaders gets to his feet with dignity: "We came here prepared to listen to any reasonable proposition," he says, "and all we have heard is double talk about legality. We resent the patronizing attitude of counsel." There is a burst of applause! Whereupon the petitioner makes for the door and drags counsel, struggling with his brief case, after him. The door slams, and the chairman declares the meeting adjourned. It takes me quite a while, as secretary of the board, to complete my minutes.

It would be hard to find a more brilliant case of communication failure. Whatever the merits of their proposal for a hospital, the petitioners committed most of the sins possible in a face-to-face group. They misjudged the temper of the group.

They disregarded the needs and wants of the townspeople there assembled, and made no attempt to put themselves in the place of a neighbor whose house was close to the proposed hospital. Counsel had no skill in presenting his case, no idea of the facts needed for a public hearing of this kind. His "perfect legality" made citizens feel suspicious and insecure, and with their insecurity came anger. He had not the faintest idea, apparently, that his problem concerned human relations more than legal formalities.

I remembered, as I wrote my notes, a leader at the Bethel Laboratory trying to steer his group in a direction it did not want to go. He felt, he said, as though he were "wrestling with a healthy bull!" In our town the bull was both healthy and angry.

"Perhaps the basic principle of the science of human relations," says Gordon Allport, "is that in order to deal effectively with any other mortal, it is necessary to find out how he feels." This principle was magnificently violated in our Town Hall—and not for the first time. By contrast, the Telephone Company had approached an earlier meeting of the Zoning Board with frankness and tact. Polite experts arrived with a roll of blueprints, all the facts, and a lively sense of how the neighbors felt, and what they would want to know about the building to house the new dial exchange which the company proposed to build.

What is a group?

There have been isolated cases where "society," "speech community," "nation," and "home" were all combined in one tribal village, where everybody knew everybody in a face-to-face relationship. The group structure of most societies, however, especially in the machine age, includes not only *face-to-face* relationships, but what we might call institutional relationships. $Adam_1$ is a member of the American nation, the Republican party, the Chamber of Commerce, the Episcopal Church, the Masons, the Bar Association, Phi Beta Kappa. He knows only a small fraction of the people in these large insti-

tutions, and communicates with them formally in writing, if
at all.

The most ancient, the most essential and by far the hardiest
of all face-to-face groups is the family. In most societies, furthermore, families are monogamous; only people who can
afford it, or stand it, practice polygamy or polyandry. In the
family group children first develop their communication skills.
Then may come play groups, school classes, clubs, gangs,
initiation classes, apprentice teams, fraternities, guilds, labor
unions, work groups in industry, councils of elders, boards of
directors, pressure groups, committees of all kinds, legislatures,
cabinets, Security Councils, the World Court—an endless list.

Two or more people in communication, over a definite time
period, with a common need, constitute a group. To be in
communication they must feel one another's personalities,
though they need not know one another's names. This implies a face-to-face relation not too large to permit ready
recognition. Face-to-face groups of strangers, not in communication and having no common goal—save perhaps a common
transportation point—are termed *aggregations*. A good example
is a packed elevator.

Theater, concert, and lecture audiences begin as aggregations, but may establish lines of communication between members if the acting, the music or the speaker really moves them.
What kind of group the Brooklyn baseball fans assembled in
Ebbets Field may constitute is something for the entire faculty
to work on. In an emergency an aggregation may suddenly become a communicating group—for instance the passengers on
an airliner which makes a forced landing.

Analyzing group behavior

Why is a group more than the sum of its members? Why
can it develop ideas, for instance, that the same people acting
alone would never think of? Because members interact, stimulate, catch fire. They develop sympathies and antagonisms, and
learn to predict one another's behavior. Many small threads of
language weave them together in a fabric of relations from

member to member, like lines of force in a magnetic field.

The variety and intensity of relations between just two people have filled many a play and novel. The unit, observe, is not either person, or both persons; it is something *between* the two—call it tension or communication. If diagrammed, it is the line from station to station—the telephone wire plus messages speeding back and forth. This *connection* is the unit.

To a two-person unit, now add one more person. The units will treble, as three people can combine in three different pairs. Add the triangle itself and you have a fourth unit. The lines of force are very apparent when, into the family unit of man and wife, a mother-in-law is introduced. With four persons interacting the minimum units of direct communication increase to ten, and the curve goes on rising by geometrical progression. The possible *minimum* combinations of a group of twelve persons have been computed at 2,102.[1] These computations demonstrate why face-to-face groups dealing with important problems should be kept small. The lesson for executives is important.

In practice, no human brain should attempt to supervise directly more than five, or at the most, six other individuals whose work is interrelated. . . . A supervisor with five subordinates reporting directly to him, who adds a sixth, increases his available human resources by 20 percent. But he adds approximately 100 percent to the complexity and difficulty of his tasks of coordination. . . .

This is all communication *inside* the group. Outside lines radiate too, and they can be very dynamic, say, in a theater panic or in the spread of hot gossip. The "bamboo telegraph" carries news at great speed in the Far East. It has been calculated that a chain letter in multiples of ten persons per day, without duplications, could reach the entire population of the world in less than ten days.

Social scientists such as Alexander Bavelas, Robert F. Bales,

[1] V. A. Graicvnas, in Gulick and Urwick, *Papers on the Science of Administration*, Institute of Public Administration, Columbia University, 1937.

Herbert Thelen are analyzing structure and function among face-to-face groups. The role of leader, for instance, has various forms. He can be in the center, with direct lines to all members, who do not communicate with each other except through him. Or he may have fewer channels than there are members—for instance, where an assistant acts as go-between. In some offices the boss's secretary relays instructions downward and reports upward. Whether the leader exerts authority by pressure, or enlists co-operation, may be more a matter of degree than of structure.

Other roles, with their communication lines inside the group, are under study by scientists. They include the special positions of players on a ball team, the different instruments in an orchestra, the assignments to children in a classroom—where many a problem child has been rescued by being appointed monitor of the wastebasket or the flower pot. The secretary, the treasurer, the membership committee of a social club, all have their special relations to each other, and to the rest of the members.

Groups at Bethel

Many of the conclusions now being reached in the study of face-to-face groups were anticipated by the Quakers. Their "laboratory," in the form of the monthly business meeting, has been operating for three hundred years. The National Training Laboratory in Group Development at Bethel, Maine, has been operating for less than a decade. The six principles we are soon to list show up strongly in both.

Bethel carries on the work inaugurated by Kurt Lewin in his classic experiments with children's handicraft classes at Iowa State.[1] He gave his studies the label "group dynamics," but as some other students object to the term, Bethel has officially dropped it. (Personally I don't care what they call it, so long as dependable results are forthcoming.) Every sum-

---

[1] For an account of these experiments see his book, *Resolving Social Conflicts.*

mer about 100 delegates report from active work in business, teaching, labor, the armed services, social work, to act as guinea pigs in a series of experimental groups. A large staff headed by Leland P. Bradford sets up the experiments and records them, with up-to-date mechanical equipment. Every group has its special observers and its statistical output. Questions of the best size of groups for various tasks, of leadership techniques, of how to suppress Napoleonic characters bent on making off with the agenda, how to "involve" shy members, how long a group can concentrate on a problem without tiring—all are studied. There may be as many as 300 two-hour sessions with some twenty persons to a group, to be observed and recorded by the staff. Financing has come from the National Education Association, the Navy, the Carnegie Corporation, and various universities. Sound and helpful conclusions are beginning to emerge. We shall end the chapter with a case of applied group dynamics conducted by a Bethel staff member.

Group analysis is focusing attention on primary sources of human energy. Like all vital new movements, the study attracts some rootless individuals looking for ideological salvation. They will hardly find it at Bethel, however, for the discipline is severe.

Until yesterday the only knowledge about a group's magnetic field was intuitive. Some individuals were obviously aggressive in dealing with others; some were hesitant and shy; nobody knew why. Some groups got their problems solved, others did not; nobody knew why. Now, thanks to Lewin, Elton Mayo, the Bethel staff, and others, we are beginning to find out. Even the Quakers are making scientific studies of their own group performance.

A woman who worked with hundreds of joint committees of businessmen and government officials during World War II summarizes the need for such studies:

We question whether . . . a man who knows all about a commodity knows all about conducting a conference. We wonder if inexperienced chairmanship is not the cause of the silence of many members. We see meetings . . . that last three hours and others on the same agenda that last two days . . . and we wonder. . . . We read a 630-page transcript that says no more than another of 65 pages. . . .[1]

Think of the man-hours wasted in those endless committee meetings and reports, hours ill spared with a war to be fought.

SIX PRINCIPLES IN GROUP COMMUNICATION

Six principles of successful group action impress me as particularly useful and important. Group leaders and group members in every corner of the country can be helped by them; committees at the United Nations can be helped.

1. Identifying oneself with the other members of the group.
2. Encouraging maximum participation by members.
3. Democratic rather than autocratic leadership. ("Permissive" is the technical term.)
4. Protecting the security of members.
5. Keeping communication lines open at all times.
6. Encouraging better listening.

Let us examine each principle in more detail.

Identifying with others

If one wants to get along with people, says Allport, find out how they feel. The effort to see things the way your listeners see them can greatly improve communication. As no two sets of personal experience are alike, it is impossible for you to know exactly how I feel, or vice versa, but just to realize that my field of perception differs from yours goes a long way to improve our relationship.

If you want to lead people or cause them to listen to you, first *discover their needs*. Do not assume that what you think desirable, they think desirable. Do not assume that what Amer-

---

[1] Ethel B. Gilbert, *What a Lot of Advice*, Washington, Office of Price Stabilization, 1952.

icans want, Iranians will want. Moral judgments as to what
people *ought* to want are no help at all, often the contrary.
The influence of any idea, says Erich Fromm, depends on the
extent to which it appeals to the psychic needs of those to
whom it is addressed. The struggle between the ideas of
"Communism" and "Democracy" revolves around the question: "Which system can best meet people's needs?"

Participation

A second important group principle is to encourage everybody to take an active part in a given decision or discussion.
The Quakers refuse to decide anything without unanimous
agreement. If a question does not produce unanimity the first
time it comes up in a business meeting of the Friends, it is put
over until unanimity is reached. When the decision comes it
is likely to stick, for there is no minority to feel aggrieved,
no majority to crow.

A group should realize that there is something to be discovered,
that one of its members cannot do this alone but that discussion
is necessary, and that the outcome will depend as much upon the
spirit in which members handle the problem before them as upon
the cogency and power with which they present their several
cases. . . .[1]

Participation, the Quakers have discovered, not only aids
agreement, but for certain types of problems produces a group
solution superior to what any member could produce alone.
If the experience of a number of persons can be pooled, the
chances of a good solution are obviously improved. The
Quakers use this idea so confidently that members seldom come
to a business meeting with a prepared solution. They expect
it to evolve out of the group discussion, and time and again
it does.

Orientation courses in the U.S. Army, to teach draftees
what democracy means, have been revolutionized by the participation principle. Instead of dozing at lectures as formerly,

[1] Pollard, *Democracy and the Quaker Method*, London, Bannisdale
Press, 1949.

the boys now pretend to be draft boards called on to decide whether to exempt baseball players, college students, businessmen, or machinists. Said one G.I., "Gee, Sarge, now I know what my own draft board goes through, back in Yonkers!" The new course was designed by Dr. William F. Russell of Columbia. Instead of fifty G.I.s in a lecture group, the men are now organized in discussion groups of ten men each.

Democratic leaders

Lewin's experiments with children's handicraft classes showed how group stability was increased by shifting responsibility from the adult leader to the children themselves. The task of the "permissive" leader is to keep things moving but allow the group to make most of the decisions.

Such an arrangement makes members feel their importance and the value of their activity. It can often increase productivity—in goods or solutions. When the girls assembling telephone relays in Elton Mayo's classic experiment were consulted by the management, and made to realize that they were part of an important undertaking, their output soared. Social scientists have pretty well demonstrated, however, that a group without any leader at all usually disintegrates. The Russian symphony orchestra without a conductor did not last beyond the stunt period.

The principle of security

People perform better in groups when they are emotionally secure. (Economic security helps too, of course.) People under tension, anxious, unsure of themselves, are likely to call names, show prejudice, impugn motives, get angry, and generally scramble communication lines.

One way to increase security is to announce plans well in advance. Experts in business management suggest, for instance, that if a shop is going to install a new machine to supplant hand labor, the working group should know about it well ahead of time. If the installation is the result of a group decision between management and union, so much the better.

Open communication lines

This was Elton Mayo's favorite prescription. Explain, explain, and explain, he said, and listen and listen. Check the channels of communication in all directions; make sure the messages are accurate, honest, and complete. Members of face-to-face groups and their leaders can make much better progress if they are trained in semantics. One road to understanding is to rely more on facts, less on opinion, not at all on rumor. Said Mayo:

> I believe that social study should begin with careful observation of what may be described as communication; that is, the capacity of an individual to communicate his feelings and ideas to another, the capacity of groups to communicate effectively and intimately to each other. This problem is beyond all reasonable doubt the outstanding defect that civilization is facing today. . . .

Better listening

Listening is semantic decoding on the engineers' diagram in Chapter 2. Talk has been under the microscope for many years, as we have seen, but scientific studies of listening are just beginning. Again the Quakers lead the way, with the intensive listening practiced in their meetings. The subject is so new and so important that we will devote the next chapter to it.

"Group dynamics," like "General Semantics," has run the danger of becoming a cult, with starry-eyed disciples and a fearful jargon. Delegates come back from Bethel, it is alleged, and let on that they have been initiated into the inner sanctum. "Now we will role-play," they say. "Now we will form buzz groups. Who will be our resource person?" They throw the words and techniques around, it is alleged, before they have located any real problem. Personally, I have never encountered such a performance, but if it is done, as alleged, it is alien to the spirit I found at Bethel.

My group leader there was Herbert A. Thelen of Chicago University. I should like to end this chapter with a specific example of how he first encountered a problem—a dramatic and difficult problem—and then applied some of the principles of group dynamics to its successful solution.

A city block becomes a group [1]

The time is 1950 and the place is the Hyde Park area around the University of Chicago. Another rumor has just exploded in the tense borderland between well-to-do white residents and Negroes, also pretty well-to-do, who are moving in to escape from ghetto-like quarters elsewhere in the city. The rumor says that a large building will be cut up and a Negro family packed into every room.

Across the street is a block of eighteen one-family houses with lawns around them, occupied by white owners. Four of these are promptly put up for sale. Fear spreads through the neighborhood. What can be done? The accepted idea is that nothing can be done; Hyde Park is doomed to become a slum.

Somebody, however, remembers an organization in the neighborhood which has advised in similar cases. On its staff is Thelen, professor of education at the university. At the invitation of several alarmed property owners he discusses the situation with them, and advises *first* a prompt investigation to get the real facts about the sale of the building, and next a meeting of all the residents in the block to hear the facts and take action. Yes, he will be glad to lead the first meeting.

Investigation shows the rumor to be wildly exaggerated; the building has indeed been sold, but not to unscrupulous speculators, and it will be remodeled into a few desirable apartments. Some Negroes are expected to rent them, but they are likely to be well-educated, pleasant people.

The first block meeting is held in a large private house. As the people arrive, they congregate in small knots to discuss their fears. An old man climbs up on the stair landing and makes a stump speech against aliens in general and Negroes

[1] To be described in Dr. Thelen's forthcoming book; see bibliography. For a shorter account, see my article in *Reader's Digest*, May 1953.

in particular. Thelen says nothing, but allows people to get acquainted and express their pent-up feelings.

After a while he calls the meeting to order and says he has been listening to the informal talk and has noted a wide range of racial feelings, from a sentimentalist to the old gentleman on the stairs. Thelen suggests that they accept the fact that everybody is prejudiced in one way or another. Whatever their feelings, they are now faced with a large, awkward chunk of reality. When the Negroes move in, there may turn out to be only three ways to deal with them:

(1) Neighbors might form an armed mob and try to drive the Negroes out of the house across the street.

(2) They might ignore them completely.

(3) They might try to establish some sort of communication with them, in the effort to prevent deterioration of property by joint action.

After two hours of discussion, the meeting adopts the third alternative and delegates a committee to call on the new neighbors as they move in.

Later, when the tenants arrive, the committee goes calling. The new neighbors receive them politely. They are very glad to hear about neighborhood standards, for they had left their old homes because of deterioration. They obviously enjoy being consulted, and agree to co-operate to the best of their ability. So instead of a gulf of fear and hostility, both groups reach an arrangement, not, you will observe, to love each other, but to work together for common specified goals—for lighted alleys, better garbage collection, more police protection, better schools.

In due course the four white owners who had put their houses on the market withdraw them. In due course the block becomes another unit in the Hyde Park Conference, ready to squelch rumors, get the facts, know the neighbors, recognize common problems, and take responsibility.

What we find here is a happy combination of grass roots democracy and group dynamics. In Thelen's approach we recognize the six principles enumerated above. Before any action was taken he punctured the rumor and got the facts. He did not call the meeting; the people who were affected themselves arranged it, and his leadership was strictly "permissive." He stated alternatives for members of the group to decide democratically. He explored prejudices and made members aware of the importance of feelings, and the distinction between feelings and logic. Participation, democratic decisions, open communication lines, careful listening, were all exemplified in that first meeting, and led later to a sense of security sufficient to take four homes off the market.

Professor Thelen saw the need and showed the group how to use some of the new techniques. The people themselves did the work and made the decisions. The contrast with our Zoning Board meeting recited earlier is startling. The group analysts may have just begun, but already they have made a solid contribution to improved communication.

Chapter 15

LEARNING TO LISTEN

Listening is the other half of talking. A message is 50 per cent sending, and 50 per cent receiving; if more than two people are present the ratio of listening increases. Thus when five people around a table are discussing a problem, and each does his share of the talking, each will be listening 80 per cent of his time. If people stop listening it is useless to talk—a point not always appreciated by politicians, among others.

Listening involves a double decoding of messages, for we must try to interpret both the literal meaning of the words, and the intention of the sender. If someone says, "Why, Jim, you old horse thief!" the words are technically an insult; but the tone of voice probably indicates affection for a friend. "When you call me that, smile," said the Virginian in Owen Wister's famous story.

Americans are not very good listeners in face-to-face groups, although hardy enough in front of microwaves. In general they talk more than they listen. Competition in our culture puts a premium on self-expression, even if the individual has nothing to express. What he lacks in knowledge he can make up for by talking fast or by pounding the table. He takes a course in personality development, hoping to learn to "sell himself." How many of us while ostensibly silent are inwardly preparing a statement to stun the company when we get the floor—and so are not listening at all? Yet it really is not difficult to learn to listen, just unusual.

Under our aggressive folkways in America, listening is regarded as a passive, almost negative form of behavior. But listening can be a very active process, something to challenge all our faculties. Here is a stream of messages coming in to be decoded: how close can we come to their real meaning? "What is this speaker trying to say? . . . What has he to tell *me*, and what can I learn from him? . . . How does he know it? . . . What has he left out? . . . What are his motives?" . . . Such questions can keep the listener anything but passive on his end of the line.

Irving Lee finds as a result of repeated experiments that only about a quarter of the class in public speaking understands clearly what a speaker has said. He arrives at this figure by asking listeners to write an abstract of the talk. The speaker himself then checks the abstract. "If the audience heard they did not seem to listen, or if they listened, it seemed with half an ear."

Various studies have been made of the way people spend their communication time. A typical division, for Stephens College girls, goes as follows: [1]

Listening—to lectures, etc.	42 per cent
Talking	25
Reading	15
Writing	18
Total	100 per cent

The efficiency of listening, in all these studies, comes out about 25 per cent, a figure which checks with Lee's experience. Students vary greatly, says Elwood Murray, in ability to comprehend, and every listener has special deaf spots where messages are blocked or distorted.

Some of this may be an emotional block. Think of the people you know who cannot listen to figures, to politics, or to accounts of their friends' operations. It is reasonable to suppose that every time an incoming message collides with an active prejudice it is distorted. To cite an extreme case, a super-

[1] Article by Donald E. Bird in *Journal of Communication*.

patriotic organization proposed in 1953 to exclude the phrase
"little red schoolhouse" from discussions of American education. The word "red" ignited the superpatriots, who gave it a
quite irrelevant political meaning.

Listening clinic

How can a listener improve his technique? The New York
Adult Education Council has inaugurated "listening clinics"
to sharpen the ears of members. One member reads aloud while
the others around the table concentrate on what he is saying.
Later they summarize what they have heard and compare
notes—often to find that the accounts are widely apart. Gradually they improve, and often find themselves transferring the
skill to business and home affairs. Here are some members'
evaluations from Clinic No. II: [1]

"In interviewing guests on the air, I have gotten much better
material from them because of really listening."

"I became aware of a new attitude developing in me of attempt-
ing to understand and interpret the remarks of my friends and
associates from *their* viewpoint, and not from my own as I had
done previously."

"I have decided that the art of questioning is dependent directly
on the art of listening. Ability to listen depends on this responsive-
ness of the communicators to each other."

"I think the Clinic demonstrated its objectives. Nevertheless I
have not learned to listen—a lifetime of not listening has been too
damaging."

Reading the contract

Some years ago, Major Charles T. Estes of the Federal Con-
ciliation Service was called in to help settle a dispute between
a corporation and its unions. They had been quarreling for
years and the emotional potential was high. The Major proceeded to invent a technique for listening that has since had
wide application, both in the labor field and in discussion

[1] Mimeographed report, June 1950.

groups. He asked delegates from both union and management
to read aloud the annual contract which was in dispute. Each
man would read a section in his turn; then all would discuss
the section read. If a dispute began to develop, the clause was
put aside for later examination.

In two days the lesson was learned. By that time the delegates really knew what was in the contract, and were competent to go back and tell their fellow managers or fellow
workers what it contained. "We had conditioned them to communicate," said the Major. The contract was not rewritten but
continued in force with very few changes. Good listening had
transformed bad labor relations into good ones.

Carl R. Rogers, of the University of Chicago, suggests a
game to be played at a dinner party which goes like this: A
political discussion breaks out—say on the French elections—
which shortly becomes acrimonious. At this point Rogers asks
the company to try an experiment. Before Nelson, who is on
the edge of his chair, can reply to the statement made by Robinson, he must summarize what Robinson has said in such a
way that Robinson himself accepts it. This means careful
listening, in the course of which emotion is likely to cool. It
means further that Nelson must put himself, temporarily at
least, in Robinson's place, assume his point of view.

The result is that everyone in the circle, by listening and
rephrasing, acquires a working knowledge of the other fellow's
point of view, even if he does not agree with it. Any attempt
to slant or distort is instantly corrected by the original speaker:
"No! I did not say that; try again!" In addition to a course
in listening, the players are quite likely to increase their knowledge of the subject—something that rarely happens in the
usual slambang argument. The experiment takes courage, says
Rogers, because in restating the other man's position, you run
the risk of changing your own.

Rogers is a leader in group therapy, where people suffering
from mental maladjustments help themselves through group
action. To be neurotic, he says, is a sign that one's internal

communication is out of order; reports are scrambled, feedbacks are not operating properly. This promptly interferes with the external network, and communication with other people is disrupted. Psychotherapy might thus be described as a service truck restoring communication lines which are down —though sometimes alive and sputtering. A neurotic person has lost outside connections, including the power to listen; he hears only the compulsion inside his head.

We recognize the neurotic as a person who is not well, and we are often sorry for him, but an aggressive opponent only annoys us. Actually, says Rogers, a man emotionally aroused in a political argument is equally out of control. He cannot listen, he cannot weigh the facts, he cannot reason.

Listening to Bill

F. J. Roethlisberger, of the Harvard Business School, in a recent study of training courses for supervisors, describes a significant contrast in listening.[1]

An executive calls foreman Bill to his office to tell him about a change he intends in Bill's department. A casting will be substituted for a hand-forged job, and the executive proceeds to explain how it should be done.

"Oh yeah?" says Bill.

Let us follow two interpretations of "Oh yeah" which the boss might make at this point. First, suppose he assumes that Bill does not see how to do the new job, and it is up to the boss to tell him. This he proceeds to do clearly and logically. Nevertheless Bill is obviously freezing up, and presently things begin to happen inside the boss. "Can it be," he asks himself, "that I have lost my power to speak clearly? Impossible. Bill just doesn't understand plain English; he's really pretty dumb." The look which accompanies this unspoken idea makes Bill freeze even tighter.

Now, says Roethlisberger, let's take the second interpreta-

[1] *Harvard Business Review*, July 1952. Rogers' and Roethlisberger's experiments both described.

tion; suppose the boss senses from the "Oh yeah" that Bill is disturbed, so he tries to find out why. He says:

"What's your idea about the job, Bill?"

"Well," says Bill.

"You've been in the department longer than I've been in this office. You probably have a pretty good idea how the change-over ought to be made. Let's have it. I'm listening."

Things now begin to happen inside Bill. The boss is not laying it on the line, he's willing to listen. So ideas come out, slowly at first, then faster, some of them excellent. The boss becomes really interested in Bill's approach. "Smarter man than I thought!" A spiral reaction is set up, as Bill begins to realize that he never appreciated the boss before. The interview ends on a note of close harmony.

Role-playing

Though Roethlisberger does not mention it, the case of Bill would have been ideal for a little role-playing by the boss. This new technique helps one to step into the other fellow's shoes and understand how he feels. It consists of a short, unrehearsed charade, and is being widely used in conference work, in schools, in training programs, in industry. It is a frequent activity at the Bethel Laboratory. It allows us to explore a coming situation without the risk which the actual situation entails. It is a free show, and this is the way it works:

When the boss knew that a drastic change had to be made in Bill's department, he might have asked his secretary to sit in his big chair and pretend to be himself, while he pretended to be Bill. He would walk through the door, hat in hand, and listen respectfully while the "boss" told him what was cooking in the department. If the "boss" began to lay it on the line, "Bill," standing there in front of the desk, would begin to feel the way the real Bill might feel. Why shouldn't *he* be consulted? He would begin to freeze up too, actively resenting the man on the other side of the desk.

You may say that the boss would have to be a talented actor

to imagine all this, but you are mistaken. Actors are not good role-players as a rule, whereas most normal persons seem to have enough thingumbobs stored away to take roles like this spontaneously without coaching.[1]

When the real interview takes place, the boss is ready to listen and to understand, because for a few moments he *was* Bill. If Bill could have role-played the boss before *he* came upstairs, so much the better. Managers in some industries, union officials in others, are now role-playing the conference in which the annual contract is to be negotiated. Some managers pretend to be union delegates, and vice versa. A C.I.O. official of the rubber workers told me at Bethel that role-playing had changed his whole outlook. "I could feel those stockholders breathing down my neck!" he said.

In role-playing you go farther than just listening to the other fellow; you put yourself in his place, and the more unreservedly you can do it, the better the results will be. The cowboy in Wendell Johnson's story was a highly successful role-player. Asked how he managed to find a lost horse so infallibly, he replied, "Well, I just ask myself, if I were that horse, where would I go?"

Critical listening

So far we have been talking about sympathetic listening in face-to-face situations, to make sure we grasp the sender's full meaning. Critical listening too is needed—not necessarily unsympathetic—in a world full of ideologists, propaganda, door-to-door salesmen, and high-pressure advertisers. Later we shall consider some of the problems of mass media, where an understanding of the machinery of newsgathering, publishing, and broadcasting can be helpful, and where ideological immunity needs to be actively promoted. We need protection, too, even at our own front doors, when we are urged to sign petitions and contribute to charities, not to mention magazine subscriptions to put young persons through college.

[1] See the author's book, *Roads to Agreement*, Chapter 10.

Sitting on a jury listening to evidence, you need a still different set of ears. Dr. Douglas Kelley teaches methods for interviewing witnesses of an accident or a crime. The witness, he says, frequently cannot tell the story because of physical or mental blocks. First the interviewer must make sure that the witness was conscious and really looking at the event; then that his eyesight was dependable; then that no gross emotional blockage interfered—for instance, fear of an armed assailant. Next, is the witness slanting his account? What is the effect of past experiences on the witness? Finally, the interviewer has to consider the ability of the witness to communicate. Can he say what he means? We have here a whole spectrum of listening techniques.

Some of Dr. Kelley's methods are applications of General Semantics. Here is a list of what a student of semantics is already equipped to do in listening to a speech or a conversation.

1. He delays his reactions and looks for motives. What is behind Bill the foreman's "Oh yeah?"

2. What level of abstraction is the speaker on? Are there any referents for his remarks? What important characteristics is he leaving out?

3. Is the speaker talking chiefly in the accepted symbols of the culture—Home, Mother, the Founding Fathers, Our Glorious Heritage—and so on, avoiding the necessity for thought, or is he really trying to think? Most political speeches are larded solidly with symbols, and the well-trained ear can identify them up to a mile away.

4. Does the speaker's personal ideology show conspicuously? The trained ear can almost immediately spot a Communist by the use of certain stock phrases—"lackeys of imperialism," for instance. Similarly it is easy to spot a hard-money man, a single taxer, or a devotee of biodynamics.

5. Is the speaker dealing in facts, inferences, or value judgments? I have trained my ear to find this distinction in political and economic talk, and to follow the shifts from one level to the next. If the facts have an authentic ring, I listen attentively,

but if the discourse is all personal opinion, I may detour the message around and out the other ear.

6. The sum of careful listening is to identify the speaker's field of perception, how he feels about events, what his needs and drives appear to be, what kind of person he is. The appraisal can only be rough but it can be a decided help in dealing with him, in giving him a fair answer. It can be a great help in deciding whether to get aboard his bandwagon, if he has a bandwagon. The listener should also consider his own attitude toward the speaker. Is he prejudiced for or against him? Is he being fair, objective, human?

Good listening aids us in sizing up a person, a meeting, a line of argument. It improves our messages going back to the speaker, deepens serious conversation, breaks up arguments over meaningless questions, reduces verbal conflict. It helps one to remain silent rather than sounding off, to choose one's radio commentators, to decide whether to go farther with a proposition presented orally—such as writing an endorsement, or buying a share of stock.

Good listening is invaluable, I find, in answering questions from the floor following a lecture. A speaker who cannot evaluate quickly and fairly the agitated gentleman in the back row is destined for a very brief career as a public lecturer. Is the questioner the town radical? The town tory? Has he an ax to grind? Is he working off a frustration? Showing off before the neighbors? Or is he honestly seeking more information? My ears work overtime up there on the platform, for I have not only the man in the back row to keep reasonably happy, but the whole audience to keep in temper. I could instantly alienate everybody in the hall by answering a question with sarcasm or resentment.

Chapter 16

FEEDBACK

A homely definition for a "feedback," given earlier, was "How are we doing?" A number of theories have been discussed in the preceding chapters, and various activities described, under the broad label of communication. What is the general direction of the studies? Are there any serious contradictions? Where should research be concentrated to continue an orderly advance? Clearly a vigorous attack has been launched along the whole communication front. What dependable conclusions are coming to light?

Six conclusions seem to me to be outstanding:

First: that communication, in the sense of messages dispatched and decoded, is a characteristic of most animal life, but only man has refined the messages into structured language, useful for evaluating his world.

Second: that two systems of communication interlock in each individual: internal lines to keep the organism stable; external lines to keep society stable. To understand communication, accordingly, one should study the human nervous system, as well as the languages developed in human cultures.

Third: we can assume that men developed their languages in order to keep the group together. They had to communicate for defense against enemies, to insure the food supply, to bring up the young in the way they should go. Language was a tool and a weapon for a relatively defenseless mammal; it sharpened his wits and taught him to reason his way out of a tight corner.

Fourth: once a language developed, the process we call culture inevitably began its geometrical progression, as one generation told the next what had been learned. The early inventions—fire, the wheel, domesticated animals, a storable grain—were widely spaced, hundreds, perhaps thousands of years apart. With the great invention of writing, the curve went up more steeply. The language we learn from the culture meanwhile shapes our "world view," our behavior, our very thoughts. In addition, some scientists, including Julian Huxley, are beginning to wonder if culture may not provide a substitute for evolution. Instead of environment modifying man, man with the help of his inventions modifies environment.

Fifth: in addition to the linguistic relativity expressed in the culture, other forms of relativity apply to language, meaning, and perception. The meaning each individual perceives is relative to his experience, and for a message to be understood, there must be some overlapping of experience between the sender and receiver. Their relation to each other helps to determine meaning. Within a face-to-face group, interrelations grow more complicated as more members are added. Logic and reason form only part of the communication process, and not always a dependable part. Really to understand a person we must know something about his feelings, needs, and motives.

Sixth: it is quite possible to bring our methods of evaluation closer to "reality." Some techniques have already demonstrated their usefulness and more will come, while international communication systems will certainly be improved. The outlook is hopeful and exciting.

So much for major conclusions. What then is the goal of communication study? Its goal, like that of any science, is first understanding, then application. Communication can be improved as we learn more about it, and improvement is long overdue. As the mass media of press, radio, television, bombard us, an understanding of the process becomes increasingly urgent. The ocean of words mounts—more messages, faster messages, everyone talking at once, and perhaps drowning out solutions to important problems. The final goal of communication study is knowledge, to direct the power of words toward survival and well-being, knowledge to check human confusion and failure.

In the foregoing chapters we have examined twelve contributions to that study. We found no serious contradictions, and considerable co-operation. The semanticists, for instance, are eagerly following the work of the linguists, the brain physiologists, the cybernetics engineers. A brief summary—or feedback—may help the reader at this point. The twelve branches, to repeat them, are: brain physiology, cybernetics, the psychology of perception, animal psychology, child psychology, the culture concept, linguistics, metalinguistics, the languages of science, semantics, General Semantics, group analysis.

1. The physiologists and neurologists

As light waves, sound waves, tactile pressures, come in from the submicroscopic world of the atom to stimulate the nerve ends, the brain decodes them, some automatically, some consciously, in various centers. A complicated system of input nerves with many alternate paths takes the message up to the brain. After action is determined, aided by stored memories, another complicated system of output nerves delivers the order to the muscles of foot, hand, or tongue. The action taken depends heavily on the "thingumbob" principle: what we perceive and do is conditioned by past experiences. If there is nothing in the memory files, a crisis may develop.

Some fifteen billion interaction points in the brain give humans great powers of flexibility and adjustment. A large fraction of these connections, says C. Z. Young, are reserved for the control of tongue, lips, and larynx. We are born without any stock of words, but with a powerful drive to learn words. Learning comes from the culture, especially the family group. "The use of words to insure co-operation is the essential feature of man."

Language operates in two interlocking networks, inside the

individual and out to the community. Dr. Young believes that the networks are capable of great improvement in their day-to-day performance. The technical equipment—as in the case of television engineering—is far superior to the programs.

2. *The cybernetics engineers*

This school popularized the term *feedback* for the control of a system by reinserting its results. Thus when the balls on the governor of a steam engine swing faster, they begin to close the throttle. The human body is interlaced with feedbacks; without them we could not stand erect, or maintain a constant body temperature, or probably go on breathing.

Cybernetics studies the messages that control action—which is also the function of the human brain. As machines become more complicated—say for guided missiles, or for operating a petroleum refinery—a binary system of choices, using the numbers 1 and 0, is found superior to control by temperature, pressure, or other physical analogue. It is now suspected that nerve impulses travel along their fibers to the brain on the binary on-or-off system, and that memories may be stored on that system. As their work progresses, the engineers increase our knowledge of the brain and nervous system.

3. *Perception theory psychologists*

A tour through the laboratories of this scientific group, including the "cockeyed room," leaves the inquiring layman exhausted if not slightly seasick. The relativity of perception is impressively demonstrated, and the thingumbob principle strongly supported. We can "know" only what we have experienced.

Furthermore, we never see "all" of any event, such as a chair, but only enough to deal with it. We "bet" that it is a chair, in the light of past experience; the probability may be high, but never 100 per cent. When we put what we see into words, we make a second abstraction. The word is not the object; and the object seen may be not a "chair" at all but an arrangement of sticks and wires.

What, then, philosophers ask, is "reality"? Your author guesses that if there were no eyes to see chairs, or to see any-thing else on earth, there would still be the cosmic process, the atoms of the submicroscopic world, weaving their knots in the plenum.

4. Animal psychologists

A study of the remarkable communicating ability of honey bees shows that humans are not alone in possessing elaborate systems. But a bee communicates by virtue of her inherited genes, and a man by virtue of his culture. It seems to be a few thousand brain connections against fifteen billion. There are no moral lessons to be learned by humans from the bee, for she operates on a different formula.

Chimpanzees come closer to us, and so do cats and dogs, but a deep gulf remains. After the age of three the human youngster leaps ahead of the chimpanzee, as he learns to talk and think with words. The fact that an animal cannot express his thoughts in language suggests that he has no thoughts on this level to express. We are not likely to learn anything by putting a camera behind the eye of a sheep, for our brains do not permit us to see what a sheep sees. Animals respond to some sounds made by humans—dogs even recognize specific words—but no animal, including the parrot, has true language.

Watching my cats, I am convinced of one considerable ad-vantage they possess over humans in adjusting to the environ-ment. Having no words, they cannot cut up nature into classes, and then forget to put the pieces together. Nature is all one piece, and Boots and Shadow react to the situation-as-a-whole, thus probably increasing their chances of survival in the long run.

5. Child psychologists and educators

Every human baby arrives on earth with a cry—not to say anything, but to clear his lungs. He has a few reflexes, a fear response to certain sounds, but no words and no experience. He begins collecting thingumbobs the instant he arrives, and a few months later begins to react to words. At eighteen months, his tongue, mouth, larynx, and thorax are developing at a furious rate; the drive to talk is on him. He talks with his whole body, and his early words are often giant molecules, signifying situation-as-a-whole.

Jerry is not born with subject-predicate statements and two-valued judgments, but they are built into him, to his future perplexity. Stage by stage the linguistic experiences are stored, and his incessant querying What? Why? How? is his only way to store them and achieve maturity. Some children have been clocked at 35,000 running words a day, and all talk fluently and understand readily before they go to school.

Parents and teachers are not generally aware of these findings. They may try to silence Jerry, or force him into ways he is not equipped to go. A great deal of research remains to be done in this department. Why does a child sometimes miss his potential and grow up a communication cripple? A few reasons are known, but not nearly enough.

6. Anthropologists and the culture concept

Every member of a society is a carrier of its culture, and on this level everybody is important. People who favor political democracy can take considerable satisfaction from this anthropological finding. History as usually written stands the social pyramid on its apex, concentrating on kings and warriors and seers. The culture concept puts the pyramid back upon its base; and some day histories must be rewritten on this firmer foundation.[1]

Culture may be displacing evolution. Instead of thicker fur, for instance, when the next Ice Age moves down, there will be more central heating and electric blankets. Culture builds from generation to generation through language and example, and writing has speeded the accumulation. Any normal infant can adapt to any culture, but once enclosed in its habits, sol-

[1] But see Muller's The Uses of the Past, and Ralph E. Turner's monumental study, The Great Cultural Traditions, McGraw-Hill, 1941.

dered into its belief systems, the child finds it difficult to imagine other ways, and is confident none can equal his own. By twelve he finds it easy to believe that "those foreigners" are slack, wrongheaded, and immoral, besides talking preposterous gibberish.

There has never been a world culture, and so never a world language. No one can enter into an alien culture short of many years' experience, but any one of us can learn to climb up the walls of our own culture and see other peoples behind theirs. It is strenuous exercise, but there is no better way to tolerance and understanding.

The frequency distribution curve is another useful tool for tolerance and understanding.

7. The linguists

This small but competent group of scholars stands at the very center of communication study. They collect the sounds of any language, derive patterns thereform, and can presently describe the basic phonetic structure. Writing does not interest linguists as much as speech, while grammar as hitherto taught in the schools fills them with apprehension. The grammarians, they say, began at the wrong end, by analyzing written words. It is quite probable that the linguists will revolutionize the study of grammar.

Linguists are not interested in how things ought to be said, but in how they are in fact said. They are interested in gestures and overtones as aids to the spoken word, and have analyzed these aids too, in a sub-science called *kinesics*. The linguists point out that while there may be tribes living in what we Westerners call primitive conditions, there are no languages to be called primitive.

8. The metalinguists

From the basic study of predictable sounds, students of metalinguistics take off into wider regions. They theorize that the language one learns exerts a powerful influence on one's thinking and behavior; and they support the theory by uncovering many concealed assumptions in Indo-European languages, such as Absolute Time and Absolute Space. Some languages which escape these handicaps have other handicaps— a fact which makes it clear that there is no "law of reason" underlying *all* languages. Each language shapes the reasoning of its speakers. Thus English enforces either-or reasoning, while Chinese does not. Indo-European languages lead to subject-predicate concepts, yet the whole trend of modern physics is away from them.

9. The physicists

We use our reason only to support our prejudices, said Bernard Shaw. In the behavior called "science" this does not happen—making it a very unique form of behavior indeed. Science requires continuous open communication between research centers. Every major development in science involves a crisis in communication, of which the latest and greatest was relativity. New languages have been developed to meet these crises—higher mathematics, multivalued logic, operational definitions, probability theory, statistics of aggregates, the concept of process, and the theory of types. The operational definition is especially useful to the student of communication for getting rid of meaningless questions.

Physicists, needless to say, are not purposely assisting communication study. Their contribution is a by-product of their severe and lofty discipline.

10. The semanticists

Major challenges to language date back to Aristotle and Zeno. Long before the word "semantics" was coined, scholars were worried about generalization, the limits of abstraction, the inconsistencies of logic, and loose meanings generally. The concern went far beyond dictionary definitions. Bertrand Russell demonstrated how most propositions are *both* true and false, depending on time and place, and called them "propositional functions." Ogden and Richards deflated a vast verbal superstructure with "find the referent," and Richards helped the linguists to break up the one-proper-meaning superstition.

Semantics is at once broader than General Semantics and less ambitious. I do not mean to make a sharp distinction between the two schools, so much as to keep the disputants separate.

11. The General Semanticists

This school was created by Alfred Korzybski, almost single-handed, and was chiefly founded on the new talk in physics. Korzybski's own contribution, so far as physical research went, was not great, but he was a great interpreter, and a great stimulator of interest in how words behaved. He "brought together a useful way of thinking and talking about human thinking and talking." He advocated five useful "stop, look, and listen" techniques to help evaluation. Out of twenty-one statements on General Semantics listed in Chapter 13, here are some of the more important:

> No two events in nature are identical.
> Nature is best understood in terms of structure, order, relationships, process.
> Any event has unlimited characteristics. We abstract only what we need.
> A word is not a thing: a map is not the territory.
> Abstract qualities are in our heads, not in nature.
> At the end of all verbal behavior are undefined terms.

12. The group analysts

Kurt Lewin was the outstanding pioneer of this school, which deals with the outer network of the twin systems. The school analyzes chiefly face-to-face groups of two or more persons, but also studies larger impersonal groups, aggregates, and institutions. Interactions between members of a group grow like compound interest, as each new member is added. (Consider a mother-in-law added to a family group of man and wife.) Among the more useful conclusions are, (1) the importance of identifying oneself with the speaker, entering his "perception field"; (2) encouraging participation, to get the advantage of pooled experience; (3) "permissive" rather than autocratic leaders; (4) establishing the security of members; and (5) the use of certain semantic principles to keep communication fluid.

Some of the group analysts are beginning to investigate listening, the reception and decoding of messages. They have organized listening clinics, experimented with labor-management groups, with college students, even with after-dinner conversations. They point out how attention to the motives, needs, feelings of the speaker improves understanding of the words he utters.

Every living creature is a kind of communication box, a walkie-talkie machine, sending and receiving signals, both conscious and automatic, continuously throughout his life. If the box fails, he will not long survive. Man shares this apparatus with other creatures, but his box has the special attachment of language. A general theory of communication must be concerned, of course, with both types of box. The task of semantics is to examine and repair the language attachment, a recent gadget as evolution goes, which still needs a good deal of servicing.

Meaning is relative to one's experience, and to every individual's "perception field." To have meaningful messages exchanged, the fields of sender and receiver must overlap. Inside a culture, overlapping is very extensive, due to a shared language and world view, as well as the customs of the tribe. But acquired prejudices and ideologies can spread a fog over verbal messages, blotting out common meanings, distorting common experiences. Perhaps the main goal of communication study is to reduce the fog; to keep shared experience in an unclouded state, to see oneself in other people.

Part Two APPLICATIONS

"The question is," said Alice, "whether you *can* make words mean so many different things."

"The question is," said Humpty Dumpty, "which is to be master—that's all."

LEWIS CARROLL

"The peoples of the world are islands shouting at each other over seas of misunderstanding."

CLEMENT ATTLEE

Chapter 17

TOOLS FOR WRITERS

The twelve approaches to communication study described in Part One were illustrated there with many cases. Part Two will deal mainly in cases. Assuming that the student of communication has absorbed some of the knowledge now available, how can he use it day by day?

The problems to be analyzed fall under the labels of "economic," "political," "medical," "educational," and so on, and are the sort which have challenged your author in recent years. Were he a lawyer by training he would include several chapters on semantic calamities in the law; were he a businessman, some concentrated attention to prose among top-drawer executives, "communication-wise." Almost any corner of the culture is susceptible to analysis, and a whole shelf of case histories could readily be compiled. Here, I have sampled some subjects which interest me, on the theory that if I am interested the reader is less likely to be bored. The reader is advised, however, to try the tools for himself in subjects which are his particular concern.

Let us start with the case of a writer attacking a literary problem.

The welfare state

Here is your author at his desk, with a tray of sharp pencils and a pad of ruled paper before him, the hills of Connecticut out the window. He is about to start writing an article on "the welfare state" for a magazine called *The Nation's Business*. The year is 1950. A reader who cares to watch him at his work may understand better how to use the tools described earlier. This yellow pad, the hand which holds the pencil, the brain which directs the hand, all illustrate applied communication theory. To be sure, he might write an article under this title even if he had never heard of semantics, linguistics, or the culture concept, but it is safe to say he would write it very differently.

To go back a little, the editor had invited me to take the affirmative in a debate by defending the "welfare state," while a distinguished conservative economist was to attack it. The invitation had two drawbacks from my point of view. First, it offered no factual basis for discussion, but called for abstractions of a high order. Second, it was specifically to be a debate.

I thanked the editor and told him that since taking up semantics I had renounced debating. The practice was, I said, a two-valued verbal combat with the effect of over-simplifying and distorting questions which were usually many-valued. Nevertheless, I said, I should be glad to discuss the welfare state from the semantic point of view, if that would interest the editor.

He seemed disappointed, but told me to go ahead. There would be no formal debate, but each of us would define and discuss the term. Thus, before even putting pencil to paper, I used a semantic tool to help make a decision.

I sit here at my desk, thinking about the term "welfare state," somewhat the way we thought about the term "communication" in Chapter 2—as a verbal tent to cover a large and active circus. I take up one of the sharp pencils and, in the first paragraph which I write, assert that no such thing as a "welfare state" exists anywhere but in our heads. No camera can find it, no radar screen pick it up; it is an abstraction with very limited usefulness.

After thus locating the term in the stratosphere, I proceed down the abstraction ladder to the solid earth. What are the referents for "welfare state"; what tangible administrative bodies and government organizations can legitimately be called welfare agencies? The American Constitution aims to provide for the "general welfare," and a great deal of legislation in the last 150 years falls under the welfare clause. How far down the ladder must I go before finding something I can take a picture of?

I jot down a few notes from memory, then swing around to the reference shelves beside my desk and consult the Congressional Directory, the World Almanac, and various other sources. After a period of fact-finding I come up with a list of nearly 100 activities which are clearly concerned with welfare and supply at collective expense needs which individuals cannot, or do not, meet for themselves. It turns out to be quite a comprehensive and interesting list, including:

The public school system	School lunch programs
The Homestead Act	Old-age pensions
Land grant colleges	Unemployment insurance
The GI Bill of Rights	The W.P.A. of the 1930's
The Public Health Service	Public housing
Pure food and drug inspection	Subsidy to the merchant marine
The Red Cross	Subsidy to potato farmers
The child labor law	Federal insurance of bank deposits
Community chests	Soil Conservation Service
Taft-Hartley labor law	Public credit agencies

This is only a sample, but enough to show what is going on under the label of "welfare state." These services are paid for by direct or indirect taxation or by voluntary contributions. Here are agencies of the utmost value to the community, and here are others, like the subsidy to potato growers, of very questionable value. Some, like the public schools, have been with us for a century or more; others, like the W.P.A., were created hit-and-miss to meet an unemployment crisis, and have been discontinued. Some, like the school lunch program, created to meet an emergency, have survived, and may or may not be needed in prosperous times. Every item demands careful scrutiny on its merits. Was it necessary when set up? Is it necessary today? Is it nice to have but too costly? What is the effect on recipients?

Nobody in his senses would object to every agency; nobody in his senses would embrace them all. Anyone in his senses, furthermore, would agree that even the most essential agencies could stand improvement in structure, or administration, or both. Nobody, except a few howling dervishes, is against the American public school system as such, but what one of us is not convinced that it needs considerable overhauling?

The list demonstrates one of the sharpest tools in the whole kit: *find the referent*. Neglecting to find it, one takes his stand "for" or "against" the "welfare state" as an entity, and presently begins to suffer from a mild form of "unsanity," to use Korzybski's term. Yet in a recent season, the scholastic debating teams of the nation went into battle on a thousand platforms, "Resolved: That the American People Should Reject the Welfare State." They might equally well have marched into the fray, "Resolved: That the American People Should Reject the Man in the Moon."

David Lilienthal, while he was Chairman of the Atomic Energy Commission, received a letter from a young student which went something like this:

Dear Sir:

Our school is debating the atom. I am taking the negative. Please send me some information.

Yours,

Johnnie

Formal debates of public questions can provide entertainment and amusement, but seldom enlightenment. We cannot hope to grasp a multivalued event with a two-valued tool. "Welfare state" has at least a hundred sides, each to be considered on its merits, and it is dubious whether the term has now any utility beyond an instrument of political abuse.

On the Town Meeting radio program, to which millions of Americans listen every week, the moderator holds up a ball and asks the studio audience what color they see. They answer "white." Then he turns the ball around and asks again. The answer is "black." He explains that every question has two sides, and what one sees depends on the direction from which one is looking. But Leo Cherne points quite another moral. The two-colored ball, he says, illustrates the distortion which ruins most radio and television debates. The world's big issues are no longer black *or* white—if indeed they ever were.

But the debates that are staged for the living rooms of America tend by their format and emphasis to reduce all of our problems to two colors. There is almost never a gray, an expressed doubt, seldom a concession that there are elements of truth in contrasting points of view. . . . There is nothing wrong with entertainment *per se*. What is dangerous is the acceptance of entertainment as news, the assumption that we have been informed when we have only been amused.[1]

My article for *The Nation's Business* concludes with a proposal to liquidate certain agencies—like the inequitable potato subsidy, to amend others like the Taft-Hartley law, turn others from government to private hands, and generally clean up the welfare clause. I end it on the note that we would do well to stop loose, emotional talk about "welfare states," and concentrate on improving or abolishing specific welfare agencies, in line with technological change and popular necessity.

By the time the article is sent off to the editor, I have picked up and used quite a variety of communication tools. Let us lay them out, including those already identified. I have:

1. Avoided a meaningless debate.
2. Distinguished between levels of abstraction.
3. Kept in mind that the word is not the thing.
4. Looked for referents—and found 100 of them.
5. Prepared an operational definition.
6. Made allowance for dates, and for the necessary shift of evaluation through time.

[1] Leo Cherne, "Biggest Question on TV Debates," New York *Times Magazine*, March 2, 1952.

7. Regarded the U.S. economy as a developing process, rather than an entity governed by absolute laws, moral or economic.

8. Tried to think in terms of relationships.

9. Drawn the distinction between facts, inferences, and value judgments.

If the reader believes that I keep a list of tools pasted on my blotter, he is mistaken. To use the tools efficiently one must build new habits in one's nervous system. In acquiring their use, a good deal of effort is required—as in learning the multiplication table, though the material is a good deal more interesting. Eventually the user reaches for these tools the way a carpenter reaches for his hammer.

Choosing one's words

There are other tools which I find useful in writing an article. One is a lively consideration of the reader and his "perception field." To whom am I writing? What is his probable feeling about this topic? How can I get him to read objectively? What is our area of agreement?

It is not difficult to imagine the feeling of an average reader of *The Nation's Business*, organ of the United States Chamber of Commerce, toward the "welfare state." He will consider it an entity and be against it. I have a problem, accordingly, but I may be able to solve it by careful attention to the words I use. The American business executive, to judge by the many I know, is a thoroughly decent, fair-minded, and intelligent citizen. He recognizes a fact when he sees one. If I can keep away from terms which irritate him, and can pose the problem in terms similar to the assets and liabilities on the balance sheet of his firm, he will be willing to take a good, hard look at it. I do not want to convert him to anything, I want him to consider referents rather than stereotypes.

Again, in writing the article, I will try to use short, Anglo-Saxon words in preference to long, Latin polysyllables; and use short sentences and paragraphs when possible. I do not follow, however, any rigorous system in this connection. The longer word is sometimes the better one. I will break up the page with side headings to catch the eye; indeed, I will give the reader whatever typographical substitutes are available for the kinesics of oral speech. Thus I do not subscribe to the doctrine of my Puritan ancestors that the more painful the effort, the better one learns. It contradicts nearly everything we know about conditioned reflexes.

Other tools could be named, but perhaps I have described enough to give the reader a general idea of what is happening on that yellow pad, marked by that pencil, guided by that particular brain. This is my usual course in writing an article, the chapter of a book, the outline of a lecture.

Can these communication tools be used by any normal person? Yes, I am positive they can, and that they will give him a new and better grip on reality. Can he then write articles which editors will be glad to print, and even pay for? Now we are getting into deeper waters. I know of no dependable research telling us why people become good writers, or painters, or composers—which may be just as well for those of us who are writers, painters, and composers.

We can say with some confidence, however, that the tools described will make a "born" writer a better communicator, and warn him of the limitations of his craft. They promise an aspiring writer a better chance of avoiding rejection slips; but they carry no money-back guarantee.

Piers to reality

We recall Alexander Leighton's happy simile of sending down piers of fact to solid earth, lest the bridge of theory collapse. After a lifetime of writing nonfiction, I have learned that locating authentic cases to support generalizations is hard, grueling work. It means halting the rhythm of writing, and ransacking memory files or library shelves, usually both, to find specific examples which honestly illustrate the point. To make them up would be cheating. The easy way is to continue writing abstractions and not to bother about referents at all.

The easy way is to assume that the reader will supply his own cases. The easy way is to coin a few high-sounding terms to cover up the obvious lack of a specific illustration.

We nonfiction writers need to be constantly jerked back to reality, lest we stray into that misty land of "nonsense fortified with technicalities," where so many promising academicians have been lost. The casework, furthermore, is not alone for the edification of the reader but also for the clarification of the writer. The reader receives a dividend, as it were, from the writer's hard-won earnings. Time and again, especially in writing economics, I have been forced to discard an inviting generalization because I could find no dependable facts to support it. If you want a case for this generalization, try wrestling with the Malthusian law, in which population *always* outruns the food supply. The law seems to apply in India at the present time, but not in the United States.

Straight reporting and casework follow the order demanded by science—first the facts, then the generalizations from them. Too much writing in the social sciences reverses this—first the hunch, then a frantic search for any stray fact which can be pummeled into supporting it. The *Economist*, observing an author in this travail, called it proceeding from an unwarranted assumption to a foregone conclusion. It is a procedure which beckons every writer as the sirens beckoned Ulysses, and, like Ulysses, we must tie ourselves to the mast. Since looking into semantics I have tied firmer knots—though it is improbable that I have never struggled out of one.

In a famous essay about the writer's craft, Somerset Maugham says: "All experience, even the most ordinary and insignificant, is grist to his mill. He should not sit around and wait for experience to come to him, he should go in search of it."

The better the writer, the larger the proportion of ordinary experience he can utilize. A poet like Keats seems to absorb enough in childhood to distill into a rich stream of lovely cadences. The rest of us have a harder time, especially if we are trying to convey information. I could "write" as a school-boy; the words came easily; but I did not have anything worth saying until I was past thirty. The things I wanted to write about—social problems—took years of personal contact with social and economic facts in all manner of situations, before I stored enough material to know what I was talking about. I could regurgitate generalizations at twenty, but it took another dozen years to know if a generalization would stand up.

I always try to go and *look* at what I propose to write about, regardless of how much documentary matter may be available. The looking, the hearing, the touching, get into the nervous system in fresh, new experience. When the time comes to write, the experience cannot fail to kindle the prose. This again is hard work. It is so much easier to sit at a desk and take notes from other people's observations than to get on a train, or a plane, and go a thousand miles to look at the factory, or the power dam, or the welfare agency. But following our familiar thingumbob principle, that is what the writer must do.

Northwest by west

There is a final point I should like to make while in this confessional mood. No matter how numerous the trips of inspection, how voluminous the notes, how well rehearsed the ideas, the final form of an article on the welfare state, or on anything else, cannot be known in advance. Something happens in the actual writing which deepens it, stretches it, often changes its path. Novelists report that their characters sometimes turn independent and go off in the most contrary directions. The writer prepares to proceed due north, but as he writes he finds himself, willy-nilly, being pulled northwest by west. Struggle as he may, he cannot return to due north—unless, of course, he is willing to turn out a hack job.

I would venture the hypothesis, based on a good many years of experience, that this strong, sometimes violent pull is the result of fresh thinking which grows out of the actual putting down of words on paper. By writing in the formal structures of one's language, one enriches and clarifies his original thoughts. The original thoughts were verbal too, of course, but scattered. When the time comes to write, they must be co-ordinated into an orderly structure, often unforeseen. All this gives further support to the conclusion that without language one cannot think—at least beyond what an intelligent cat can do.

In whatever way this unfolding process may be explained, I am at a loss to know what a writer would do without it. It gives to the craft of letters part of its fascination and unending adventure.

Chapter 18

ECONOMIC TALK

"The besetting sin of the economists," said a British jour-nalist, F. S. Oliver, "was their preference for argument over observation."

Economic theory has been dominated by philosophical systems—Adam Smith, Ricardo, John Stuart Mill, Karl Marx, Henry George. Very few dependable laws based on controlled experiments have been established. The "law of supply and demand," for instance, is so loose and imprecise that it cannot be compared with a law in natural science.

Economic talk has been of many kinds, but only rarely the scientific kind that helps to advance knowledge. Practically all the semantic offenses have been committed by economic writers. The high abstractions might have been more closely analyzed—as we tried to do in the previous chapter with "welfare state"—but they were not. The unstated assumptions and philosophic theories might have been tested and shaped by observation into better tools. Instead, raw untested theory has been seized upon as a weapon for political controversy; and whatever edge it originally possessed has been blunted. "Free enterprise" is a good example of an economic term which has been practically talked to death.[1]

Business cycles

Consider the "business cycle," about which so many millions of words have been written. "Cycles" should go around

[1] Well documented in W. F. Whyte, *Is Anybody Listening?*

with some measurable regularity—at least they do in physics and astronomy. Every time this one has been around, however, it has ground under its wheels most of the economists bold enough to try to predict its course. They cannot even foretell the general direction. For example, as I write, the perennial argument is raging as to whether the American economy is headed for more inflation, for a recession, or for an old-fashioned depression.

It would be illuminating to compare the actual course of the American economy since 1900 with the prophecies made about it—not by crackpots but by serious students of economics. One revealing collection, dealing only with forecasts before the depression of 1929, was published by a cynical journalist under the title of *Oh Yeah?*. He found nearly every prophet either seriously or totally wrong, the majority firmly convinced that prosperity would continue long beyond 1929.

The years of Franklin Roosevelt's "New Deal" were sown with prophecies of national bankruptcy, runaway inflation, the end of enterprise, with grass growing in the streets, dictatorship, chaos and ruin—prophecies which never came to pass. Part of the foreboding was political, to be sure, but a good deal of it was sober economic judgment. I remember debating the danger of inflation with Lewis Douglas at the Economic Club of New York in 1935—before I gave up debating. Mr. Douglas, an honest student of economics if ever there was one, convinced the entire audience, and came perilously close to convincing his opponent, that the financial policy at Washington would lead straight to a runaway inflation. Washington did not mend its ways, but the inflation failed to come as announced.

In 1940, a contemplated national debt for America of $100 billions was enough to make an economist of any stripe turn pale, while a total much beyond that figure was synonymous with the end of the world. Yet the debt went sailing up to $279 billions by 1946, and the economy went sailing into unheard-of prosperity. Meanwhile the postwar depression, so confidently prophesied by practically everybody, including your author, never arrived.

From time to time the American economic system has been solemnly declared on the verge of ruin because of protective tariff, because of free trade, taxation policies, the abandonment of gold, labor unions, trusts, foreign agitators, Wall Street manipulators—what a list of total calamities could be compiled since 1900! Yet the American economy in sober fact, save for small setbacks in 1907 and 1921, and the large one in 1929, has grown like a green bay tree, to become today the wonder and envy of the world. The helpful indexes have gone up—population, production, output of inanimate energy, output per man hour, literacy, health, longevity—all up, while the curves of disease, slum-dwelling, poverty, have gone down. More than half of all American farmers are now enrolled in conservation districts, with the result that we are even beginning to save our soil. This comparison is given not to show that American economic problems are solved, only that the facts have consistently belied the predictions of the economists.

Perpetual-motion machines

Before the laws of thermodynamics were developed, many inventors busied themselves with perpetual-motion machines. In 1660, the Marquis of Worcester contrived a wheel fourteen feet in diameter, rigged with forty sliding weights of fifty pounds each. Even Leonardo experimented with quicksilver to turn a wheel forever. But by 1775 the Paris Academy of Sciences refused to accept any more schemes for *perpetuum mobile*. Physics had advanced to the point of proving their impossibility.

Unfortunately economics is still plagued with perpetual-motion machines. Every man is still free to propound his own economic plan to save the world. A major difficulty is that economics is so completely interwoven with human behavior that reliable theory cannot be formulated unless the economist takes both psychology and anthropology into account. Thorstein Veblen, Wesley C. Mitchell, John Maynard Keynes, a few others, have been aware of this; but most economists have stubbornly held to prescientific assumptions about human behavior.

The statistical output of the economists, however, is often excellent.[1] W. W. Leontief at Harvard is now working on a new statistical method to describe the interrelations of the whole American economy.[2] He employs electronic computers to plot the production figures of each industry against the consumption of material by every other industry, thus weaving the economy into one integrated pattern, with almost every ton accounted for. Professor Leontief believes that government statistics are now good enough to warrant the operation, and he calls it "Input-Output Economics." It may help economics become a genuine science.

Economics as philosophy, sometimes as theology, heretofore has been the dominant note. The dialectic of the Marxians has a good deal in common with medieval disputations about the angels on the pin; while the grim morality of the *laissez-faire* classicists is not much more helpful. After the Russian revolution a group of Marxian purists proposed that their nation's railways be torn up as a vile bourgeois product, and replaced by good proletarian roadbeds! There are still capitalist theologians in America who believe that kilowatts produced by government dams are as malevolent as kilowatts produced by private power companies are beneficent.

Ideologists have had the field, and the average citizen has failed to get a workable map of the economic territory, either present or past. With some justice he has called economics the dismal science. Linguistic difficulties have made the map even more inaccurate by personifying abstractions, especially in the form of an absolute "Capitalism" opposed to an absolute "Socialism," with no intermediate points of view allowed. Dreadful battles over words have ensued, sometimes leading to bloodshed. German "Communists" and "Fascists" staged sanguinary riots in the 1930's, while many young people changed from side to side, convinced that one theory must be entirely right, but uncertain which theory it was.

[1] For example, F. Dewhurst, *America's Needs and Resources*, Twentieth Century Fund, 1947.
[2] *The Structure of American Economy 1919-1939*, Oxford, 1951.

In addition to these struggles between philosophical systems, there have been even fiercer battles between factions for control of the same system. Thus "Trotskyism," "Titoism," and "Stalinism" violently compete for the one true faith of "Communism." Will "Malenkovism" last, or be soon replaced in another theological split?

"Capitalism" vs. "Socialism"

The war between these two words is perhaps the greatest verbal block in the world today. Do you devoutly believe in "government ownership" or in "free enterprise"? No middle roads, no compromises are recognized in this war. Yet the actual space-time world is full of middle roads, halfway measures, whether in the West, or in Russia itself. People in factories, offices, shops, are carrying on day by day in ways which bear no relation to the two-valued talk. But the talk cannot fail to confuse their day-by-day acts and hinder needed corrections. We may blunder into them, as we blundered into the "New Deal" reforms. More often we lose our way in a morass of dogma. "Which side are you on?" asks a left-wing song, and to millions of people on either side, that is all that matters.

Disregarding the words and observing any considerable segment of economic behavior, it is immediately apparent that activities are mixed, sometimes inextricably tangled. The Tennessee Valley Authority, for instance, is owned by the federal government, but encourages new private enterprises throughout the Valley, sells much power to private power companies, co-operates closely with state and local governments. Great corporations take on functions closely resembling governmental powers, as Peter Drucker has pointed out, while many private businesses are subsidized by governments—for example, trucks on the highways.

The closer one looks at economic realities today, the clearer it becomes that both "Socialism" and "Capitalism" are old-fashioned concepts, useless to explain what is taking place. An intelligent visitor from another planet would be unable to make head or tail of them. Terms like "Wall Street profiteers" and "Creeping Socialism" can generate plenty of heat but no enlightenment. The world of tangible behavior is moving into a new and dramatic dimension, which the old words cannot describe or explain.

New dimension in Puerto Rico

What, for instance, can the standard theorists, right or left, make of the economy of Puerto Rico? I have studied it at firsthand and found a situation calculated to drive either a "Capitalist" or a "Socialist" to despair.[1] An American engineer, long in residence, summed it up for me soon after my arrival:

They haven't any ideological principles, or if they have, they don't show. Their only commitment as far as I can see is the well-being of the whole island. They are not tied up in either Marxian or free-enterprise straitjackets. They can think without looking it up in the book; they are flexible and mentally free to think out what needs to be done. If business can meet a need, fine. But if business cannot, then let the government do it, or a cooperative, or a non-profit association. The main thing is to get it done. They have achieved what you once called "ideological immunity."

This is the more surprising because when Governor Luis Múñoz Marín came into power in the early 1940's his party was frankly socialistic. No good Socialist trusts businessmen, any more than good businessmen trust Socialists. The first reforms were along doctrinal lines. Government corporations were set up to operate new projects in both agriculture and industry. The object was to shift from a one-crop sugar economy to diversified agriculture plus diversified light industry.

It was clear, too, that certain essential utilities and services could not be organized at all unless government set them up.

[1] See my report, *"Operation Bootstrap" in Puerto Rico,* National Planning Association, Washington, 1951.

The island government could borrow money more cheaply in the States; private business feared to take the risks. In addition to power plants and water systems, five industrial plants were built and operated by the government—cement, clay, glass, a shoe factory, a paper mill.

Before long the program ran into difficulties. Some of the agricultural corporations were badly managed, and losses continued in four of the five industrial plants. Only the cement mill showed a profit. One trouble, of course, was union labor. A socialist government is supposed to be on labor's side, which gives the unions heavy leverage in all managerial decisions. Collective bargaining becomes a feeble instrument to protect the interest of consumers.

As the impasse was reached, strange things began to happen. The Governor and his economic staff, instead of standing on their socialist principles, sold the five manufacturing plants to private business. The Ferré interests, who bought four of them, were the leading industrial group on the island, and had long experience in dealing fairly with union labor. They put the factories on a paying basis. The government used the $10,-000,000 received from their sale to build hotels, factories, shops, for lease or sale to other businessmen. When these properties were sold in turn, the government reinvested again—and went on repeating the process as a means of bringing new industry to the island.

As far as I could determine, this move toward co-operation with businessmen was the result of direct experience; no theories were involved. The Governor and his staff did not rush from the bosom of Karl Marx to the bosom of Adam Smith—after the fashion of a number of American intellectuals in recent years. No. After some harsh administrative experience, the top command was flexible enough to move with the facts, while never for an instant losing sight of its goal, the economic well-being of the island. They cared more for Puerto Rico than for dogma. Perhaps some of the staff found it painful to discard their ideology, though no one mentioned it to me. Perhaps some retained their fear of "wicked capitalists" and "profiteers." I found many of the staff, however, busily entertaining the wicked capitalists, taking them around to factory sites, and showing them how to make more money.

Under this treatment, local businessmen in the island, and even businessmen from the mainland, began to build up ideological immunity. They lost their fear of the wicked "State," and came to look on government men as their friends rather than a nest of bureaucrats determined to tax them to death. The remission of taxes on new enterprises for ten years also contributed to a tolerant point of view.

I asked Luis Ferré, whose firm had bought the government plants, where he thought the line should be drawn between government and business. This is his reply:

> We can produce cement more cheaply than the government and outsell our competitors all over the Caribbean; but the government must take the risks of launching new enterprises at this particular time in Puerto Rico. After they are fully launched, the government should not try to operate them indefinitely, but should allow business men to have the headaches and make the decisions. I think the government should get out of the municipal telephone business, but it is doing a good job with slum clearance and housing. It should provide most of the utilities—power, water, drainage, transportation. It should build more schools and hospitals but fewer baseball parks.

New dimension spreading

After the ideological warfare at Washington, where "free enterprisers" were locked in struggle with "planners" and "New Dealers," I found it refreshing to listen to Mr. Ferré. His mind ranged freely to attack the practical problems of the island. What agency could best find the capital? Who could best take the risk? Who could best manage a specific enterprise? Instead of growing angry about abstractions, he was finding referents on all sides and drawing practical conclusions from the facts.

How different on the mainland! The first atomic explosion in Russia in 1949 provided both the *Wall Street Journal* and the *Daily Worker* with a text for a rousing editorial. The *Journal* said that the Administration in Washington was using the blast as a new excuse for "Stalinizing" America. The Stalinist *Daily Worker* said that the Administration in Washington was using the atomic explosion as an excuse to give "Wall Street" control of the country. "Which side are you on?"

The people of Sweden, with their famous "middle way"— between Socialism and Capitalism—resemble the people of Puerto Rico in economic maturity, although traces of dogma are still to be found in the Social-Democratic Party.

The British Labor Party after World War II faced a semantic crisis revolving around the word "nationalization." As a party devoted to Socialism it had to be for the "nationalization of the principal means of production." But while the coal industry had to be nationalized if the British people were to get coal—private business having refused longer to take the risks— the nationalization of the steel industry made very little sense. The program of nationalizing for the sake of nationalizing ran into the gravest difficulties. More mature thinking by British leaders was called for, and at last accounts the leaders were in a reflective mood.

Even Tito of Yugoslavia, a professed Marxist, is questioning traditional slogans. Asked by an American journalist if his order to go easy on collectivizing the farms was a new interpretation of Marx, Tito replied:

> For us, the collective farms are not a matter of dogma. We are not concerned about whether the farms are called socialist or not. What we need is more agricultural production—*more bread*. We are trying to find means of getting it.

Bread before dogma sounds like another landmark in the new dimension.

Every modern economy, whatever the talk, is a mixed dish— with government ownership stewed up with private ownership, garnished with labor unions, co-operative societies, resale price maintenance laws, and huge nonprofit organizations like colleges, churches, and foundations.

In addition to the "Socialism" versus "Capitalism" semantic confusion, there is another only less serious between "Socialism" and "Communism." Many Americans resolve the problem by saying that the two doctrines are identical. Thus, Arthur Summerfield, President Eisenhower's Postmaster General, was quoted as saying that Socialists and Communists are indistinguishable, and both are "inchworms, responsible for the state of affairs we are in today." Mr. Summerfield did not seem to realize that he himself, though no Communist, was presiding over the second largest piece of "Socialism" in America.

The Atomic Energy Commission is the largest chunk of "Socialism" in the U.S., but twenty-five private companies are now co-operating to build the first full-scale atomic energy plant; "the beginning," says the New York *Times* editorially, "of a partnership between government and private enterprise."

Most of our allies in the so-called "Free World" have strong socialist parties, yet are as bitterly opposed to Communism as we ourselves. The difference between the two doctrines is profound, for the Socialists favor peaceful change under political democracy, while the Communists favor violent revolution to establish the dictatorship of the proletariat. Yet because both favor government ownership, millions of Americans believe that the programs are identical, with the result of misjudging our allies, and weakening the front against Moscow.

Countervailing power

Fortunately some new economic theory is being developed to fit the new economic facts of middle roads and mixed economies. J. K. Galbraith, in his arresting study of the American system, succeeds in bringing map and territory into reasonable agreement.[1] Socialism, far from a growing menace, is old hat, he says, while the free market of the *laissez-faire* classicists is pretty well buried under the technology of mass production and mass distribution. A monopoly of national power by organized labor is extremely improbable, especially after

[1] *American Capitalism.*

the revealing experiences of the labor government in Britain.

What the United States now enjoys in effect, says Galbraith, is an economy based on the principle of "countervailing power," where five great institutions strenuously interact, compete, and limit each other's ambitions. If one of them gets too far out in front, the other four unite to drag it back. The five are:

1. Big business—primarily mass production.
2. Big distribution—the chain stores, mail-order houses, the great department stores.
3. Big labor—the A. F. of L., C.I.O., and the Railway Brotherhoods.
4. Big agriculture—including the farm lobby.
5. Big government—swollen through the advance of technology, and by reason of wars, hot and cold.

If big business raises its prices too high, it will run into pressure from large distributors threatening to set up captive plants; into pressure from government threatening antitrust suits; into angry farm organizations and angry unions. If labor leaders play fast and loose, businessmen, farmers, and government will combine against them; and so on, for all five power centers.

Few Americans understand this pressure game. It is new, and it does not fit the accepted stereotypes. There is no "side" to be on; and two-valued judgments give way to a five-valued situation. The theory of countervailing power goes a long way to explain the economic stability of America in recent years. Older theories, by contrast, could not explain it. Galbraith has set a pattern of the kind of mature, objective thinking we should expect from our economists in the future.

On not warring with history

"The legitimate object of government," said Lincoln, "is to do for a community of people whatever they need to have done, but cannot do for themselves." Puerto Rico is a good example of following this counsel, and so are Sweden, Denmark, New Zealand. Even Marshal Tito is beginning to be aware of it.

In the age of the atom, superimposed on the age of the machine, we need flexibility to survive. There is no flexibility in dogma which says that business is always "bad," and government is always "good," or vice versa. The crucial question is who can do what needs to be done.

There is much I might have said about word trouble in economics—consider the semantics of money alone. Instead I chose to devote most of this chapter to what seems to me to be the outstanding economic trouble today. Somehow we have to break through the 'isms and 'ologies and see our economic problems in their true dimensions. They are severe problems, but I think they are soluble. To people blinded by old words they are insoluble.

Senator Milliken of Colorado gave us a fine example of breaking through.[1] Although a vigorous conservative, he voted to make atomic energy a government monopoly. What caused him to act against his established economic principles? The facts converted him. After careful study he came to the conclusion that the U.S. government was the only possible enterpriser, at that time. If the government did not pour in the billions to develop atomic fission, nobody else in the United States would or could. That would leave Russia in sole possession of the most powerful engine ever discovered. Said the Senator: "I do not war with history. I cooperate with the inevitable."

[1] *The Reporter*, April 1953.

Chapter 19

MOSCOW TALK

Politics can be defined as the art of gaining power, and holding it once gained. With the decline in the divine right of kings, two chief methods now remain for gaining supreme power in a nation. The candidate can shoot his way in, as in the case of Lenin, Hitler, and other modern dictators, or he can talk his way in, by cajoling the voters.

The student of semantics has here a rich mine to work, for many politicians do not say what they mean if they can help it. When their messages are connected with personal power, it is not easy to factor this out. The task of the semanticist is to find the real meaning in the geyser of words.

In this chapter we will examine a famous exhibit in propaganda among the dictators, and in the next chapter an exhibit of campaign oratory among the democracies. Modern dictators are seldom silent. With their left hand they build armies, with the right hand propaganda machines, using either or both, as circumstances warrant. Hitler hoped to conquer Europe by words alone.

Propaganda machine

A brisk setting-up exercise in the morning for a Moscow politician, describing a group with whom he does not see eye to eye, sounds something like this: "They are Trotskyites, spies, wreckers, Titoists, fiends, cannibals, enemies of the people, murderers, *agents provocateurs,* diversionists" . . .

Pausing for breath, he continues: "lackeys of imperialism, union-smashers, stool pigeons, renegades, Fascists, liars, profiteers, warmongers, aggressors, Wall Street blood-suckers, stooges of a moribund crisis-ridden capitalist society!" This puts him in a good mood to enjoy his breakfast.

The Moscow propaganda machine has two tasks: to talk inside the country to the Russian people; to talk outside to the world. Inside, the aim is to build loyalty to the Kremlin and to get people to work harder. Outside the country, the aims are four, according to Edward Crankshaw: [1]

1. To broadcast ideas of revolution and revolt in other countries.
2. To break up coalitions against Russia by exploiting differences between allies.
3. To weaken individual Western nations by sowing internal dissension, setting group against group.
4. To paralyze the will of the opposition by building up a picture of the Soviet Union as an invincible power based on an invincible idea.

Crankshaw says that following World War II, Moscow selected Britain as her main propaganda target, hoping that the United States would retreat again to isolation. But the Truman Doctrine in Greece, followed by the Marshall Plan, caused the target to shift to America. The United States has been in the zone of heavy verbal fire since 1946.

In Kremlin circles an arch-enemy is a very precious thing, to be built up and cherished. It is the scapegoat to be blamed for all the ills of the world, including the harsh consequences of the Kremlin's own domestic policy. The line in such matters, too, is always that what now is, must always have been. [A is A.] Thus it is not enough to call President Truman a cannibal; it has to be proved that cannibalism is a long-time American tradition. President Wilson was also a cannibal. . . .

Cold war talk from Moscow insists that "Wall Street" rules America, while "millionaires," "monopolists," "profiteers," and

[1] "Stalin Turns His Hate Battery On Us," New York *Times*, August 17, 1952.

all officials connected with corporations, banks, and government departments are *ipso facto* members of American "ruling
circles." "Peace-loving" peoples co-operate with the Kremlin,
"aggressors" and "warmongers" do not. Governments that co-
operate are "People's Democracies," non-co-operators are
"Fascist States." The word "democracy" was not stolen by
the Russians from the West, but given a special meaning—
"economic democracy," where the livelihood of citizens is
underwritten by the State if they toe the line. "Political democracy" Moscow calls a raw and hypocritical scheme for insur-
ing capitalist control. Russia has rejected the goals of the
United Nations, but is glad to use it as a sounding board for
propaganda.

The machine is a powerful one. Tens of thousands of propaganda experts are graduated from the 6,000 schools, which
train nearly 500,000 native and foreign students. In 1950, the
Russian government spent $928 million, and satellite govern-
ments $481 million, for propaganda—not including the outlays
of communist parties outside the iron curtain. (France has an
enormous party with five million votes.) The $100 million
spent by the United States in 1950, with only 10,000 persons on
the propaganda payroll, was insignificant by comparison.[1]

Through United Nations debates the Russians convert their
propaganda into "news" which gets disseminated throughout
the world.

Their lies about germ warfare, atrocities against prisoners of
war, breadlines and soup kitchens in the United States, always
make the headlines even though they are branded as lies; yet many
well-informed readers may begin to suspect that where there is so
much smoke there must be some fire.

On January 21, 1951, a special "Hate-America" campaign
was launched by the Kremlin. Its ammunition consisted of piles
of "documents," faked photographs, "eyewitness accounts,"
"historical records," and "statistics"—the kind which come

[1] Report by Professor Mark A. May of Yale, House Document 94,
83rd Congress, 1953.

after "damned lies." Thirteen books appeared in Russia, including novels and plays, about the unspeakable Yankees. Broadcasting stations burned the air with the theme, and new textbooks were placed in the schools. In addition to the usual line of vilification, three new stories were introduced: (1) The United States had cheated Russia out of Alaska; (2) American troops at Archangel in 1919 had buried Russian civilians alive; (3) Posters advertising Coca-Cola in the United States show Christ on the cross, asking for a bottle.

Picture book

Harry Schwartz, Russian expert for the New York *Times*, has assembled a choice album of American life today, as retouched by Moscow, and from there beamed to both the Russian people and the world at large. *Izvestia* discovers that the annual meeting of the National Association of Manufacturers is held for the sole purpose of formulating directives for government policy, "directives which are then followed exactly by the President, the State Department and Congress." This while Mr. Truman was President!

The Russian *News Times* reports that out of a class of 750,000 United States college graduates in 1950, "only one-fifth have managed to find jobs—as waiters, street cleaners, cemetery employees. The rest are doomed to a life of semi-starvation unless their parents can support them." *Soviet Radio* adds that capitalists are so greedy for profits from collegiate sports that injured football players "are often carried to the hospital or even straight to the cemetery at the University of Michigan."

In *Pravda* a Russian seaman reports from Brooklyn that "decently dressed Americans came up to our sailors and begged a penny for food." *Molodaya Cardia* declares that American businessmen stop at nothing. In Alabama, they stole a steel bridge worth $25,000 while the police obligingly shut their eyes.

In the 1948 presidential campaign, Thomas E. Dewey, the Republican candidate, was photographed with a group of businessmen in a small town in Oregon. They were dressed in animal skins and waved assorted bones, calling themselves the "Cavemen." They thus hoped to attract some visitors to the local caves. You can imagine what Moscow did with this picture! It proved conclusively the savage and barbaric character of Americans—a presidential candidate being made an honorary member of a society devoted to drinking blood and eating raw meat!

During the water shortage in New York in 1950, a Moscow broadcast received in England said that many people were dying of thirst in the streets. Meanwhile day in and day out, the coming Great American Depression is announced.

Ends and means

Russian propaganda attacks America but is not addressed to Americans. When a Russian delegate at the United Nations looks at a United States delegate and proceeds to charge Washington with the most dreadful crimes, he is not really talking to the United States delegate and is well aware the charges are untrue. He is talking to a ragged peasant listening to the village radio somewhere in Burma or Iran. He is trying to fix in that peasant's mind a list of evils which will thereafter be associated with "America." Moscow, fighting the cold war, is seeking to turn every non-American mind against America—her morals, her coming economic crisis, her treatment of Negroes, her jobless college graduates, her germ warfare, her Coca-Cola posters, her blood-drinking cavemen.

The propaganda is double-barreled; for along with belittling America, it elevates Russia to the skies. Russians made all the important inventions, from the lever to the transistor tube; Moscow is the natural home of the sciences and arts—where "Marxian" physics flourishes side by side with anticapitalistic string quartets. To Western minds this boasting seems childish—until we recall that Burmese peasant. The idea is to impress *him* with American vice and Slavic virtue—Russia the fountainhead of civilization and human knowledge.

Moscow propaganda takes account, too, of the peasant's wants and needs. Most peasants in Asia today want three things: (1) land, (2) relief from usurers, (3) the end of Western domination. Moscow promises all three, regardless of ability to make good.

Lenin said: "It is necessary . . . to use any ruse, cunning, unlawful method, evasion, concealment of truth." The end justifies the means. Hitler said: "On a given signal, bombard him with a regular drum fire of lies and calumnies. Keep it up until his nerves give way."

In America an ex-Communist screen writer named Richard Collins testified that when he was following the U.S. "party line" he found himself cheering for Earl Browder one day, and denouncing him as a "betrayer of the working class" the next day. "You have to keep your hatreds flexible," says Collins. To follow the corkscrew course of the party line requires the surrender of all consistent reasoning. The Hitler-Stalin pact of 1939 was the prize example.

Achilles heel

It is a waste of time and emotion to look for facts, logic, reason, in this kind of political talk. The dictatorships specialize in it, but it is not unknown elsewhere. It is also a waste to attempt to answer it with logic or reason. Having analyzed it to the extent of knowing what the aim is, and the audience aimed at, the best answer is to get to that audience with some concrete acts.

Here is an example. The Soviet delegate at a United Nations meeting in Indonesia delivered the standard tirade against the United States. Whereupon the delegate from India arose and said: "The Soviet Union has done practically nothing to help this region, and has attributed malicious motives to other countries that have." Thomas Wilson, who told the story in the *Reporter*, points the important moral. While American counterpropaganda has been feeble compared to the blasts from Moscow, he said, the tangible *acts* of America, expressed in the Marshall Plan and the Point Four programs, have done more to hold our friends than all the propaganda ever heard of. "In the final analysis, the Communist system cannot deliver what it promises to deliver, and therein lies the fundamental weakness of the propaganda."

Some observers seem to believe that propaganda can do anything—up to making water run uphill. If people are once exposed to it, as to typhus or cholera, they are done for. This is simply not so, and our study of communication shows why.

In the first place, propaganda is still far from being a science. There are too many variables in the picture. Leonard Doob of Yale, who did notable work for the O.W.I. in the European theater of World War II, lists fourteen questions to be answered in analyzing the effectiveness of a single piece of propaganda, beginning with the existing opinions of the group aimed at. Failure to focus on a specific purpose causes a good many expensive campaigns to be wasted.

In the second place, propaganda cannot exist indefinitely on words alone, as the delegate from India made plain. There must be *acts* to reinforce the words, which is another way of saying that referents must be found from time to time. For thirty years now, the Kremlin has been promising the Russian people a great improvement in their standard of living as soon as the productive plant was built. It has been built well enough to show a great improvement in the output of tanks, artillery, and bombers, but much less in food, shelter, and clothing. Researches by Clyde Kluckhohn and his staff of the Russian Research Center at Harvard indicate that the Russian people are becoming increasingly skeptical about those consumer goods which have never come. The propaganda is losing its bite. This comes under the law of diminishing returns, and it applies to all kinds of propaganda.

Moscow discovers semantics

The masterminds in the Kremlin have collided with semantics, but rather than twisting it to their uses have backed off in horror. An article in a philosophical journal in Moscow

attempts to demolish the entire school, including Wittgenstein, Carnap, Korzybski, and your author. A quotation translated by Rapoport (*ETC*, Autumn 1948) gives the flavor of
Moscow's consternation:

Semantics will not save the capitalist beast. . . . Chase, the
bourgeois economist . . . has lost the last remnants of common
sense and come forward with a fanatical sermon . . . a belief in
the magical power of words. All his strivings are directed to keeping the people in economic, political and spiritual slavery. This is
the goal which is served by the clownings of the semanticists. . . .

It is an honor to be selected for special excoriation by the
intellectual elite of Moscow, but the reason is not far to seek.
A general understanding of semantics would utterly deflate
Moscow's propaganda.

Chapter 20

CAMPAIGN ORATORY

Wendell Willkie, caught in a certain discrepancy between deeds and former words, excused himself by saying that the words had been "just campaign oratory." The dictatorships have no monopoly on political double talk, but in the democracies, when the verbal carnage is over, the loser sends the winner a telegram of congratulations. In the democracies politics is a game, though often a costly one. In the dictatorships it is war without quarter.

Listening to both the Republican and the Democratic presidential conventions in Chicago in 1952, one had the feeling that most of the speakers had attended the same school of oratory and graduated well before 1900. Their voices were forced to a uniform theatrical pitch, in which the stock phrases, "your Great State," "the Great Party of Abraham Lincoln," "the Great Party of Thomas Jefferson," kept reappearing like wooden horses on a merry-go-round.

The speeches, the parades up the aisles, the banners, the singsong of the balloting—"Oklahoma casts three votes for Governor Stevenson"—the demonstrations measured in minutes, all fused into a kind of formal ballet, where nobody seemed to be doing any thinking, and everybody was following an automatic pattern generations old. An anthropologist would have no difficulty in comparing it to a Polynesian tribal dance. A great spectacle, yes; but what it had to do with the selection of leaders competent to face the mounting problems of the modern world remained obscure.

Clinical samples

During the campaign it was my privilege—in the clinical sense—to listen attentively to a local speaker who was a master of extreme tory dialectic. He was a tall, bald man with heavy tortoise-shell glasses and a deep, resonant voice which he knew how to use. He talked about Democrats somewhat the way Moscow talked about profiteers. He began by saying that the United States was balancing on the knife-edge of ruin. The New Deal, he said, was the embodiment of the welfare state, which was "creeping socialism," and in the last analysis Communism. It was all part of a deliberate conspiracy, he said, plotted years ago by a group he called the "welfare revolutionaries."

History proves, he said, that all welfare states begin as idealistic movements—the Red plotters seemed to have momentarily disappeared—and end as brutal dictatorships. You can't change human nature, he said, especially labor union human nature, and that of bureaucrats. You give them an inch, he said, and they take an ell. It always happens.

America must choose and that soon—his voice became sepulchral—between Constitutional Government and the Slave State. There is no middle ground; those who are not with us are against us.

American capitalism, he said, is the wonder of the world, but at the same time it stands in hideous danger. It is on its way to collapse because of unbalanced budgets, staggering debts, the crushing burden of taxation, runaway inflation, the destruction of incentives, government interference, tinkering with the currency, handouts to foreigners, and Reds in the State Department. The graduated income tax, he said, is a Communist plot and unconstitutional as well. The British Labor Government was a communist government in disguise, with not a pin to choose between it and the New Deal. Midnight has struck, he said, and more.

From my notes, I reconstructed some of the patterns in this standard campaign oratory of the Upper Mississippi, or Early

Devonian, school. The speaker repeatedly used guilt by association and spurious identification, as in equating the "New
Deal" with "Communism." He played the conspiracy note for
all it was worth—plotters undermining our liberties both inside
and outside the nation. He leaned heavily on those well-worn
phrases, "history proves," "you can't change human nature,"
"the thin entering wedge," and "America must choose." He
did not hesitate to work both sides of the street by declaring
that American capitalism was all-powerful, and at the same
time almost as badly undermined as claimed by Moscow.

The talk proceeded in a series of high abstractions, omitting
any facts which might be subject to verification. Value judgments dominated the discourse. What he said made no more
sense than what *Pravda* said, literally interpreted, but the inner
meaning was equally obvious. He was saying he did not like
Democrats. His technique was to associate unpleasant terms
with Democrats—"bankruptcy," "debt," "spending," and especially "Communism"; and to associate pleasant terms with Republicans, such as "economy," "tax reduction," "freedom,"
"home," "the flag."

Speakers for the Democratic Party operated on substantially
the same formula. Being in office, however, they had to assume
the defensive and refer now and again to a few facts, which
always weakens propaganda. They did their best, however,
building up an idyllic picture of life in America under the
Democrats. "You never had it so good." Their prophecies of
what would happen in the event that the Republicans came
to power were just as gruesome as the statements of the Republicans about what *had* happened while the Democrats were
in power. "Big business" and "the interests" were given a
thorough going over, the Taft-Hartley labor act was called
the "slave labor law," while the protective tariff was taken out
of moth balls and given a vigorous airing reminiscent of the
days of William Jennings Bryan.

Democratic as well as Republican speakers pretty well
agreed on the following categories of good and evil words.

The "good" received a kind of ceremonial obeisance; the "evil" a ceremonial curse.

Good words: The Constitution, the American Way of Life, Free Speech, Free Enterprise, Little Business, the Founding Fathers, et cetera.

Bad words: Unbalanced Budgets, Big Government, Taxes, Monopoly, Bureaucracy, Aggression, Appeasement, Lobbyists, Gangsters, Communists, et cetera.

These terms dilated like the swaying monsters in Macy's Thanksgiving parade up Fifth Avenue, until they blocked the sky. Like Macy's monsters, too, they were filled with gas.

Exception noted

There was, however, an extraordinary exception to the standard run of campaign oratory in the speeches of Democratic candidate Adlai Stevenson. He said when nominated at Chicago that he was going to try to "talk sense"; and for the first time in my long and painful recollection of campaign speeches, he actually did talk sense, at least a good part of the time. If he had not been obliged to make so many speeches (more than 200), he might have talked sense all of the time.

The point is not that he was right, but that he tried to consider the event under discussion in a civilized, grown-up way, with proper qualifications. Time and again he said he did not know the answer, which stunned citizens accustomed to candidates who knew all the answers to everything. One can only hope that Mr. Stevenson's unique performance marks the beginning of a trend in American political talk.

The Russians staged an election in 1950 in Berlin, and gave the world a magnificent example of not talking sense. They began by defining a "free election," as "voting which is free from contest." The Soviet Army newspaper *Taegliche Rundschau* went on to say:

These elections will be the most free Germany has ever had. Free from anti-Soviet agitation, free from demagoguery of opposition parties, from all bribery by monopolistic capital, from all pressure and terror of foreign taskmasters.

And free, though the paper omitted to say so, from any reason for voting.

Real issues and phony issues

Apart from Stevenson, the real issues before the country and the world might be mentioned in the American campaign but were seldom dealt with. What were the real issues in 1952 as against the phony ones? Here are some of them:

The issue of atomic energy, especially the H-bomb, how we could neutralize it, and if worse came to worse, how we could defend our cities against it.

The issue of the growing pressure of population on food supply over much of the world, as modern science drives down the death rate, leaving the birth rate practically unchanged.

The issue of the future of Korea, as a tongue of land encircled by three great powers—China, Russia, and Japan.

What to do about Japan's economic future, and about Formosa.

What economic steps to take to halt depression when defense orders should slacken.

A new program for agriculture, as subsidies based on an unrealistic "parity" made less and less sense.

The baffling problem of the aging population of America, as applied science prolongs the life span.

The issue of the definition of loyalty, and how Anglo-Saxon justice can be upheld against the inroads of Congressional committees.

The urgent problem of how to change the political structure in Washington so that Congress and the White House, instead of being continually embroiled, can co-operate for effective government.

The crisis in American schools was a real issue, and so was the future of sixty million motorcars on congested roads.

Perhaps the greatest issue of all was how to break the deadlock of cold war, especially an exploration of ways and means for possible negotiation.

Live and looming issues either were not discussed at all, or were talked about disingenuously as the crimes of the opposing party and its leaders. The billions of words assaulting the air waves and filling the papers in the fall of 1952 contained almost nothing to nourish the mind of a mature citizen—Mr. Stevenson's words excepted. The politicians brushed this off by saying that grownups were "egg-heads," and they, the politicians, were talking to Joe and Mac who had the votes.

The sovereign voter

What did Joe and Mac think about the Niagara of words? Nobody knows—not even the Messrs. Gallup and Roper. The *Reporter*, however, gathered some straws in the wind by interviewing television owners and viewers in New York during the campaign. The TV viewers continually spoke of someone called "they"—as though the government belonged to other people. Said a fat man in a candy store: "They're all a bunch of crooks, makes no difference who gets in. We're still loused up. When you have to work for a living, nothing can change anything." Said a war veteran: "That stuff drives me mad. . . . I shut the damn thing off. They can make a fool even of a man like Eisenhower!" Said a bartender: "You can't go by what they say in the speeches. It's all bull to attract the voter; then they do what they want."

"Political campaigners," observed a woman voter writing in the New York *Herald Tribune*, "had better climb out of their cocoons and look around. The customers these days want to do the talking and the thinking . . . that old-fashioned-preacher method of political oratory is interesting to no one except the preacher."

A fundamental rule with American politicians is that the voters above all else want their taxes reduced. Yet Elmo Roper found a substantial majority of the American people (June 1953) against cutting taxes "at the expense of external or internal security."

Perhaps the sovereign voter is not so bemused by campaign oratory as the politicians believe. Perhaps if not an orator had opened his ample mouth from June to November of 1952, General Eisenhower would have been elected by the same comfortable margin. Perhaps Joe and Mac and their wives in their perplexity were primarily looking for a real leader and were not much interested in a mess of stale words.

Perhaps, at this particular period in history, it is time to talk sense and face real issues; just as in the field of economics it is time to abandon the meaningless debate between "Socialism" and "Capitalism" and get on with the job of production. To spend so much energy and money arguing questions of little or no importance is bad enough. What makes it worse is the angry emotions aroused over questions of little or no importance. At a period when national unity is badly needed, an artificial battle of words disrupts it. Perhaps it is time to gaze outward at what is really happening in a world of unprecedented change rather than inward at ideas which have not changed for fifty years.

Chapter 21

GUILT BY ASSOCIATION

After Benjamin Franklin invented the lightning rod, the principle was widely accepted but there was much discussion whether sharp points or round knobs made better conductors. In the absence of conclusive experiments, the discussion became heated. Franklin favored points. King George III, however, belonged to the knob school, and urged the Royal Society to rescind its resolution in favor of points and come out for knobs.

The argument the King used was guilt by association. He said Franklin was a leader of the insurgent American colonies and that to adopt his type of lightning rod would be to uphold a rebel. The scientists of the Royal Society, unimpressed by the case against guilty lightning rods, refused to budge.

The *Economist* of London, listening in considerable astonishment to the charges coming from investigating committees of Congress in 1952, proceeded to apply their logic to Winston Churchill. As a member of the Church of England, said the *Economist*, Churchill was automatically associated with an admitted fellow traveler, the "Red" Dean of Canterbury. As a member of Parliament, Churchill for fifteen years shared the House of Commons with a card-carrying Communist, William Gallacher. As a member of the Big Three in World War II, Churchill sat at conference tables with Joseph Stalin. Therefore Churchill must be a Communist. Q.E.D.

The notion of guilt by association arises in part from the structure of the language we speak, in part from the association process in the memory patterns of the mind. It takes two forms, physical association and verbal. Churchill was physically associated with the Red Dean, though of course he was not contaminated thereby. The case of King George and Franklin, however, was purely a verbal trick. Franklin favored pointed lightning rods; Franklin was a traitor. Therefore anyone who favored pointed lightning rods was a traitor.

This spurious identification is one of the major roadblocks in human communication. No animal could be guilty of it, for it is uniquely a phenomenon of language. It has operated so persistently down the ages that elaborate legal defenses have been erected to protect innocent citizens. Spurious identification flourishes when times are out of joint. If citizens feel insecure, frightened, frustrated, they are in the mood to blame somebody for their troubles. Whereupon demagogues and fanatics create scapegoats out of other citizens, condemning them on the principle of guilt by association.

The Spanish Inquisition rose to great heights in such a period. The "heretic" was the scapegoat then, and Protestants were convicted by the Ecclesiastical Courts and subjected to horrible punishments on the flimsiest grounds. The standards of admissible evidence were relaxed to allow extra-judicial confessions, the evidence of accomplices, of the excommunicated and the perjured, of sons against fathers, spouse against spouse.[1]

. . . the beliefs of relatives were held to be presumptive proof of the guilt of the accused. In one case, the charge against a man was that his mother was a heretic, that she often used to visit him, and sometimes helped him out when he was in need. The standard of judgment was that a strong suspicion should be sufficient to condemn a man as a heretic.

Dictators and tyrants use guilt by association to give a pretense of legality when they remove persons in their path. In the United States during the cold war with Russia charges of subversion were widely circulated, chiefly by political demagogues in Congress and state legislatures. Nobody was immune; even the loyalty of General of the Army George Mar-

[1] Eleanor Bontecou, *The Federal Loyalty-Security Program.*

shall was attacked by Senator McCarthy in a long speech on the Senate floor. Instead of "heretic," the scapegoat was "Communist," but the verbal patterns were very similar.

In America, at least, nobody was burned at the stake, though some books were burned. Many loyal citizens branded as "Communists" were ruined for life, and a few committed suicide. The morale of the government services, especially the State Department, was alarmingly reduced at a time when a strong government was needed to stand up against the maneuvers of Moscow. Perhaps worst of all, Americans began to wonder who could be trusted. If not General Marshall, why anybody? "Perhaps your best friend . . . perhaps your minister . . . perhaps your wife's brother . . . you can't be sure."

This unprecedented situation was due almost entirely to twisted communication. First the modern inquisitor misuses the language; then the mass media, especially the newspapers, carry the scrambled results into every home. It would be hard to find a situation where the tools we have been discussing were more needed. The evaluation by Americans of other Americans was distorted out of all resemblance to the facts; map and territory were far out of line.

Legal guilt

One does not need to study law to understand the nature of legal proof. Readers of detective stories know that without evidence that will stand up in court, the "private eye" is stopped in his tracks. He cannot convict his man on the fact that his name is Jones, and recent crimes have been committed by a party named Jones; verbal identity is not enough.

Anglo-Saxon legal rules, going back a thousand years to Magna Charta, and enshrined in the American Bill of Rights, insist that the accused is innocent until proved guilty by evidence acceptable to judge and jury. The rules of evidence were designed to circumvent purely verbal condemnations, such as those of the Inquisition. Trial by jury, presumption of innocence, suspicion of circumstantial evidence, outlawing bills of attainder, specifying *acts* rather than threats to act, and other safeguards have been introduced over the years to defend citizens from being put away by tyrants, inquisitors, and personal enemies.

But in certain Congressional investigations these legal safeguards were ignored. The hearings, viewed on television, looked judicial enough. Actually they constituted a legal no man's land, with no cultural tradition behind them and no dependable rules. An accused person might be absolved by one committee and promptly summoned by another, or recalled by the first committee. Abe Fortas, a Washington lawyer, has described how such proceedings could appear legal, though the traditional safeguards were missing.[1] He explained how frustrating the process was for counsel, giving a lawyer the sensation of a nightmare, for the victim was rarely charged with a specific act.

If the victim had been called an "atheist" or an "anarchist," it would only have been insulting. But he was labeled a "Communist"—a small matter in the 1930's, but a terribly serious matter in the 1950's. For it meant that the accused was in effect an agent of a hostile foreign power, and so by implication a spy and a traitor. It meant that he could be ruined for life, with little or no recourse.

Find the syllogism

The charges, whether by legislative committees or by persons outside, could usually be reduced to a simple but fallacious syllogism, allowing the verbal trickery to come out clearly, thus:

Adam$_1$ believes in free public schools.
American Communists quote the *Communist Manifesto*, which demands free public schools.
Therefore Adam$_1$ is a Communist.

We might more properly call this guilt by *verbal* associa-

[1] "Outside the Law," *Atlantic Monthly*, August 1953.

tion. We will consider physical association in a moment. Here is another example from a nonpolitical field:

> My grocer has cheated me.
> My grocer is a Yankee.
> Therefore all Yankees are cheats.

Every person has almost unlimited characteristics. He may be white or colored, tall, short, Catholic, Baptist, Buddhist, banker, butcher, Socialist, individualist, and so on. Cattell has drawn up a list of 171 personality characteristics in alphabetical order: "alert, acquisitive, affectionate, alcoholic, ambitious, amorous, argumentative, arrogant, ascetic . . ." Every organization may also possess a large number of characteristics.

The trick is to locate *one* characteristic which both parties share, and then leap to the conclusion that other characteristics, perhaps all, are interchangeable.

> The Pope favors child labor laws.
> The Politburo favors child labor laws.
> Therefore the Pope is a Communist, or therefore Stalin was a Catholic.

It can work either way, you see. With this monstrous logic it is possible to "prove" anybody guilty of anything. Just find *one common characteristic;* you will have no difficulty because of the thousands available.

Missing dates

In another gross semantic distortion, the modern inquisitors are careful not to date their accusations, but assume "once a subversive always a subversive." The most glaring case I can remember is when Senator McKellar smeared David Lilienthal with a "Red taint" because his parents came from Czechoslovakia, now a satellite of Moscow. The fact that they came to the U.S. in the 1880's, when Czechoslovakia was part of the Austrian Empire, was not brought up, nor was the fact that David was born in Illinois. This masterpiece of guilt-by-association-through-time made headlines all over the country.

The committees have read into the record excerpts from a victim's books, poems, articles, written five, ten, twenty years earlier—often torn from their contexts. To aid them in this dateless research, they have called to the stand professional ex-Communists, being careful however to apply dates to them. He was a Communist, yes, in 1940, and knew everybody in the ranks; now in 1953 he is cured. But the victim was not often considered cured.

Physical association

We can all agree that if your neighbor is repeatedly seen in the company of second-story men it is a good idea to lock the windows. Physical association with subversives, as with criminals, is a warning signal, but in itself it does not constitute guilt. Association may, and often does contaminate; the test, however, is not association but contamination. If contamination can be proved by specific acts of the accused, the warning signal has been useful; if the court finds no evidence, it is irrelevant. The late Judge Woolsey once said: "Before judging a man by his associates, remember that Judas Iscariot traveled in the best of company."

What did the accused steal, whom did he strike down, what acts did he commit in aid of a foreign power? Here lies the final test of guilt under Anglo-Saxon law. Very few who came before the committees were guilty by this test.

Procession of the "guilty"

The Russian state, whose state religion is Communism, has been an avowed enemy of the American state since the inauguration of the Truman plan in Greece. Active members of the Moscow-controlled Communist Party in America are, in effect, agents of a foreign power, with whom the United States is fighting a "cold war." They can be a serious threat to the national interest, and it is one of the main tasks of the Federal Bureau of Investigation, the FBI, to watch them.

From this foundation, the investigating committees take off

in a kind of formal procession, a daisy chain of guilt by association. Each link may be weaker than the last in fact, but
verbally all are equally strong. Let us review this parade, for
the like of it has never been seen in America before. The in-
vestigators attack:

1. Any member of the Communist Party today. He is suspect, and rightly so.

2. Any former member of the Party. Careful investigation
is needed; but most ex-Communists in America got out because they could not stand it any longer. The Stalin-Hitler
pact terminated the allegiance of many of them.

3. Any "fellow traveler" at any time. This group also needs
checking, but few are now left. Most of them are faddists who
join popular movements and drift away when the fad declines.
Communism as a fad was at its height during the Spanish Civil
War in the late 1930's.

4. Any Marxist at any time. But anti-Stalin Marxists call
themselves the only true Communists, and hate the Russian
brand with a great hatred. Thus, wrongheaded as they may be,
such Marxists are *not* agents of a foreign power.

5. Any Socialist. But most Socialists today, as we noted
in Chapter 18, are implacable enemies of the Stalinite Communists. They are against violent revolution, against dictators,
in favor of parliamentary government. Norman Thomas is no
more an agent of a foreign power than Bernard Baruch.

6. Any New Dealer. The New Deal, as we have seen, has
been prominently labeled "Creeping Socialism."

New Dealers favor old-age pensions.
Socialists demand old-age pensions.
Therefore, the New Deal is Socialism.

7. Any liberal or any reformer, often described on Capitol
Hill as a "parlor pink." He is usually described, too, as "soft
toward Communism."

8. Any advocate of racial and religious tolerance. Here the
anti-Semites, the Negro-haters, the storm-troopers generally,
rally behind the inquisitors.

9. Any supporter of the United Nations, and especially of UNESCO. The fact that President Eisenhower is a pillar of the United Nations seems to make no difference.

10. Anyone with reservations about the omniscience, military, political, and spiritual, of Generalissimo Chiang Kai-shek. The syllogism here often takes the form:

Communists are against Chiang.
The State Department is dubious about Chiang.
Therefore the State Department is run by Communists.

11. Any American rash enough to have ideas—about education, crime, slums, diet, housing, health. He is probably guilty of "communist type thinking."

From here on let us carry the procession to its logical conclusion.

12. Anyone who can read. This is not as absurd as it sounds. Senator Mundt opposed the appointment of Dr. James B. Conant for High Commissioner of Germany, on the grounds that the President of Harvard University was "too bookish a sort of fellow." Considerable evidence was introduced that Conant was indeed literate, and worse, he had written a book. The attack on Harvard, however, was not exactly new. In 1723 Cotton Mather urged a committee to inquire whether the Harvard College library was not full of "satanical books."

13. Anyone the inquisitor does not like—a convenient method of blasting opponents or competitors out of the way. It is assumed that a citizen who criticizes an inquisitor on any grounds must be a Communist, and that the inquisitor is the final judge of who is a loyal American.

Guilt is briskly transferred back and forth along these categories, usually on the principle of verbal association. Specific acts are almost never proved. Citizens stationed at any point along the line can readily be identified as Communists, or at least as communist sympathizers. The procession is fluid, flexible, and beyond legal reach. Even Senator Taft was not immune to this revolving march of calumny. When he sponsored a bill for public housing, the real-estate lobby, in opposition, announced to the press that he was "lined up with Communism."

> Communists favor public housing.
> Senator Taft has introduced a bill for public housing.
> Therefore Senator Taft is a Communist.

Judge Learned Hand summed up the situation when he said:

I believe that that community is already in the process of a dissolution where each man begins to eye his neighbor as a possible enemy, where nonconformity with the accepted creed, political as well as religious, is a mark of disaffection, where denunciation, without specification or backing, takes the place of evidence. Risk for risk, for myself I had rather take my chance that some traitors will escape detection than spread abroad a spirit of general suspicion and distrust, which accepts rumor and gossip in place of undismayed and unintimidated inquiry.

Two mainsprings

How did such a phenomenon ever get started? Why have so many good Americans been misled by it? Here is perhaps the central problem for the student of communication.

The irresponsible character, to use no harsher term, of the gentlemen who have the movement in hand, does not explain it. Probing deeper, we find two reasons which go far to clarify the situation: widespread feelings of insecurity, and the performance of the mass media. McCarthyism would never have got off the ground without popular unrest, and without the newspapers, radio, and TV.

How profound is this unrest? The American people have been uniquely secure economically, but confused and uneasy politically. They are worried about atomic energy and Russia's possession of the H-bomb, about their country's new role as banker and leader of the free world, about the Korean adventure, the huge military outlays. They want a leader who can explain their troubles, find whatever culprits are to blame for them, shoulder the responsibility. McCarthyism was an understandable response to the needs of a great many Americans—good people, with intelligence far exceeding their information, but unused to evaluating the world much beyond their immediate surroundings.

Great, however, as might have been their need, the movement would have been lost without the newspapers. News in America has come to be defined as a fight. An aggressive Senator has but to clap his hands, and the newshawks come running, hoping that somebody—preferably a celebrity—is about to be put upon the rack. Alan Barth, the author of *The Loyalty of Free Men*, and a newspaperman himself, makes the point far better than I can:

> For some time past the press has been conveying to the American people some fantastically misshapen pictures of their country and their fellow-citizens. It has allowed itself to be used by demagogues as a vehicle for the exploitation of anxiety. Day after day it has reported—with an "objectivity" that treats with perfect even-handedness the character assassin and his victim—allegations that the government of the United States is overrun with Communists and subversives. . . . The constant repetition of such charges, the incessant sowing of suspicion and distrust, could not fail to affect men's minds in time of tightening international tension. . . . The newspapers . . . have been the carriers of hysteria in much the same way that the mosquito has been the carrier of malaria. . . . When the news pages have created a panic, the editorial pages are likely to be powerless to quell it.[1]

Another reason why the Congressional committees gain such leverage is that they take advantage of public confusion between "Russia" the state, and "Communism" the philosophy. The two are not identical. Imperial Russia is marching with heavier boots than ever did Peter the Great, and uses "Communism" as a fifth column. The weakness of the American

[1] Speech before the School of Journalism, University of Minnesota, December 1952.

communist movement is hidden behind the military strength
of Russia. The public bewilderment was dramatically shown
by those definitions of "Who is a Communist?" which we
quoted in Chapter 12.

Confusion is increased by the fact that Marxism used to be
a strongly internationalist philosophy, not tied to any one nation, and that Socialists generally were passionate advocates of
peace. But Germany, with the "National Socialism" of Hitler,
and now Russia, with "Stalinism," have tortured the old international concepts out of all recognition. Moscow gives them
another twist by setting up huge slave labor camps in the
workers' paradise.

What is a Communist?

With these points in mind, let us attempt a short semantic
definition, being especially wary of our dates. It is possible to
identify at least three classes of people who deserve the name
"Communist":

$Communist_1$—a member of the Party *today*, here or abroad,
who follows the Moscow directives.

$Communist_2$—a sympathizer or "fellow traveler" *today*, not
a member of the Party, who follows the Moscow directives.
This does not mean favoring public schools or child labor legislation, but shifting when the party line shifts—for example,
changing from an isolationist to an advocate of intervention
when Hitler attacked Russia; praising Beria until he was
purged, then denouncing him.

$Communist_3$—a subscriber *today* to the system of Karl Marx,
as set forth in the *Communist Manifesto*. A better label for this
group would be "Marxist," for Communist₃ does *not* follow
any Moscow directive. On the contrary, he is in violent opposition to it. Members of the U.S. Socialist Labor Party,
"Trotskyites," "Titoites," are such Marxists. Some, like Tito,
are U.S. allies.

I believe this covers the territory. Note particularly the
word *today*—now in 1953 as I write. The names of individual
members will change, as converts come in and the disillusioned

drop out. They are now leaving, in the United States, considerably faster than they are coming in. The fortunes of the Party are at an all-time low.[1]

But isn't it true that "once a Communist always a Communist"? It is no more true than once a Baptist always a Baptist, or once a Democrat always a Democrat. Communism makes serious inroads on one's integrity, to be sure, but recovery is not impossible.

Will the American culture absorb this outbreak? I think it will, but much depends on events, and on the time required to replace public confusion with understanding. On the whole, the popular feelings of insecurity are shallow compared with the insecurities of the German people which brought Hitler to power. They had lost a war and we have won one. They were at the bottom of the pile and we are at the top. They had been ruined by a runaway inflation, and we have suffered only a mild creeping inflation.

The internal menace of Communism in America is real enough, but it is the menace of potential saboteurs and spies. The prospect of the Party overthrowing the government is about as likely as Holy Rollers becoming the state religion. It would take twenty million unemployed, with no hope in sight, to bring a threat of revolution. Prosperity and Communism do not mix. The way to catch potential spies, according to J. Edgar Hoover, is to let the FBI experts do their subterranean work. The Congressional hearings often make such work harder because of their noisy publicity, and confusion of the innocent with the guilty.

McCarthyism is a product of the cold war. The times being what they are, supersonic characters were bound to arise. But if enough citizens were armed with the tools of communication, supersonic careers, one suspects, would be brief and unhappy. Semantics is the demagogue's worst friend.

[1] Herbert A. Philbrick, an FBI undercover man, in the New York *Herald Tribune*, May 3, 1953.

Chapter 22

THE MASS MEDIA

I can sit here at my desk in Connecticut and hear a wounded soldier in Korea say how wonderful it is to be free again after a year in a prison camp. I can sit here and watch him being carried from his plane to a waiting ambulance in California, and see the expression of wonder on his face.

Before the machine age, the size of a community was limited by the area over which messages could be delivered. Without messages, government and law were impossible. The empires of Persia, Peru, Rome, were held together by the roads over which not only legions marched but swift runners or horsemen could carry orders and information.

Today, radio and jet plane can take the orders of the ruler —or the management if you prefer—to the ends of the earth in practically no time at all. "It is even possible to maintain," says Norbert Wiener, "that modern communication has made the World State inevitable." Archibald MacLeish strikes a similar note when he observes that technology has produced the means for world-wide understanding at the moment when world-wide understanding is the only possible means for lasting peace. The mass media and the atomic bomb have coincided in the march of applied science.

All the varieties of talk recited earlier stand ready to be amplified by the mass media. A recently developed machine can magnify a spoken word one billion times, in decibels. Yet while the talk exhibits its present uncertain quality, how does a billion-fold amplification improve it? Or does amplification make it worse?

In this chapter we will try to describe and define the mass media as integral parts of the communication process. We shall be concerned not so much with casework as with the extraordinary extension of the communication field. We will strike a preliminary balance sheet of liabilities and assets, with sidelights on propaganda and politics.

The day-by-day performance of press, radio, and television, as reported in the last two chapters, indicates that the mass media are not an unalloyed boon. Could Hitler and Mussolini have seized power, could Stalin have continued in power, could any dictatorship survive today without control of communications? The early morning targets of a *coup d'état* are now the radio station, the telephone exchange, and the airport, in that order. Would it be possible, on the other hand, for a candidate to run for high office in a modern democracy without radio and television, let alone posters and sound trucks? Where would our modern inquisitors have been without the newspapers?

The ocean of words rises higher, and we get our information fast and fresh, though not always pure. The news of the world which Socrates received might have been slow and not too accurate; but he got it without a plug for the beer that is dry as a beer can be.

What are the mass media

Mass media can be defined as technological inventions which amplify a message, usually a message from some person or group. Instead of reaching one individual or a face-to-face group as in the old days, the message now reaches a thousand, a million, or a billion persons, far more rapidly and much louder. The Emperor Augustus could appear and read a message to the Roman Senate, and that was as far as it went. Winston Churchill arises to speak in the House of Commons and the whole world, wherever a hook-up is installed, can listen to his voice. The speech may be no better than the

Emperor's, but the audience has grown from a handful to half the population of the world!

The media can be classified and named as follows:

Words for a mass audience to read

Newspapers and tabloids	Paper-backed books
Mass magazines	Billboards
Pamphlets and leaflets	Neon signs
Best sellers	Skywriting
Textbooks	Market and news tickers

Words and music to hear

Radio	Sky broadcasting
Public-address systems	Records
Sound trucks	Music piped to offices and factories

Pictures to see (with words on the side)

Moving pictures	Newsreels
Television	Photographs
Documentary films	Comics

The above list does not include such outstanding media as the telephone, telegraph, cable, airmail, because messages normally go to one person, not to a mass of people. Telephone wires, of course, can be employed for a link in radio transmission and news can be cabled.

There are at least twelve uses for the mass media:

Straight news dissemination	Advertising of products
Education	Institutional advertising
Entertainment	Publicity, for persons and places
Propaganda	Electioneering
Indoctrination	Warning signals
Religious broadcasting	Military action, up to the sei-
Psychological warfare	zure of a state

With advancing technology, societies become more complex, and communication between the local sections becomes increasingly necessary. The process spirals as a complex society requires faster communication, and mechanized communication makes the society more complex. The media, in the words of W. Lloyd Warner, furnish a common core of understanding, known and used by everyone. But a demagogue can manipulate the common symbols, not for understanding but for personal power.

Roots

Three hundred years ago there were no newspapers in the modern sense, no telephones, telegraph, or radio. Scientists, who were in an active phase, realized that if their knowledge was to progress, the findings of one group had to be made known to other groups. Into this communication void moved a number of public-spirited men who came to be called "intelligencers." They were well-educated amateurs rather than professional scientists, and their task was to provide a clearinghouse for scientific information. Samuel Hartlib of London was such a one in the days of Charles I. He made it his business to transmit scientific information from Europeans to Englishmen, and vice versa.

As the intelligencers, with goose quill and courier, helped weave the scientific world together, scientists themselves began to lay the groundwork for the mass media. The printing press had already been invented, but it was a slow, clumsy affair. Clerk Maxwell was a pioneer student of the behavior of microwaves. His studies of magnetic fields, with which the waves are associated, cannot be described in words, only in mathematical equations. Yet out of these wordless symbols have come verbal hurricanes. Hertz produced electromagnetic waves based on Maxwell's equations; Marconi developed a practical way to send wireless signals. Finally the vacuum tube made it possible to send shorter waves and led to the first radio station.

Television

More than 100 television towers span the United States today, and engineers see microwaves displacing wires for the communication systems of the future. Such waves are particularly effective to reach so-called backward areas—"a cable that can't be cut." Microwaves could give excellent communication to the moon or to any of the planets, by apparatus already developed. The trouble is that the space-ship boys must first make an installation at the far end! If a satellite ship were devised to circle the earth above the atmosphere—a not impossible project—it could be used as a microwave relay point for round-the-world television.

The transmitting machinery is highly refined, but what about the messages? Statements duly qualified and guarded seem to have difficulty in adjusting themselves to vacuum tubes. Though television holds great promise, especially in its eventual round-the-world phase, nobody knows how long it will be before responsible and intelligent minds take hold of the programs. The irresponsible, and those whose intelligence is subject to flicker, have the matter pretty well in hand now in America, where the broadcaster is at the whim of his sponsor.

Significant by-products, however, are beginning to appear. Television may remodel the elaborate ballet of U.S. political conventions, and change the course of presidential campaigns. In 1948, when television was in the experimental stage, no conclusions were possible; but by 1952 more than eighteen million sets were in operation, and four out of ten families could simultaneously see and hear a candidate. It was estimated that 14,272,000 Americans witnessed the dramatic call of successful candidate Eisenhower on unsuccessful aspirant Taft immediately after the final vote.[1]

It is argued that the citizen, sitting before his television screen, can now participate more directly and intimately in the political life of the nation. The vast canvas is reduced to the dimensions of the home. Radio did this in part by introducing the sound of the candidate's voice. "But television," said Mr. Paley, "did it even more; it showed the glint in his eye, the mole on his cheek, the smile that revealed sincerity or disingenuousness—the cast of his character and personality."

Again, it was actually easier for a citizen to follow the con-

[1] William S. Paley before the Poor Richards Club of Philadelphia, December 1952.

vention while relaxing at home than for an official delegate in the hall at Chicago to follow it. The television audience saw and heard not only the smoke and roar of the big hall, but what was going on in committee rooms, in frantic hotel conferences all over town. In front of the screen, the citizen can form a judgment in relative tranquillity. He can form it at firsthand, not filtered through the evaluation system of a newspaper reporter, a radio commentator, or an editorial writer.

Television created new personalities in 1952 with unprecedented swiftness. Senator Estes Kefauver of Kentucky was relatively unknown to the general public. He held a series of television hearings on crime which made him famous overnight, and elevated him into the position of a strong contender for the presidential nomination. Governor Adlai Stevenson was brought to public attention and respect in record time.

Many observers think that television is destined to bring a marked decline in the quantity of political talk, and a considerable improvement in its quality. It could shorten the electioneering period, and moderate the candidate's promises, especially to local voters. The demagogue, the phony, it is claimed, cannot long survive the cold hard look of the television audience. The phonyness will come out in their faces, where it does not come out in their voices on the radio. If television can discourage the enemies of the people, so much the better—though a pretty good crop of demagogues survived 1952. A view of a demagogue's face six feet away, in the act of saying what he does not believe, and solemnly affirming what he knows to be untrue, conceivably could have a quite educational effect on the voter. "Television confronts ordinary citizens with the very ordinary citizens who happen to be politicians," says Paley.

Ex-Senator William Benton is another optimist. Remarking that 113,000 letters were received as a result of the Kefauver hearings, 80 per cent of them handwritten by "little people," he suggests that we have here "a key, a hope, a chance to get at the basic problem of our time, which is the understanding

and education of our fellow citizens." But if sponsors continue
to control the programs, says ex-advertising man Benton, we
may find that serious and controversial subjects will either not
be discussed at all, or be watered down to become "entertainment."

The late cartoonist H. T. Webster, an outstanding con-
tributor to mass media himself, once sketched a man slowly
twisting the dials on his television set, to get the following
composite message: "Ask the man for— Don't be *half*-safe—
All you have to do is to tear off 50 box tops— Are you a victim
of dishpan hands?— No sticky oil to trap dust— I can't go,
Otto, not with this nagging backache— Go to your friendly
neighborhood dealer— Big economy size— Tangy, locked-in
goodness—"

Practically all of this microwave communication goes in one
direction. Behind the local broadcasting station is the giant
network, and behind the network the giant sponsor. The receiver of the message can rarely talk back. There are, to be
sure, "panels," fan mail, pan mail, Hooper ratings; but no tech-
nician has yet devised a method for the audience really to get
into the act. When some day the audience does, it may become
a different and more rewarding act.

Perhaps it will be done in connection with public opinion
research. Already Elmo Roper broadcasts every Sunday over
a big network what a scientific sample of Americans—sometimes Englishmen, Frenchmen, Germans—think about current
questions. He may give, for instance, the percentage of the
population in favor of NATO (the European Army), the percentage opposed, and what some respondents say about it.
Thus the people really talk back, though this talk is not a true
conversation piece.

Meanwhile a great deal of intensive thinking by educators
and social scientists, as well as by TV technicians, must go into
the preparation of television programs before they can raise
popular understanding of big basic issues—issues like the future
of Japan, or how to stop a depression. Sponsors, by the nature
of their function, are interested in entertainment ahead of

understanding—several light years ahead. They believe that it sells more beer, and probably it does. Television in America is still devoted to selling beer. Many broadcasters keep hoping the audience will demand something better.

Gilbert Seldes even raises the question whether microwaves furnish the proper channel for a discussion of serious issues. "Is it possible," he says, "that all broadcasting is the wrong medium for communicating ideas above the lowest order of complexity, with television even more wrong than radio?" The issue of the "mess in Washington" goes over readily; but such a subject as "fighting Communism without endangering civil liberties" is much more complicated, perhaps *too* complicated. After monitoring the 1952 campaign with expert ear, Seldes found that the most successful programs were untheoretical and surrounded by clusters of symbols—prejudices, stereotypes, traditions.

Voice of America

The report on foreign information by Mark A. May's committee strikes a more hopeful note. It concludes with seven major propaganda issues now being fought around the world. People everywhere, the committee finds:

1. Want to know the facts, the truth about domestic and foreign affairs. *Who is telling it? What station can we rely on for straight news?*

2. They want peace; a universal desire in every country. *Who is furthering it sincerely?*

3. They want better living standards. *Who is promoting them? Who, per contra, is exploiting the poor?*

4. They want political independence; no more foreign masters. *Who are the imperialists?*

5. They want their own religious customs. *Who is undermining our religion?*

6. They want to know more about other peoples, to travel abroad if possible. *Who is afraid of letting us go?*

7. Finally, they want to be on the bandwagon, the winning side. *What is the wave of the future—freedom or authority? Which way shall we jump?*

Russia is winning the propaganda contest on some of these issues, the Free World on others. Russian propaganda on Number 6 is particularly effective, hammering home the restrictions against visitors to America. The McCarran Act, it seems, has been a generous gift to the voice of Moscow.

These seven wants exemplify the wisdom of people in the mass, whatever their culture. The things they need, the questions they ask, are direct and human, the answers they often get are slippery, slanted, inhuman. One hopes that the Voice of America will take account of this list in every future program.

BALANCE SHEET

The mass media cover far too much ground to be adequately discussed in one chapter. There is room, however, to draw up a preliminary schedule of failures and achievements to date. The evaluation will have to be mine, but I stand ready to be corrected. We will set down the liabilities first, contrary to accounting practice, because it is more cheerful to end our discussion with the assets. (This might be an idea for accountants too.)

Liabilities of the mass media

1. They are invaluable to modern dictators. Characters like Hitler can rise to great heights by capitalizing mass insecurity through their use.

2. Demagogues in political democracies can do likewise—though without the prospect of rising quite so high.

3. Mass media can damage our foreign relations through misleading and harmful pictures of life in America. A symbol system has been created in which U.S. citizens are portrayed as money-mad gangsters or romantic dolts. Any nation exporting films can produce a similar deformed picture of its home culture, but so far there is only one Hollywood. The Mark May report proposes a treaty between Washington and Hollywood to improve the picture of America produced for export.

4. The media create stereotyped patterns of behavior, and tend to speed up the evolution of a given culture. In wise hands this form of education might be valuable. Instead, the invariable happy ending dripping with sentiment, the cops and robbers story, the bang-bang-you're-dead motif, the view of history as a series of plots—all such standard products of film, television, radio, make it harder for people to deal with the world they find outside on the street. In some cases the stereotypes may be a specific incitement to crime and violence. It is arguable that America suffers from legislative spy hunts more severely than any other democracy, because Americans suffer more from spy drama in the mass media.

5. Entertainment tends to crowd out knowledge, as we noted in discussing television. Sponsors are not easily persuaded that knowledge sells more beer.

6. Knowledge when permitted to come through is packaged in easy capsules, to be swallowed at a gulp. Says John Hersey with a fine irony: "If we must read, we demand brevity, generous typography, mean paragraphs, philosophy that has been run through a chewing machine and been eased with editorial pepsin and bile."

7. Conflict is played up; peace and harmony are not news. We hear instantly about all the fights in the world, more slowly, if at all, about techniques of agreement.

8. Advertising, like the movies, builds a dream world, full of beautiful women and luxury cars. Artificial wants are created; people are encouraged to get into debt and live beyond their means; a number of the less amiable traits of Homo sapiens are sharply stimulated.

9. Publicity becomes a salable product. "Shine, mister?" "Build you up, mister?"

10. Both city and country, but especially the latter, are made hideous with billboards. More traffic accidents are a by-product.

11. The night is often rendered sleepless by competing radio and television sets. The decibel rate is everywhere going up, with sound trucks, sky broadcasting, canned music, jukeboxes.

More ear troubles are one by-product, more nervous troubles another.

12. The phenomenon has appeared, new to history, of a "captive audience." Listeners just have to sit and take it.

13. Mass media, with their one-way traffic, cater to "spectatoritis." To play tennis is fun and good for the system; to watch it in the open air at Wimbledon is a step back; to see it on a screen is one more remove from reality.

14. The effect of many comic books is probably a liability. The appeal to youngsters is very great. Habits can be built into the nervous system, however, which make it harder to read sensible material and perhaps easier to draw a gun.

Now for the other side of the balance sheet.

Assets of the mass media

1. They can blanket the world at approximately the speed of light with news of what is happening anywhere. The press can follow the radio with the full story, via airplane editions. The planet is now vulnerable to complete news coverage, and assuming an honest source, the preliminary step to One World is an accomplished fact. This was MacLeish's point.

2. Following honest news, the media can inform the people of one culture about the customs, beliefs, and human interests of another. Although most moving pictures make intercultural understanding more difficult at the present time, they could make it easier. A documentary like "Nanook of the North" helps the whole world to understand an Eskimo family.

3. The media are beginning, just beginning, to influence education. School topics can be made more interesting and learning can be helped by visual aids, documentary films, television for current events. Children of the next generation may increase their stock of meaningful experience very considerably over the past generation. They may learn to use a larger fraction of that magnificent instrument, the human brain.

4. The networks can warn us of approaching storms, floods, disasters, send out S O S signals at sea. The radio told a few

million of us along the New England coast in 1944 to get back
at least a mile from the sea. In the 1938 hurricane, 600 people
were drowned in New England, many because there was no
warning.

5. Appreciation of good music has shown a spectacular increase, thanks to radio and records. All the media can be used
to further popular appreciation of the arts.

6. Despite the extravagance of much advertising, one effect
has been to speed invention and mass production. Keeping
up with the Joneses creates more factories and more prosperity—as well as more ulcers and nervous breakdowns.

7. News stories and advertising combine to spread discoveries in medicine and other sciences. The cause of scurvy was
found by a Captain Lancaster of the East India Company in
1605, but it was not until 1795 that the Royal Navy required a
regular issue of citrus juice to protect sailors from the dread
disease. Compare this with news about penicillin today.

8. Television, according to the experts, is going to scourge
the phonys out of politics. We await the demonstration with
breathless anticipation.

9. Soap opera, says W. Lloyd Warner after commendable
research, strengthens the symbol systems of American housewives in the middle income brackets.[1] They identify their frequently limited lives with the heroine of the story and get a
healthy emotional release. Dr. Warner hints that other mass
media may have similar effects on various classes, and that the
intelligentsia, instead of always looking down their noses,
might well take another look.

10. Mechanical communication is a blessing to many invalids
and other lonely people.

On balance

Taking it all in all, I would say that the net effect of the
mass media on human well-being to date is negative. They
have caused more misery and misunderstanding, I would guess,

[1] *American Life; Dream and Reality.*

than happiness. Consider the melancholy career of Hitler alone, unthinkable without radio.

The greatest asset is, I believe, the unchallenged fact that communication gets around on a scale and to a depth never before dreamed of. Granted that most of it is now unhelpful, and some of it actively destructive, it may be that there is a kind of reverse Gresham's Law in operation, where good communication ultimately drives out bad. It may be that truth will prevail, not so much because it ought to, as because people weary of old lies. There is hunger for the truth—John Dewey called it the "quest for certainty"—operating on all levels, and sometimes pathetically among humble people in despair against being fooled all the time. We saw it in the seven basic issues of the Mark May report.

How many Germans still believe the tall stories of Goebbels? Lies spread by mass media often begin with an appalling massiveness, but they erode through time. Science progresses on the principle that truth accelerates through time. Where are the myths about the nature of fire and water, so potent up to a century ago? The technical equipment to broadcast truth to the world is here, now. The skill, and the will to use it for humanity, are still to come.

Chapter 23

GOBBLEDYGOOK

Said Franklin Roosevelt, in one of his early presidential speeches: "I see one-third of a nation ill-housed, ill-clad, ill-nourished." Translated into standard bureaucratic prose his statement would read:

> It is evident that a substantial number of persons within the Continental boundaries of the United States have inadequate financial resources with which to purchase the products of agricultural communities and industrial establishments. It would appear that for a considerable segment of the population, possibly as much as 33.3333 * of the total, there are inadequate housing facilities, and an equally significant proportion is deprived of the proper types of clothing and nutriment.
>
> * Not carried beyond four places.

This rousing satire on gobbledygook—or talk among the bureaucrats—is adapted from a report [1] prepared by the Federal Security Agency in an attempt to break out of the verbal squirrel cage. "Gobbledygook" was coined by an exasperated Congressman, Maury Maverick of Texas, and means using two, or three, or ten words in the place of one, or using a five-syllable word where a single syllable would suffice. Maverick was censuring the forbidding prose of executive departments in Washington, but the term has now spread to windy and pretentious language in general.

[1] See bibliography. This and succeeding quotations from F.S.A. report by special permission of the author, Milton Hall.

"Gobbledygook" itself is a good example of the way a language grows. There was no word for the event before Maverick's invention; one had to say: "You know, that terrible, involved, polysyllabic language those government people use down in Washington." Now one word takes the place of a dozen.

A British member of Parliament, A. P. Herbert, also exasperated with bureaucratic jargon, translated Nelson's immortal phrase, "England expects every man to do his duty":

England anticipates that, as regards the current emergency, personnel will face up to the issues, and exercise appropriately the functions allocated to their respective occupational groups.

A New Zealand official made the following report after surveying a plot of ground for an athletic field: [1]

It is obvious from the difference in elevation with relation to the short depth of the property that the contour is such as to preclude any reasonable developmental potential for active recreation.

Seems the plot was too steep.

An office manager sent this memo to his chief:

Verbal contact with Mr. Blank regarding the attached notification of promotion has elicited the attached representation intimating that he prefers to decline the assignment.

Seems Mr. Blank didn't want the job.

A doctor testified at an English trial that one of the parties was suffering from "circumorbital haematoma."

Seems the party had a black eye.

In August 1952 the U.S. Department of Agriculture put out a pamphlet entitled: "Cultural and Pathogenic Variability in Single-Condial and Hyphaltip Isolates of Hemlin-Thosporium Turcicum Pass."

Seems it was about corn leaf disease.

[1] This item and the next two are from the piece on gobbledygook by W. E. Farbstein, New York *Times*, March 29, 1953.

On reaching the top of the Finsteraarhorn in 1845, M. Doll-fus-Ausset, when he got his breath, exclaimed:

The soul communes in the infinite with those icy peaks which seem to have their roots in the bowels of eternity.

Seems he enjoyed the view.

A government department announced:

Voucherable expenditures necessary to provide adequate dental treatment required as adjunct to medical treatment being rendered a pay patient in in-patient status may be incurred as required at the expense of the Public Health Service.

Seems you can charge your dentist bill to the Public Health Service. Or can you?

Legal talk

Gobbledygook not only flourishes in government bureaus but grows wild and lush in the law, the universities, and sometimes among the literati. Mr. Micawber was a master of gobbledygook, which he hoped would improve his fortunes. It is almost always found in offices too big for face-to-face talk. Gobbledygook can be defined as squandering words, packing a message with excess baggage and so introducing semantic "noise." Or it can be scrambling words in a message so that meaning does not come through. The directions on cans, bottles, and packages for putting the contents to use are often a good illustration. Gobbledygook must not be confused with double talk, however, for the intentions of the sender are usually honest.

I offer you a round fruit and say, "Have an orange." Not so an expert in legal phraseology, as parodied by editors of *Labor:*

I hereby give and convey to you, all and singular, my estate and interests, right, title, claim and advantages of and in said orange, together with all rind, juice, pulp and pits, and all rights and advantages therein . . . anything hereinbefore or hereinafter or in any other deed or deeds, instrument or instruments of whatever nature or kind whatsoever, to the contrary, in any wise, notwith-standing.

The state of Ohio, after five years of work, has redrafted its legal code in modern English, eliminating 4,500 sections and doubtless a blizzard of "whereases" and "hereinafters." Legal terms of necessity must be closely tied to their referents, but the early solons tried to do this the hard way, by adding synonyms. They hoped to trap the physical event in a net of words, but instead they created a mumbo-jumbo beyond the power of the layman, and even many a lawyer, to translate. Legal talk is studded with tautologies, such as "cease and desist," "give and convey," "irrelevant, incompetent, and immaterial." Furthermore, legal jargon is a dead language; it is not spoken and it is not growing. An official of one of the big insurance companies calls their branch of it "bafflegab." Here is a sample from his collection: [1]

One-half to his mother, if living, if not to his father, and one-half to his mother-in-law, if living, if not to his mother, if living, if not to his father. Thereafter payment is to be made in a single sum to his brothers. On the one-half payable to his mother, if living, if not to his father, he does not bring in his mother-in-law as the next payee to receive, although on the one-half to his mother-in-law, he does bring in the mother or father.

You apply for an insurance policy, pass the tests, and instead of a straightforward "here is your policy," you receive something like this:

This policy is issued in consideration of the application therefor, copy of which application is attached hereto and made part hereof, and of the payment for said insurance on the life of the above-named insured.

Academic talk

The pedagogues may be less repetitious than the lawyers, but many use even longer words. It is a symbol of their call-

[1] Interview with Clifford B. Reeves by Sylvia F. Porter, New York *Evening Post*, March 14, 1952.

ing to prefer Greek and Latin derivatives to Anglo-Saxon. Thus instead of saying: "I like short clear words," many a professor would think it more seemly to say: "I prefer an abbreviated phraseology, distinguished for its lucidity." Your professor is sometimes right, the longer word may carry the meaning better—but not because it is long. Allen Upward in his book *The New Word* warmly advocates Anglo-Saxon English as against what he calls "Mediterranean" English, with its polysyllables built up like a skyscraper.

Professional pedagogy, still alternating between the Middle Ages and modern science, can produce what Henshaw Ward once called the most repellent prose known to man. It takes an iron will to read as much as a page of it. Here is a sample of what is known in some quarters as "pedageese":

Realization has grown that the curriculum or the experiences of learners change and improve only as those who are most directly involved examine their goals, improve their understandings and increase their skill in performing the tasks necessary to reach newly defined goals. This places the focus upon teacher, lay citizen and learner as partners in curricular improvement and as the individuals who must change, if there is to be curriculum change.

I think there is an idea concealed here somewhere. I think it means: "If we are going to change the curriculum, teacher, parent, and student must all help." The reader is invited to get out his semantic decoder and check on my translation. Observe there is no technical language in this gem of pedageese, beyond possibly the word "curriculum." It is just a simple idea heavily ververbalized.

In another kind of academic talk the author may display his learning to conceal a lack of ideas. A bright instructor, for instance, in need of prestige may select a common sense proposition for the subject of a learned monograph—say, "Modern cities are hard to live in" and adorn it with imposing polysyllables: "Urban existence in the perpendicular declivities of megalopolis . . ." et cetera. He coins some new terms to transfix the reader—"mega-decibel" or "strato-cosmopolis"—and works them vigorously. He is careful to add a page or two of differential equations to show the "scatter." And then he publishes, with 147 footnotes and a bibliography to knock your eye out. If the authorities are dozing, it can be worth an associate professorship.

While we are on the campus, however, we must not forget that the technical language of the natural sciences and some terms in the social sciences, forbidding as they may sound to the layman, are quite necessary. Without them, specialists could not communicate what they find. Trouble arises when experts expect the uninitiated to understand the words; when they tell the jury, for instance, that the defendant is suffering from "circumorbital haematoma."

Here are two authentic quotations. Which was written by a distinguished modern author, and which by a patient in a mental hospital? You will find the answer at the end of the chapter.

(1) Have just been to supper. Did not knowing what the woodchuck sent me here. How when the blue blue blue on the said anyone can do it that tries. Such is the presidential candidate.

(2) No history of a family to close with those and close. Never shall he be alone to be alone to be alone to be alone to be alone to lend a hand and leave it left and wasted.

REDUCING THE GOBBLE

As government and business offices grow larger, the need for doing something about gobbledygook increases. Fortunately the biggest office in the world is working hard to reduce it. The Federal Security Agency in Washington,[1] with nearly 100 million clients on its books, began analyzing its communication lines some years ago, with gratifying results. Surveys find trouble in three main areas: correspondence with clients about their social security problems, office memos, official reports.

[1] Now the Department of Health, Education, and Welfare.

Clarity and brevity, as well as common humanity, are urgently needed in this vast establishment which deals with disability, old age, and unemployment. The surveys found instead many cases of long-windedness, foggy meanings, clichés, and singsong phrases, and gross neglect of the reader's point of view. Rather than talking to a real person, the writer was talking to himself. "We often write like a man walking on stilts."

Here is a typical case of long-windedness:

Gobbledygook as found: "We are wondering if sufficient time has passed so that you are in a position to indicate whether favorable action may now be taken on our recommendation for the reclassification of Mrs. Blank, junior clerk-stenographer, CAF 2, to assistant clerk-stenographer, CAF 3?"

Suggested improvement: "Have you yet been able to act on our recommendation to reclassify Mrs. Blank?"

Another case:

Although the Central Efficiency Rating Committee recognizes that there are many desirable changes that could be made in the present efficiency rating system in order to make it more realistic and more workable than it now is, this committee is of the opinion that no further change should be made in the present system during the current year. Because of conditions prevailing throughout the country and the resultant turnover in personnel, and difficulty in administering the Federal programs, further mechanical improvement in the present rating system would require staff retraining and other administrative expense which would seem best withheld until the official termination of hostilities, and until restoration of regular operations.

The F.S.A. invites us to squeeze the gobbledygook out of this statement. Here is my attempt:

The Central Efficiency Rating Committee recognizes that desirable changes could be made in the present system. We believe, however, that no change should be attempted until the war is over.

This cuts the statement from 111 to 30 words, about one-quarter of the original, but perhaps the reader can do still better. What of importance have I left out?

Sometimes in a book which I am reading for information—not for literary pleasure—I run a pencil through the surplus words. Often I can cut a section to half its length with an improvement in clarity. Magazines like *The Reader's Digest* have reduced this process to an art. Are long-windedness and obscurity a cultural lag from the days when writing was reserved for priests and cloistered scholars? The more words and the deeper the mystery, the greater their prestige and the firmer the hold on their jobs. And the better the candidate's chance today to have his doctoral thesis accepted.

The F.S.A. surveys found that a great deal of writing was obscure although not necessarily prolix. Here is a letter sent to more than 100,000 inquirers, a classic example of murky prose. To clarify it, one needs to *add* words, not cut them:

In order to be fully insured, an individual must have earned $50 or more in covered employment for as many quarters of coverage as half the calendar quarters elapsing between 1936 and the quarter in which he reaches age 65 or dies, whichever first occurs.

Probably no one without the technical jargon of the office could translate this: nevertheless, it was sent out to drive clients mad for seven years. One poor fellow wrote back: "I am no longer in covered employment. I have an outside job now."

Many words and phrases in officialese seem to come out automatically, as if from lower centers of the brain. In this standardized prose people never *get jobs*, they "secure employment"; *before* and *after* become "prior to" and "subsequent to"; one does not *do*, one "performs"; nobody *knows* a thing, he is "fully cognizant"; one never *says*, he "indicates." A great favorite at present is "implement."

Some charming boners occur in this talking-in-one's-sleep. For instance:

The problem of extending coverage to all employees, regardless of size, is not as simple as surface appearances indicate.

Though the proportions of all males and females in ages 16-45 are essentially the same . . .

Dairy cattle, usually and commonly embraced in dairying . . .

In its manual to employees, the F.S.A. suggests the following:

Instead of	Use
give consideration to	consider
make inquiry regarding	inquire
is of the opinion	believes
comes into conflict with	conflicts
information which is of a	
confidential nature	confidential information

Professional or office gobbledygook often arises from using the passive rather than the active voice. Instead of looking you in the eye, as it were, and writing "This act requires . . ." the office worker looks out of the window and writes: "It is required by this statute that . . ." When the bureau chief says, "We expect Congress to cut your budget," the message is only too clear; but usually he says, "It is expected that the departmental budget estimates will be reduced by Congress."

Gobbled: "All letters prepared for the signature of the Administrator will be single spaced."
Ungobbled: "Single space all letters for the Administrator." (Thus cutting 13 words to 7.)

Only people can read

The F.S.A. surveys pick up the point, stressed in Chapter 15, that human communication involves a listener as well as a speaker. Only people can read, though a lot of writing seems to be addressed to beings in outer space. To whom are you talking? The sender of the officialese message often forgets the chap on the other end of the line.

A woman with two small children wrote the F.S.A. asking what she should do about payments, as her husband had lost his memory. "If he never gets able to work," she said, "and stays in an institution would I be able to draw any benefits? . . . I don't know how I am going to live and raise my children since he is disable to work. Please give me some information. . . ."

To this human appeal, she received a shattering blast of gobbledygook, beginning, "State unemployment compensation laws do not provide any benefits for sick or disabled individuals . . . in order to qualify an individual must have a certain number of quarters of coverage . . ." et cetera, et cetera. Certainly if the writer had been thinking about the poor woman he would not have dragged in unessential material about old-age insurance. If he had pictured a mother without means to care for her children, he would have told her where she might get help—from the local office which handles aid to dependent children, for instance.

Gobbledygook of this kind would largely evaporate if we thought of our messages as two way—in the above case, if we pictured ourselves talking on the doorstep of a shabby house to a woman with two children tugging at her skirts, who in her distress does not know which way to turn.

Results of the survey

The F.S.A. survey showed that office documents could be cut 20 to 50 per cent, with an improvement in clarity and a great saving to taxpayers in paper and payrolls.

A handbook was prepared and distributed to key officials.[1] They read it, thought about it, and presently began calling section meetings to discuss gobbledygook. More booklets were ordered, and the local output of documents began to improve. A Correspondence Review Section was established as a kind of laboratory to test murky messages. A supervisor could send up samples for analysis and suggestions. The handbook is now used for training new members; and many employees keep it on their desks along with the dictionary. Outside the Bureau some 25,000 copies have been sold (at 20 cents each) to individuals, governments, business firms, all over the world. It is now used officially in the Veterans Administration and in the Department of Agriculture.

The handbook makes clear the enormous amount of gob-

[1] By Milton Hall. See bibliography.

bledygook which automatically spreads in any large office, together with ways and means to keep it under control. I would guess that at least half of all the words circulating around the bureaus of the world are "irrelevant, incompetent, and immaterial"—to use a favorite legalism; or are just plain "unnecessary"—to ungobble it.

My favorite story of removing the gobble from gobbledygook concerns the Bureau of Standards at Washington. I have told it before but perhaps the reader will forgive the repetition. A New York plumber wrote the Bureau that he had found hydrochloric acid fine for cleaning drains, and was it harmless? Washington replied: "The efficacy of hydrochloric acid is indisputable, but the chlorine residue is incompatible with metallic permanence."

The plumber wrote back that he was mighty glad the Bureau agreed with him. The Bureau replied with a note of alarm: "We cannot assume responsibility for the production of toxic and noxious residues with hydrochloric acid, and suggest that you use an alternate procedure." The plumber was happy to learn that the Bureau still agreed with him.

Whereupon Washington exploded: "Don't use hydrochloric acid; it eats hell out of the pipes!"

Note: The second quotation on page 254 comes from Gertrude Stein's *Lucy Church Amiably*.

Chapter 24

MEDICAL TALK

Fluorine in drinking water has been shown to reduce tooth decay, especially in children. Certain fluorides also are used in rat poisons. Newburgh, New York, among other cities, had voted to try fluoridation in an effort to improve its children's teeth. The opposition to the project, after vigorously publicizing the rat poison argument, had been defeated.

A day was announced when the chemical would be added to the water supply. The day dawned, and before it was over, the city fathers received many telephone calls from citizens, complaining that the water was causing dizziness, nausea, headaches, and general debility. The city fathers replied that owing to a technical delay, no fluorine had yet been added, and that it was the same old water.

Words can make us sick, and sometimes make us well. The practice of medicine has often been close to word magic; the grosser forms of pre-scientific days are still with us in some patent medicine advertising. The word "arthritis" is said to cripple as many people as the disease itself, while to tell a patient he is suffering from "pernicious anemia" can make him a good deal sicker than he needs to be. Some medical men still spend much time trying to find diseases to correspond to words, rather than framing words to describe the condition.

Up to the eighteenth century, medicine had not progressed much beyond the days of Galen, 2,000 years earlier. Doctors were still called "leeches," and it was widely believed that disease was caused by evil spirits, and that countermagic was the way to cure it. In 1662 Dr. Bryan Rossiter, of Hartford, Connecticut, performed an autopsy on a little girl, to find his worst suspicions confirmed—she had indeed died of witchcraft!

Sympathetic magic was much in favor. *Eyebright*, a plant marked with a spot which looks like a human eye, was used as a specific for ocular diseases. *Bugloss*, which looks like a snake's head, was of course good for snakebite, and *celandine*, with its yellow juice, was just the drug for jaundice.[1] "Like by like is to be cured, similar ulcers by similar forms." The great Dr. Stafford of London prepared the following prescription for smallpox and gave it to Governor Winthrop of Connecticut:

In March take some live toads. Putt them in an earthen pott. Cover with iron plate. Overwhelm it, putt charcoales around it and burn. Remove toads and pound well. Moderate does according to the strength of the partie.

The party would have to be pretty strong. George Washington, doctors now believe, was not strong enough to survive the practice of bleeding, so popular in his day.

A reputable physician would not now recommend well-pounded toads for smallpox. But a Massachusetts ex-druggist, reported by Albert Deutsch in 1948, attracted thousands of people to his farm with the announcement that he had discovered a "master living cell." He claimed he could impregnate cement disks with these cells. Customers were to soak the disk in water, and thus put the master cell into solution. The fluid could then be sprayed on crops to make them grow, or be administered internally to cure all the ills of man or beast. The disks sold like oil leases until the U.S. Food and Drug inspectors caught up with the ex-druggist.

At the period when scientists were writing books about the "properties of matter," doctors were writing books about the "properties" of various diseases. Every case of malaria was

[1] T. J. Wertenbaker, *The First Americans*, Macmillan, 1927.

supposed to be like every other case. A is A. Once an ailment was classified, its essence known, the standard specific could be applied. But often in reality it was not known, and dreadful mistakes resulted from this pigeonhole method of diagnosis.

We realize today, says George Boas,[1] that a patient may have a common disease in his own very personal way. It may be less important in some cases to know *what* he has, than *how* he has it. An allergy to eggs which will cause one sufferer to sneeze may make another deathly ill. Remedies prescribed solely from the name of the disease can be disastrous—as if a judge should decide a case from the name of the crime. A person in good physical condition, bitten by a rattlesnake *after* the snake has had a full meal, may be but little inconvenienced. A person in bad condition, bitten *before* the snake has eaten, may die of it. How dependable then is one standard dose for snake bite? $Adam_1$ is not $Adam_2$; $rattler_1$ is not $rattler_2$.

The scientific attitude was slow to penetrate medicine, especially before Pasteur; but its introduction in "mental" disease was even slower. Only within the last few years have "psychosomatic" conditions been widely recognized. Only now are most doctors admitting that "mind" and "body" are inseparable parts of a single organism. Some of us who find nothing funny in a young man stricken with polio may still smile at the eccentricities of a patient in a mental hospital, though he is just as ill and helpless.

Mental patients until recent times were regarded as possessed of devils, and were often beaten and tortured. This horror of misevaluation was followed by a period of either-or diagnosis—either "mind" or "body." Now we are realizing the shortcomings of such two-valued medicine and beginning to understand that mental worry can produce peptic ulcers, and that a pain in the back can affect the mind.

We can classify medical communication failures in six ways:

1. Word magic. "Indian Bear Oil" for every human ill.
2. Maintaining a rigid distinction between "mind" and "body."

[1] *Our New Ways of Thinking.*

3. Defining a disease as an entity with absolute properties.
4. Treating the name of the disease, rather than the patient.
5. Frightening the patient with words like "pernicious anemia."
6. Delay in treating a disease because its name is under a taboo.
In "syphilis," for example, doctors were ready to act, but until recently the public was not. The idea of sickness as a punishment for sin dies hard.

Dr. Hervey Cleckley, of the University of Georgia School of Medicine, tells of a schizophrenic who looked down at the floor during the entire time he interviewed her. Again and again he asked her to look up at him, and she always replied, "Why certainly, doctor," but never lifted her gaze. Finally, her eyes still on the floor, she exclaimed impatiently, "I'm looking right at you, doctor!"

"The interest of the schizophrenic," says Dr. Gregory Zilboorg, "is concentrated on the word itself and it is the word that he endows with all the qualities which the so-called normal person sees mostly in things. . . ." Mostly but not exclusively—for we have described many situations in the preceding pages where whole populations of so-called normal persons mistake the word for the thing, as in guilt by verbal association. Schizophrenics carry this latent "unsanity" to its logical conclusion, believing that *only* words are real.

The Grace Clinic

Medical men are waking up to the power of words. I should like to describe briefly a clinic for preventive medicine where a strenuous and successful effort is being made to counter the communication failures just recited.

The Clinic of Dr. Edwin J. Grace in New York was founded twenty years ago, with clients or members from all walks of life. A dozen specialists represent the major skills, and a psychiatrist, a psychologist, and a dental specialist are regularly consulted. The laboratories include X-ray rooms, facilities to make careful bacterial cultures, as well as the usual chemical analyses, equipment for electrocardiograms, basal metabolism tests, and so forth. The Clinic is also equipped to practice a few limited kinds of special therapy. The medical achievements offer a story in themselves, but our interest here is in applied communication.

Clients or patients join the Clinic as "members," and receive a yearly check-up. One large bank, among other firms, retains the Clinic to examine all its employees, and notes a measurable improvement in their health and work. The staff appraise a patient as if they were decoding messages, many of them non-verbal, transmitted through the patient's gait, skin texture, X-ray pictures. (Probably every skilled diagnostician employs this sort of decoding.)

Staff members think their method of evaluation is unique in several ways: the appraisal conference, in which they study a patient's assets as well as his liabilities, and form a picture of his whole personality, is unique. They follow this by one or more conferences with the patient. In an X-ray viewing box they may show him graphically the condition of his spine or his stomach, and how it compares with a healthier specimen. They try to show him to himself as he is, and as he may become under proper treatment. They give him a future goal for his "whole self," with a program for reaching it, and follow this up with stiff persuasion to carry it out. This calls for co-operation by the patient, and by his family doctor at home. "We got her to reduce her weight," a staff member says casually, and the remark opens vistas of changed habits, self-denial, and achievement.

When you first come as a member of the Clinic, you are interviewed at length and encouraged to tell about your problems and worries as well as about your health. You are then given the first physical examination, an extremely thorough one, with special X rays and laboratory tests as indicated. The results are filed in concise records for periodic comparison. A special optical perception test may be given. This measures the time required to respond to flicker or pulsation in a beam of light; it is found to correlate closely with nervous tension. One of the staff is selected to become a sort of liaison officer and communicate findings to the individual patient and to his family doctor back home.

On a later visit, you confer with the various specialists, who explain what they have found, and encourage you to ask questions; presently you begin to feel a part of the investigating team. The staff doctors take care not to frighten you with what the examination has disclosed; but they speak a good deal more frankly than is usual between doctor and patient.

There are three novel communication systems operating in the Clinic. (1) The staff is in a perpetual series of group discussions about policy, and about individual patients. Clerical employees are an integral part of the discussions. (2) Group dynamics is practiced between staff and patient, while (3) a special two-person relationship is established between patient and one individual doctor.

In talking with patients, doctors at the Clinic are careful of their words, especially with names of diseases which stir emotional fears. Dr. Grace particularly distrusts the indiscriminate use of the word "cancer." There are many types of cancers, he says, some like skin cancer with a high probability of complete cure. The indexing device can be very useful here: never think of a person as having "cancer," but rather as having $cancer_1$, or $cancer_2$, or $cancer_3$ . . . Use the plural wherever possible, "cancers," thus indicating varieties of abnormal cell action instead of one absolute menace.

The formula developed by Dr. Grace and his staff, though it resembles other exhibits in group medicine, adds certain special features. It combines communication skills with medical and social science. It builds up the patient's sense of emotional security, while keeping costs per patient low and contributing to the public health of the community through its vigorous preventive methods.

A hundred clinics experimenting with this formula in different parts of the world might uncover much useful knowledge about patients' behavior, and suggest a more economical and effective use of available medical facilities. They might show a way, by utilizing social science and communication, to tap the patient's own energy and build positive health, which in turn would reduce the demand for repair service. The need for better medical care is widespread and politically strong. Somehow the need must be met, for it ranks in importance with food, shelter, clothing, and education.

SEVEN THOUSAND NERVOUS BREAKDOWNS

Now let us turn to an even more dramatic case of applied communication. Dr. Douglas M. Kelley, psychiatrist and semanticist, used the methods to cure nervous breakdowns in combat during World War II in the European theater.[1] More than 7,000 patients were treated in his hospital. Some of them would probably have gone back to their units without any treatment beyond sedatives and rest, but a good many were in serious need of the therapy Dr. Kelley and his staff had to offer. From the fall of 1944 until the end of the war, soldiers were pouring into the hospital from the front lines, speechless, paralyzed, violent, in an agony of mental and often physical pain.

At the outset we encounter a semantic problem in labeling the breakdown. In World War I army doctors called it "shell shock," but thereafter they gradually discarded the term and replaced it in World War II with such terms as "combat exhaustion," "neuro-psychiatric evacuations," and "battle fatigue." One U.S. divisional commander, arguing that the right name was "cowardice," issued a flat order that there were to be no "combat exhaustion" cases in his division. The doctors solved this by diagnosing hundreds of "concussion cases." In one day at a single battalion aid station, 85 soldiers were evacuated for "acute abdominal cramps," 70 for "severe frontal headache," 12 for "acute leg pains." The doctors had substituted symptoms to conceal the fact that men do crack up.

Every man has his breaking point, and the causes which

[1] See his report in the *Journal of Nervous and Mental Disease,* September 1951.

contribute to it are complex. Dr. Kelley tells of a young soldier who was brought up by his parents in deadly fear of pneumonia. If he got wet they said he would die—just like his Uncle John. Overcoat, rubbers, umbrella were standard gear. In the Army he received the usual pup-tent treatment and presently got soaked—no rubbers, no raincoat. This frightened the poor fellow so that his muscles became paralyzed; he could move nothing but his eyes and mouth. Asked what the trouble was, he whispered: "I am dead; I died of pneumonia."

The reality of these pains and paralytic seizures to the individual is beyond all doubt—despite the generals who think psychiatry is a lot of bosh. The soldier has ceased to function as definitely as though he had been hit with a shell fragment, and no amount of "will power" can restore his control. The Army can shoot him, or leave him on the field, or evacuate him and try to heal his trouble. The U.S. Army fortunately did the last. Dr. William C. Menninger was in over-all command, and Dr. Kelley, then a major, was assigned to develop techniques in the field.

Group therapy

In the early stages of the war, men who came back from combat with neuroses were given drugs, followed by individual psychotherapy. Anyone who has been analyzed knows the time it takes; the Army simply did not have the time—or the psychiatrists. As the war grew fiercer and the load of wounded increased, so did the cases of breakdown. Something had to be done in a hurry, and in January 1944, group therapy was tried. Instead of one man on a psychiatric couch, fifteen to twenty-five men were treated simultaneously by one therapist. The technique was developed by American doctors in a hospital at Stafford, England, and later a 1,000-bed hospital was established by Dr. Kelley in Ciney, Belgium. Other hospitals also used the Stafford methods. The results were spectacular, both in the high percentage of cures and in the greatly reduced cost per patient.

The two major remedies come right out of our tool kit:

semantics and group dynamics. The work of Alfred Korzybski and of the group analysts helped restore thousands of shattered men to sanity. In the beginning, groups were formed of patients with similar complaints, but it soon appeared that mixed groups did better. They permitted the doctor to demonstrate at firsthand the different patterns of emotional stress. (Mental defectives, together with aggressive and hysterical patients, were excluded from the groups.)

First session

A group has gathered in one of the rooms of the Ciney hospital. The doctor begins by telling them that every man who ever lived has his breaking point. In Guadalcanal, he says, nearly every member of a tough Marine division cracked up. It is not your "fault," he says, if you break under stress. It is the result of many complicated causes, a whole process, probably going back to your childhood. He tells about the boy who got wet and thought he was dead of pneumonia. The therapist drives home the idea that it is no disgrace to be in this hospital; anybody might be here. Thus he attacks the initial antagonism of patients to both the special hospital and the doctors. This antagonism is part of that cultural lag we mentioned earlier, where a physical injury is regarded as a serious matter, but a nervous injury is both comic and disgraceful. It takes some time to dissolve the "nut factory" idea.

Each lecture brings out a few simple points, using informal, colloquial language, with plenty of homely illustrations and frequent use of the blackboard. After half an hour, the therapist becomes a "permissive leader." He organizes a general discussion and stimulates the men to participate by describing their own experiences. This continues as long as interest remains keen, sometimes for an hour or more. At the end of the first session, everyone is asked to write a short autobiography, describing his family, friends, schools, jobs, sicknesses, sex problems, Army problems, religion, and his picture of his future.

The value of group therapy becomes almost immediately

obvious. Soldiers suddenly realize that they are not alone in
their misery. "As the individual merged into the group, the
immediacy of his symptoms receded, and to a degree he became desensitized to them." He began to come out of the ex-
clusive concentration on himself. Such extreme suggestibility
was built up in the discussion period that when one soldier
offered a testimonial to his own improvement—as often happened—a general feeling of well-being pervaded the whole
group, as if one man's advance were everybody's.

To the benefit that individual therapy can accomplish, group
therapy thus added a powerful new element. Furthermore it
was an easier method, for any doctor in the hospital, once he
mastered the content of the brief lectures, could take his turn
as therapist. He was only one part of the total pattern; "the
group did the job itself." (This reminds me of my own experience in a workshop group at Bethel, Maine. We ejected
our leader one day and took affairs into our own hands, with
very satisfactory results.)

"The development of group enthusiasm," says Dr. Kelley,
"was as important as the lecture content itself." The individual
in many cases had come to the hospital feeling guilty for
what had happened, and for what his buddies might think of
him. Now his group became a new unit which understood him,
and his feeling of guilt began to melt away, relieving tension.

The semantic approach

Korzybski was not mentioned in Dr. Kelley's "course," but
sooner or later the group of soldiers would discuss the fact
that words are not things, and the map-territory idea would
then be introduced. Dr. Kelley had the semantic approach in
mind as he prepared the course. He deliberately sought to
break up spurious identifications, misevaluations, and acute
conditioned reflexes, so that the patient could apply his own
mind to his own problem. Kelley is sure that General Semantics
provided a specific for treating combat cases. Combat, he says,
is a kind of mass production factory for turning out conditioned reflexes.

In the first lecture soldiers were asked to imagine two automobiles, both apparently in fine condition. The first, however, has a broken differential; the second, a crankcase filled with glue. Neither car will run, but they call for very different treatment. The first car represents a battle wound; the differential must be repaired, as a broken arm must be set. The second car represents *your* condition, soldier. You have no parts broken, but your nervous system is blocked up. We have to drain out the glue and put in good oil, and you have to help, soldier. Then you can go. Our emotions can so affect our bodies that we get all crossed up with ailments as serious as broken bones.

Our bodies and minds, the therapist continues, were developed as one organism tens of thousands of years ago. This organism had to be ready to defend itself when a man had no weapons, and in a crisis must either fight with hands or run. If we find ourselves in a situation today where we can neither fight nor run—say we are pinned down by mortar fire—this ancient and powerful stimulus will assert itself and get us into an emotional, perhaps a physical, jam. A whole battery of responses are touched off; the glandular system pours adrenalin into the blood, rapid breathing increases the oxygen supply, blood sugar develops more energy; the blood's clotting time is shortened in anticipation of injury; digestion stops, permitting more blood to go to arms and legs for quick action. *But pinned down we can't act.*

Our childhood experiences, too, have built up conditioned reflexes and reactions—here the doctor describes Pavlov's famous dogs with the aid of the blackboard—and when a stimulus is given, the reflex tends to follow. Troops in combat who have been repeatedly dive-bombed often develop stomach cramps—a perfectly natural reflex. Later, in noncombat areas, just the sound of a friendly plane overhead can produce a cramp.

Past experiences, the therapist says, are never forgotten by your nervous system. Everything that happens, everything you hear and see and feel, is filed away. If the experiences are strong enough they set up conditioned reactions, some of which may not appear for years. Suppose you saw your father die of a heart attack when you were a small boy and it made a profound impression. Now you are in the Army; you exercise strenuously, your heart begins to pound—and suddenly the memory of the day your father died returns in a flood! You faint dead away, though there is nothing wrong with your heart.

The original reaction to a crisis situation is usually bearable, provided you do not set up a *secondary* reaction. If you do, you have two emotions churning away, which may be enough to induce a wonderful crack-up! Thus the first time you are in combat, you are afraid. So what? Everybody is afraid the first time. But if you become afraid that you will show your fear, you set up a secondary reaction—the fear of fear, and then the emotion may spiral. You become fearful of symptoms rather than of the outside danger—like the poor soldier who thought he had to die if he got wet.

The therapist warns the group to be careful of the words "always" and "never"—which is another way of saying Beware of Absolutes. Be careful, he says, of your use of dates; what occurred at one time need not occur next time. You are not a coward, soldier; what has happened to you has happened to many others. You are not marked for life; you will get over it just as thousands of brave men, caught in the vise of a conditioned reflex, have got over it. Think of those Marines on Guadalcanal.

Every human being is different from every other human being, but all are influenced by three great forces: (1) their inherited characteristics, (2) their past experiences, (3) the present situation. The most effective single statement made in the whole course of treatment, says Kelley, was that *every man has his breaking point*—as conditioned by these three forces. This statement pulled the patient back into the human race! He began to think: "Sure, everyone can break at some point, and everybody's point is different. My point is different—and out there I hit it. Other guys have snapped out

of it; I'll snap out of it." Thus the soldier was removed from
the moral frame which tortured him, and put in a scientific
frame where he could breathe again.

"Employed in this manner," says Kelley, "General Semantics
ceases to be lecture material, and becomes a living dynamic
system, formulated in response to an expressed need." Toward
the end of the treatment the therapist always told the soldier
the eight steps that had been taken to get him back to duty:

First, your physical injuries, if any, have been repaired.

Second, your tensions have been relaxed by rest and sometimes
by narcosis.

Third, insulin and other chemicals have been given to you when
it seemed advisable.

Fourth, we have tried to get a picture of your past experiences,
in the discussion periods, through personal interviews, and in your
written autobiography.

Fifth, we have tried to help you see through fixed ideas and false
beliefs, and make you more critical of the things you feel and
hear and witness.

Sixth, we have tried to explain how the nervous system works,
and how everyone is subject to conditioned reactions.

Seventh, we have shown you that your symptoms are universal,
but occur in different people in different ways at different times.

Eighth, your body is stronger now, you are beginning to understand what happened to you and why. If you have learned these
things, Soldier, you are ready to return to duty.

Ninety-six per cent of Dr. Kelley's soldiers returned to duty.
Did they stay on duty? The percentage which came back to
the hospital was no greater than the percentage among new
soldiers.

Chapter 25

SCHOOLROOM TALK

The time has come to take the roof off the schoolhouse, as we promised, and look with some care at what is going on underneath. Did the author ever qualify as a teacher? No, but he qualified as a student—by spending eighteen years in schoolrooms of various kinds. I did not enjoy it much, nor was I supposed to in those sterner days. I emerged from the ordeal none too well prepared for the life I had to live within the American culture. In retrospect, it seems that I might have been better prepared for that life, in a good deal less time. The outstanding mood, as I look back, was apathy, tinged occasionally with terror. I can still feel my heart pounding as the examination papers were passed out. But there were bright moments too; I remember a few excellent teachers who excited me.

My school was much better than Tom Sawyer's school, with its rote learning, birch rod, and flying spitballs. Everyone tells me that American public schools are doing much better now than when I was in them; and if there is one man to thank, it is John Dewey. Well, that's fine; but let's take a look just the same. Not at the whole curriculum, but at three kinds of talk inside the schoolroom. There is (1) talk among the children themselves, (2) talk between teacher and class, and (3) talk about talk in the sense of learning "English," or grammar, or how to write and speak correctly. Students must communicate about communication, and use it in order to learn it.

Jerry in grade one

We are now going to visit an elementary school, not the worst but still not the best of the thousands which dot America. This is where the children begin their formal language instruction. We shall find our little friend Jerry where we left him at the end of Chapter 7, still full of the drive to talk. He is in grade one, listening to the teacher tell the new class what school means. She is a friendly, conscientious girl, anxious to give her charges a good start and turn these illiterate little individuals into a well-behaved class. Since this is not the early 1900's, she does not make them sit in rows or keep strict silence. She says:

"In school we talk quietly at the tables or when it is our turn. Who will tell me what he sees in this picture?" A dozen voices answer: "A kitty," "A pussycat," and one voice—is it Jerry's?—continues with a nonstop account of the kitty next door. He has to be shushed. (A useful new word, at last in the dictionary.)

All the children want to talk, and they speak fluent English (except one little Puerto Rican girl who speaks fluent Spanish). They have many questions to ask and many stories to tell. One of the hardest things they must learn is to answer questions instead of asking them.

Before many weeks have passed, Jerry and his classmates are a co-operative group and relatively subdued. They no longer ask so many questions; they answer better. Later, Jerry is proud when he can take home a page he has written, and he likes to read stories about animals to his mother. Only at home can he still talk freely and ask all the questions he wants.

We go on down the school corridor. In the third grade we see a teacher up front talking, two or three hands waving briskly, and most of the children gazing dreamily out the window. In the fourth-grade room, the pupils are reading aloud in singsong voices a story about Paul Revere. Progress is slow, and desk copies of the story book have their margins covered with doodles, initials, and sketches. Boredom shows in the slumped shoulders, the fidgeting, the dull faces.

Almost every room along the corridor has a teacher up front, working hard, while the children behave like an audience. Those who are listening show little interest; the others are killing time in more or less ingenious ways. They remind us of Tom Sawyer's virtuosity in that direction.

Hopi boy

We can find classrooms like Jerry's in all civilized countries. I have seen their counterparts in England, France, Germany, Mexico, Russia, Puerto Rico; and have heard about them elsewhere. They form a cultural bond among the civilized as contrasted with more primitive societies. Children in simpler cultures do not go to formal schools; they learn their language easily because it is spoken and not written; they are never tortured with spelling bees. Like Jerry up to age six, they absorb their culture directly by communicating with their families and community. The older people help the children and answer their questions as they come—not systematically. By the age of six, the children know the main outlines of the culture, including prejudice against the out-group, "those foreigners," as well as the language. "Even the children," as the explorer observed, "talk Eskimo here." Often they have a large amount of practical knowledge and skill. Gesell and Ilg quote a Hopi child:

By the time I was six, therefore, I had learned to find my way about the mesa and to avoid graves, shrines, and harmful plants, to size up people, and to watch out for witches. . . . I could help plant and weed, went out herding with my father, and was a kiva trader. I owned a dog and a cat, a small bow made by my father, and a few good arrows. . . . I could ride a tame burro, kill a kangaroo rat, and catch small birds, but I could not make fire with a drill and I was not a good runner like the other fellows. . . .[1]

Children are a good deal brighter than we think. "Civilized" children are no less bright than Hopi children, as would be clearly seen if they could do something equally important to

[1] Leo W. Simmons, editor, *Sun Chief*, Yale, 1942, as quoted in Gesell and Ilg, *Infant and Child in the Culture of Today*.

them—go herding with their fathers, for instance, or ride a burro. Only recently have anthropologists told us about children in simpler cultures, and the implications for our schools are just beginning to be worked out.

Why are they bored?

"Education," they say at Antioch College, "is the only commodity that the customer tries to get as little of as he can for his money." Of all the criticisms one hears concerning American school children, the most universal is the complaint about their "apathy." Parents and teachers agree, and so do the children themselves. So do I, remembering those eighteen years.

One reason may lie in group structure, where teacher is up front, telling them. Another may appear when the teacher, herself a product of the system, also finds a given subject dull. A third reason may be textbooks, especially those which fail to give children credit for their built-in knowledge, or to show the connection between what they already know and what they must learn. It is only natural for children to find grammar, for instance, complex and unnecessary.

Now and then the real energy of a child comes out, sometimes in sports, sometimes in mischief, sometimes in a group undertaking. In a public school I know the eighth grade sat glassy-eyed week after week until the teacher proposed a trip to Washington to see the government in action, as part of "current events." The idea was like a firecracker under their chairs! The children set to work with enthusiasm to overcome all obstacles. They got up a dinner to raise funds, sold tickets widely, and served the meal themselves. They planned every detail of the trip in co-operation with their teachers. En route, their behavior was admirable; the dull faces were now shining with anticipation.

If such energy is available for trips to Washington, why is it not available for the history lesson or the science class? If it were available, might it not start the children earlier on their careers, with better spirits, wider knowledge, and clearer heads?

Seven defenses against boredom

There are certain recognized ways to modify the boredom of children in classrooms, though the antidotes can hardly be a complete cure. Most of them utilize the child's own feelings and experiences. With these methods, the best modern schools have shown that children can enjoy their work if it is carefully related to their needs and interests, again a matter of communication.

1. Give children credit for more sense, more seriousness, more knowledge at every age.

2. Build the school curriculum on what children already know, especially in language. It is easier to show them how the structure of their own sentences carries meaning—their meaning—than to make them parse sentences in the book.

3. Get the children to talk more to each other about their work, and let the teacher talk less. Even in colleges the lecture system is losing ground to the seminar with student participation.

4. Organize the class on democratic lines rather than autocratic or anarchistic. The teacher should neither be czar, nor abdicate.

5. Keep language in its place as *means* rather than end. The accent should be not on studying English, but on using English to study history.

6. Give school children interesting nonverbal activities to offset the heavy emphasis on language. Give them chances to express their feelings, let off steam.

7. Count on their spontaneous curiosity, which is always there unless it is suppressed. The greater their desire to learn, the less the teacher needs to teach.

These seven offsets to boredom have been often tested, and they work. In the three million classrooms of America, one ought to find almost every possible combination being applied. Some of the semantic tools discussed in Chapters 12 and 13 have also been found to work, in arousing children's interest. General Semantics, which is less a formal subject than a series of mental habits, could help every teacher of every subject, but especially language. If the teacher has a good map of the verbal jungle, he or she is less likely to lose the youngsters.

Among the semantic tools for children is the warning to be careful of absolutes, careful of using such words as "always," "never," "all," "only," "same." Teach them to be wary of either-or choices. Let them practice, with many examples, the fact that words are not things; one cannot ride in the word "car." Let them practice finding referents, and building simple abstraction ladders, and so build some immunity to prejudice, fixed ideas, and high-pressure arguments. They should learn to separate a fact, from an inference, from an opinion, and to recognize each in any talk or piece of writing. The three pails of water (page 117) could instruct them that "hot" and "cold" are relative terms, and so start them thinking in terms of relations, a habit so essential to an understanding of their world.

"If you can teach children," says Dr. Douglas Kelley, "to make proper evaluations, to develop methods of recognizing proper structure and order, you will have probably done more for them than by any other single preventive method you can offer."

A prime aid to learning is found in group study, which can tap the mysterious energy discussed earlier. According to Gans, Stendler, and Almy:

> There is a degree of redundancy in the question "How shall I group the children in my class?" [1] It is a most unusual class that does not soon form its own subgroups and cliques. The teacher's job is to encourage and develop the groups that will be effective. . . .

If a group is underground, its business carried on by whispers, secret notes, and caucuses outside the class, the teacher is in danger of losing control. If it is open and co-operative, however, the informal group may greatly aid him in his task. The important point is to center activity within the group— not focus it on the teacher, up front, but let the pupils interact among themselves for maximum interest and energy. Elton Mayo found similar informal groups in factory work.

[1] *Teaching Young Children.*

Language lessons

Jerry may be bursting with the drive to talk, but he has no drive at all to diagram sentences on the blackboard. "Why do we have to learn English?" he asks. "We know English." Dr. C. C. Fries, in his new kind of grammar book, makes the same complaint. He says the children do understand structural signals in the language before they ever go to school. If you say "The man bit the dog," they know who was bitten. Even if you say "A woggle ugged a diggle," they are aware of the structure of such a Jabberwocky sentence.

Nevertheless they have plenty to learn before they can communicate clearly and accurately. The child talks, said John Dewey, as effortlessly as he runs, and he can learn to read and write effortlessly in time. The hard part of teaching language is to convert the common speech of children into a "conscious tool of conveying knowledge and assisting thought"—remodeling habits that concern ordinary affairs into habits that concern precise notions.[1]

It seems easier for teachers to go on treating grammar as a subject standing by itself, with no relation to the children's everyday talk. Teaching it takes a great deal of time in all its formal details, and arouses much resistance, which in turn takes more time. In secondary schools particularly, specialized teachers go into vast scholarly detail about correct writing, thus getting farther and farther from the true vital stuff of communication.

Various authorities have been experimenting with the important transition from language as everyday talk, to language as a conscious tool. Fries has a fresh, new approach which shears off centuries of accumulated barnacles. He begins with tape-recordings of spoken language, and emphasizes how much meaning in English depends on the order of words. His ap-

[1] *How We Think.*

proach connects with the idea of structure and order so cardinal in semantics.

Pilot plant

When I went to primary school in Boston, the teacher would dictate a sentence and we would try to write it correctly, each at his little desk screwed to the floor, with inkpot in the corner. Today in a New York school, the pupils dictate, and the teacher does the writing—on the blackboard.[1]

"You tell me the story," she says, "and I will put it down. What do you think is the first thing to tell?"

"That we took a trip," says one child.

"Let's start this way," says another. " 'We took a trip to the park to see if we could find any community helpers.' "

"Good," says the teacher, and writes it on the board. "Now, think of the next sentence."

" 'We saw the park man,' " suggests a little girl. " 'We asked him for information.' "

Teacher writes again, but takes time out while the children discuss what "information" means. When they have finished the story of about ten sentences, they all read it aloud, feeling some of the pride of authorship, and then copy it into their own books. I am sure that this is a big improvement on my school.

Observe the processes involved: first, the children are making a record of an experience they enjoyed; telling a simple story that happened to them, very much as they would tell it to the family at home. They are shown how the spoken story can be arranged in sentences, and how it looks when written down. They go over each sentence at least three times. This is not a lesson in "reading" or "writing" or "spelling" or "discussion," though all are included. *It is the total communication process.*

Here in another school, where "reading readiness" is not standardized, is a class of seven-year-olds. Instead of many copies of a standard reader, several dozen different books are

[1] Reported by Benjamin Fine, New York *Times*, April 7, 1953.

distributed according to the teacher's estimate of each child's own progress. If a youngster finds the book too hard, he asks for an easier one. As Madeline Semmelmeyer [1] reminds us, "the child does not get 'meaning' from the printed page. . . . He puts 'meaning' into the printed page," depending on his experience.

Spelling, too, in these modern schools is related to the needs of the children. If they want to write something, spelling goes along with it. Sometimes they drill each other in pairs. A recent textbook has blank pages at the end headed: "My spelling demons." The language arts may include listening and public speaking as well as reading, writing, and spelling. Learning the sequence of the alphabet is deferred, to let the children pick it up casually as they need it.

Teaching semantics

General Semantics can be taught directly to secondary and college students, either by itself or as part of the study of communication. The speech faculty of the University of Denver say about their courses in this field:

> Human relations thus becomes the core of the Basic Communication course, with General Semantics as the principal method for training in appropriate evaluative reactions. . . . The program is concerned first with the communication skills—reading, writing, speaking, listening—secondly with the integration of the personality of the communicator, and thirdly with the social responsibilities of the speaker and writer as a member of society. In reading and listening, we are interested in making the student less naively susceptible to the suggestiveness of language. . . .[2]

Wendell Johnson, of the University of Iowa, has used General Semantics for years in guidance interviews with students, and in remedial work for stuttering. The work of Irving Lee at Northwestern and of S. I. Hayakawa at Illinois Tech is well known. O. R. Bontrager uses it to train teachers at one of the

[1] Mimeographed report, Institute of General Semantics, c. 1947.
[2] Wilson B. Paul, Frederick Sorenson, and Elwood Murray, "A Functional Core for the Basic Communications Course," *Quarterly Journal of Speech*, April 1946.

Pennsylvania state colleges. Lou LaBrant, of the Department of English Education at New York University, presents General Semantics in a graduate course called "The Nature of Language." This professional work especially should be much expanded, with action research and many experimental workshops. There is now a text available for teaching General Semantics in high schools.[1]

Backward boys

My friend James Saunders, a retired naval officer much interested in semantics, undertook to coach some "backward" boys in the local Maryland high school. They had all failed in one or more subjects. The project particularly appealed to him because he had taught himself how to study at Annapolis, boosting his rank from 193 to 14 in his class.

His basic assumption was that the "backward" boys were as smart as the average, but their interest had not been aroused. They suffered from scholastic apathy and classroom misunderstandings. His chief task was to get their feelings and interests involved in the school work.

He showed the boys that invaluable rule of priority: (a) things to learn only well enough to pass examinations, (b) things to learn permanently. He helped them fashion a series of memory ticklers; encouraged them to establish closer relations with their classroom teachers, asking a lot more questions. He taught them how to get the meaning of something which at first seemed incomprehensible by finding an association with something familiar, thus tying in to their own experience.

His techniques were exploratory, but he proved that these backward boys were not backward at all when approached more imaginatively; and he demonstrated the value of General Semantics in that approach. Every boy in the group made up his deficiency in less than six months, and those who went on to college did better than the average of their classmates.

[1] Catherine Minteer, *Words and What They Do to You.*

College themes

Most freshmen themes are literary shipwrecks, not because the student is stupid, but because he is bored. He is writing on a subject chosen by somebody else, aware that whatever he writes will be met with a hostile eye. So he grinds out some words trying to guess what will please the prof, and hoping to get a B minus instead of a C.

Certain teachers of English composition have found a means to remedy this sad situation. Here is a university instructor projecting on a screen a theme by a young woman student. It describes making an oyster stew at a party. The class is asked to discuss it, sentence by sentence. First, do they understand it?

"What does she mean by 'simmer'?" a boy inquires. The girls enlighten him with scorn.

"She doesn't say how many guests there were."

" 'Biscuits' is misspelled," somebody points out.

"The last sentence is a mile too long."

"Shouldn't that comma be a semicolon?"

The author of the theme is communicating directly to her own group of classmates, rather than writing a private letter to the instructor. In no time at all the group is taking a real interest in "clarity, coherence, and emphasis," even an interest in spelling and punctuation!

This method shows one way to release group energy *through* communication, to *improve* communication. When students write themes for each other, rather than for the prof, many educational things begin to happen. But it presents a challenge to the teacher. He must steer the class just enough to allow its group energy to develop, while at the same time completing specific assignments so examinations can be passed.

Class in insurance

A high school at Winnetka, Illinois, was having a plague of broken dishes in the cafeteria.[1] Meals were punctuated with

[1] National Education Association, *Action for Curriculum Improvement*, Washington, 1951.

resounding crashes, and many students had to pay for replacements which they could ill afford. In an arithmetic class studying insurance, somebody suggested organizing a model company to insure against broken dishes. A parent who was an insurance broker contributed advice, and presently the Skokie School Mutual Insurance Company was set up by the class and chartered by the school council. Any student, teacher, or school employee was eligible for membership, at ten cents a year.

The company is booming under an elected board of directors, who run it on sound actuarial lines. Rates were high at first because the crash rate was high, but recently a five-cent dividend was declared. Reserves are carefully maintained. A chief adjuster and his assistants are on the alert at lunchtime. When a crash echoes through the hall, one of them hastens to the scene to survey the damage and prepare the "adjuster's report." If the crasher is a member, he fills out a form and pays nothing; if he is not a member the adjuster collects the damages. The cafeteria manager is paid in full for the loss.

A more interesting way to teach insurance—not only to the arithmetic class, but to the whole school—is difficult to imagine. It goes far beyond information with which to pass an examination, for these youngsters will encounter problems of life insurance, fire insurance, social security, automobile liability, throughout their lives.

The Morovis plan

My last story comes from Puerto Rico, a simpler culture, where education is valued somewhat differently. I find the story touching.

A hill town named Morovis had no high school and badly wanted one. A small building, two teachers, and a few books were acquired. That was all the town could afford; what could they do with it? Lacking teachers, the children would have to teach themselves, *which they proceeded to do*. A group of eight or ten took turns reading the single copy of an assigned book on history. They then met around a table and quizzed the member who had read the chapter, arguing about colonial

days in Puerto Rico under Spanish rule. When their turn came
to meet with one of the two teachers, they had many questions
to ask, and presently they were prepared to pass the test he
gave. Groups studied economics, languages, and mathematics,
using the same self-help method, faster learners assisting the
slower ones. The youngsters tackled science without laboratory equipment, but one of the teachers managed to get hold
of a few chemicals and test tubes, and the class collected speci-
mens in the woods and fields.

Students who went on to the university held their own with
high-school boys and girls from San Juan and all over the
island. Thereupon the Department of Education with its limited funds decided to duplicate the idea. Today the "Plan
Morovis" is operating in more than a dozen high schools, and
has attracted international attention. The implications are broad
and dynamic, not so much in cutting costs—which of course
it does—as in a demonstrated method to tap the students'
energy, defeat apathy, and give a real education.

The goal of our schools should be to get Jerry and his friends
as ready for their life as the Hopi boy was made ready for his
life out on the mesa. The first rule seems to be to arouse the
children's interest. "They ought to learn; they must be made
to learn," is not good enough.

Every year our culture grows more complex, the sheer volume of knowledge heavier. Children have more and more to
learn to keep abreast; and they have a grim world to adjust to
in the middle of the twentieth century. Is this the penalty of
literacy, one sometimes wonders, these expanding libraries and
specialties, this growing weight of words that hangs over every
child as he faces the future? To children of this generation we
owe every tool and every aid we can muster.

More than that, we need the direct, fresh insight of children.
They are wiser than we think. Schools should not only aid
them to enter the culture in which perforce they must live,
but should preserve and strengthen their original clear gaze.
Never have straight-thinking youngsters been more needed
than in this confused and explosive world.

Chapter 26

THE UNUSED POTENTIAL

The second part of this book has shown how communication principles can be put to work on both long range and day-to-day problems. We have looked at an author writing an article, and at various aspects of current economic talk—especially the battle between the words "Capitalism" and "Socialism," and how Puerto Rico is trying to resolve it by its program of Operation Bootstrap.

We held our semantic decoders up to the propaganda streaming out of Moscow, to American campaign oratory, and to charges of high crimes based on guilt by association. We listened to lawyer talk, academic talk, doctor talk, and the gobbledygook of bureaucrats, public and private. We took the roof off the schoolhouse and saw Jerry at his desk, often reduced to lassitude by what he was hearing.

We struck a preliminary balance sheet of the mass media and concluded that up to now the liabilities have exceeded the assets, but tomorrow the advantage might shift. If One World is an imperative in the years to come, the mass media offer indispensable tools by which it may be achieved—"the cables which can't be cut."

The cases cited were designed to give the reader running samples of more or less topical problems, and suggestions of ways in which he might apply the findings set forth in Part One. The net effect, I hope, is to convince him that application is possible and often helpful. The reader can use these tools around the home, in his business or profession, in making decisions as a citizen and a voter, in foreign travel, in many phases of human relations. As writer, lecturer, consultant, citizen, I can testify that I have used them every day for many years. They have aided me in getting on with people, in saying what I want to say more clearly, in listening more carefully, in avoiding arguments over meaningless questions, in sizing up political and economic problems, and in identifying the things —the very large number of things—which I don't know, and am not competent to discuss.

In Part One, some twelve approaches to communication study were examined, with a chapter given to each. They will not be summarized again here. The reader is referred to the "feedback" in Chapter 16. No harm will be done, however, by repeating the six outstanding conclusions of that chapter.

1. Communication, in the sense of messages sent and messages decoded, is a characteristic of all animal life, although only man has developed true language.

2. Twin systems of communication interlock in every human being: the internal network, with its feedbacks to hold the organism stable, and the external network of signs and language, to hold society stable.

3. The primary function of language is to keep contact within the group, and promote the survival of a relatively defenseless mammal. Having no fangs or armor, he must reason his way out of tight places, or plan in advance to avoid them.

4. By means of language, what we call culture begins its portentous march, growing like a compound interest curve. Is it to become a substitute for evolution?

5. Meaning is relative to experience, and for a message to be understood, there must be an overlapping of experience between sender and receiver. To understand the sender, too, we must know something about his feelings, needs, motives.

6. The work done to date has demonstrated that it is possible, without changing human genes, or overturning the culture, to improve the linguistic apparatus. It is possible to lock up a good many verbal monsters now at large.

Paradox

The reader is bound to feel a certain paradox in the material under study. Words are what make us human, their value is transcendent. At the same time, words are full of traps, distorting evaluation, leading to pain and misery beyond all sense and reason.

There is no escape from this problem: words are helpful, harmful, neutral; in all shades and at all levels. The attitude to take, I believe, is thankfulness for the power and utility of words, and determination not to misuse the gift. Words are like a sharp new ax, invaluable for the pioneer as long as he does not let it slip. Today, however, sharp axes are flying in all directions.

The paradox runs throughout the study. People are similar— far more similar the world around, yes, and back to the Stone Age, than is generally supposed. But every individual is different: $Adam_1$ is not $Adam_2$. Absolute similarity is as untenable as absolute difference.

To achieve true evaluation one must hold these seemingly contradictory ideas in the mind at once. He must develop a view which is dynamic, not static; flexible, not fixed; a moving balance like a rock climber's. Some of the trouble, as we have seen, is due to the structure of the language we speak. Chinese, Hopi, according to the linguists, have a structure which makes multivalued events easier to grasp.

Perhaps Indo-European languages could be given more flexibility; but there is another difficulty. Every language tends to be temporal and linear; one word must follow another. But the space-time world we are driven to comprehend, the world out there, is curved; a spiral process of events. So the fit is not too close. It is like those arbitrary yet necessary classifications of nature in our heads, while nature is actually arranged on the principle of insensible gradations.

Mathematics, linguistics, semantics, help us to improve the fit and to make allowance for the arbitrary classifications. Beyond and above these disciplines, will a process some day be devised to bring us closer to what is going on out there; an easier method of dealing with the insensible gradations; a really dependable evaluation apparatus? It is not too much to hope.

More light

Some day, the accumulated research in support of communication theory is going to answer a great many questions now beyond us. Here are a few suggestions for research badly needed now:

A design for a simple, easy to learn, and widely acceptable international language.

Continuation of UNESCO's study on the improvement of international conferences. How to understand "foreigners." How to re-educate diplomats.

When does propaganda lose its appeal and why?

Continuation of Whorf's work, especially an analysis of the "world view" built in by the structure of English and other Indo-European languages.

Historical study of how cultures change, with sidelights on possible ways to change them deliberately.

How children learn to talk, an all-out study.

Misevaluations built into children, preschool and early school. This study should be based on nationwide samples.

Practical method for teaching semantics to young children, older children, adults.

How memories are stored in the brain, and how recalled.

How does a dog or a cat "think"? Compared with a wasp or a man.

More research—and it will be tough—on verbal versus nonverbal reflection. Do we always use words in thinking?

Study of the nonverbal languages of science; how messages are handled in these languages.

A careful list of meaningless questions—those now much discussed with a great waste of time and emotion.

More research in how to listen.

How can the unseen audience of the mass media talk back?

History of ideologies once widespread and now defunct.

Guilt by association, an all-out study. (The Fund for the Republic has announced one.)

The techniques of demagogues. How far are their word patterns similar?

A study in the correcting of lies and defamation. Does one ever catch up?

More research on rumor, following Gordon Allport.

Study of the patois of specialists. How far are these special languages necessary, and how much do they block communication?

The outstanding problem

Early in our study we saw the grim probability that a slip in the meaning of the Japanese word *"mokusatsu"* prolonged a bloody war, blasted Hiroshima, and upset world history.

My friend Richard C. Tolman, the late physicist, once told me of another communication failure on an equal scale in international affairs. As a member of the United Nations Atomic Energy Board in 1946, he tried to persuade the Russians to accept the Lilienthal-Acheson-Baruch plan for the control of atomic energy. They refused to entertain the idea because, said Tolman, they could not believe that such a generous proposal, involving some surrender of sovereignty by the United States, could be sincere. There must be a joker in it. Had we been able to convince them of our sincerity, had the message got through to the receiver, the world might not be shivering with apprehension today.

The Russians in 1953 exploded a hydrogen bomb. This message had no difficulty in getting through. The delicate decoding instruments of the U.S. Atomic Energy Commission picked it up promptly, though it came from halfway around the planet. Both the great power centers are now equipped to blow each other's cities to kingdom come.

The Russian people, the American people, all the people on earth, except severe mental cases, are against being blown to bits. Their wants, needs, desires, are at the farthest pole from the technological possibility. How can these fearful forms of energy be neutralized? This is far and away the most important question before mankind today, and it is largely a problem of communication. How can the passionate desire of two billion human beings find tangible expression? How can they tell each other, and tell their leaders what they want? How can the messages get through and the mandate be obeyed?

Assuming a policy universally agreed upon for peace and protection against atomic attack, how should the machinery be set up? All the findings we have discussed, from brain connections to listening clinics, are applicable to these questions. They give no final answers, but suggest a strategy for attack. They offer the kind of training and the maturity a person should possess to lead in the attack.

It may be that civilization is too much for Homo sapiens altogether. It may be that his biological equipment is better designed for pastures, steppes, and forests, than for subways, skyscrapers, and supersonic propulsion. But such an assumption has no force until man has used his full potential on the new environment which technology has built. That potential is now neutralized, due to avoidable failures of communication. Scientists like Dr. Young tell us that the power to think has never been utilized at anywhere near capacity. Of those fifteen billion connections in the brain many are unused; others are constructing phantoms. We suffer, all of us, from an imposed infantilism. We were born, all of us, with greater powers.

Mankind is a company moving across a plain. It has been moving for perhaps half a million years. Individuals are born and die; the company moves on. Civilizations rise and fall; the company moves on. When the terrain becomes too hot, too dry, too dangerous, the company, after many individuals have perished, draws away. There is drama and tragedy as established customs clash with the necessities of environment. But the company overrides the cultural lag and moves on to safer ground. How do we know this? Because we are here. The company will draw away from the lethal aspects of atomic energy in due course. But will it move in time? This is more dangerous ground than any ever traversed before.

Many languages have been developed as the company moves, group by group. Most of the words have reflected homely matters, small talk, humor, folk tales, poetry. But man is not only the talking animal; he is, by the same token, the reasoning animal, the creature alone capable of objective, impersonal thought. Many of his words must carry accurate messages— exact directions, recipes, formulas, for the crafts, the arts, for building pyramids and temples, even long before Aristotle or the beginnings of recorded science. Most of us are not too logical, most of the time. Words run into feelings, feelings into words; the line is none too sharp. But now and again we delay our words; deliberately summon experiences and associations before we take action.

It is the power to think things out which has created not only the vast body of modern science, but the stupendous arti- facts of the modern world, until now we are committed—com- mitted up to our necks. Comfortable as it might be to retreat into a less exacting environment, without a clock or an equation, it is too late. We have to go on with it, though not necessarily in precisely the same direction. The voice of reason cannot be quieted, or its consequences avoided. What does this mean? I believe it means that a relatively larger number of plain citi- zens in all cultures, and a considerably larger number of their leaders, must learn to develop a power of thought hitherto unexercised.

This study is not an attempt to remake good, human talk; it is an argument for a somewhat greater proportion of talk devoted to human survival. If we had to begin at the begin- ning it would be harder. Fortunately, as I have tried to show, a series of disciplines in communication have been clearing the way. Men of good will, I believe, should help with the clear- ing, for it may well mark the road along which the company must now go.

Perhaps the next great revolution, following the industrial, will be the revolution in communication. This book is a small contribution to that end.

Selected Bibliography

BOOKS

Allee, W. C., *Cooperation Among Animals, with Human Implications*, Henry Schuman, 1938, 1951. Many studies of group behavior among insects, fish, birds, mice, elephants, and other creatures.

Allport, Gordon, and Postman, Leo, *The Psychology of Rumor*, Holt, 1947. Case studies and interpretation.

*Ashby, W. Ross, *Design for a Brain*, Wiley, 1952. Mechanical means of adaptation, in animals, machines, people, analyzed by the director of a psychiatric hospital. The first half of the book is expressed in words, with many clarifying illustrations; the second half repeats the material in mathematical terms.

Bales, R. F., *Interaction Process Analysis*, Addison-Wesley Press, 1950. Group observation and experiment, using Harvard's special observation room with a one-way window.

Beardsley, Monroe C., *Practical Logic*, Prentice-Hall, 1950. Textbook by a Swarthmore professor of philosophy. It is also available in a shorter version, same publisher and date, called *Thinking Straight*.

Bell, E. T., *The Search for Truth*, Reynal and Hitchcock, 1934. A mathematician describes the scientific method.

Berkeley, Edmund C., *Giant Brains or Machines That Think*, Wiley, 1949.

Bernays, Edward L., *Public Relations*, University of Oklahoma Press, 1952. By a noted publicist and teacher of the "science of public relations." Contains a long bibliography on various phases of communication.

Blake, Robert R., and Ramsey, Glenn V., editors, *Perception, An Approach to Personality*, Ronald Press, 1951. Papers delivered at the Clinical Psychology Symposium of 1949-50 at Texas University, including contributions by Carl Rogers, Norman Cameron, Jerome Bruner, A. Korzybski, and nine others.

Boas, George, *Our New Ways of Thinking*, Harper, 1930. Good statement of scientific communication.

Bodmer, Frederick, and Hogben, Lancelot, *The Loom of Language*, Norton, 1944. Scholarly analysis of differences in the various Indo-European languages, with the last third of the book devoted to the "world language problem."

* Of special importance for this book.

Bontecou, Eleanor, *The Federal Loyalty-Security Program*, Cornell University Press, 1953. By a New York attorney with varied experience in government service, written as one of the *Cornell Studies in Civil Liberty*.

Bridgman, P. W., *The Logic of Modern Physics*, Macmillan, 1932. Describes the revolution in language that accompanied relativity. Excellent discussion of the operational definition.

Brin, Joseph G., *Introduction to Functional Semantics*, Tudor Press, 1949. Lectures from the author's popular course in semantics at Boston University.

Britton, Karl, *Communication, A Philosophical Study of Language*, Harcourt, Brace, 1939. A British publication in the International Library of Psychology, Philosophy and Scientific Method.

Bryant, Margaret M., *Modern English and Its Heritage*, Macmillan, 1948. Introductory college textbook in linguistics and etymology. Good bibliography.

Buchanan, William, and Cantril, Hadley, *How Nations See Each Other: A Study in Public Opinion*, University of Illinois Press, 1953. Part of the UNESCO study of "Tensions Affecting International Understanding." Nine national surveys were conducted.

Cantril, Hadley, and associates, *Gauging Public Opinion*, Princeton University Press, 1945.

——, *The "Why" of Man's Experience*, Macmillan, 1950. Some implications of the perception studies at Hanover and Princeton, developed by one of their leading exponents.

Carnap, Rudolf, *Introduction to Semantics*, Harvard University Press, 1942. Highly technical theory by a German philosopher at the University of Chicago.

*Carroll, John B., *The Study of Language: A Survey of Linguistics and Related Disciplines in America*, Harvard University Press, 1953. An objective inventory of the present state of linguistics and metalinguistics.

Chase, Stuart, *Men at Work: Some Democratic Methods for the Power Age*, Harcourt, Brace, 1945. Contains some early reports on group dynamics.

——, *Roads to Agreement: Successful Methods in the Science of Human Relations*, Harper, 1951. Conference technique, mediation, and other tested methods.

——, *The Proper Study of Mankind: An Inquiry into the Science of Human Relations*, Harper, 1948. With valuable co-operation by specialists in many fields, the author here attempted to chart the broad field of social science and see its main departments in perspective. One chapter on communication, several on the culture concept.

——, *The Tyranny of Words*, Harcourt, Brace, 1938. Described the author's discovery of semantics as a tool of communication for a writer, and gave perhaps the first popular explanation of the subject.

Childs, Harwood L., editor, *Pressure Groups and Propaganda*, American Academy of Political Science, 1942. Yearbook containing papers delivered at the annual symposium.

Corey, Stephen M., *Action Research to Improve School Practices*, Teachers College of Columbia University, 1953. Calls for group action and democratic methods among teachers.

Cunningham, Ruth, and associates, *Understanding Group Behavior of Boys and Girls*, Teachers College of Columbia University, 1951. Patterns of interaction in classrooms.

Davis, Robert G., and associates, *Direct Communication, Written and Spoken*, Heath, 1943. Practical handbook for students, by faculty members at M.I.T. and Harvard.

DeLaguna, Grace, *Speech, Its Function and Development*, Yale University Press, 1927.

Dewey, John, *Experience and Nature*, Open Court Publishing Co., 1925. A series of philosophic lectures under the Paul Carus Foundation.

——, *How We Think*, Heath, 1910, 1933.

Dollard, John, and Miller, Neal E., *Personality and Psychotherapy*, McGraw-Hill, 1950. Discusses and illustrates some important verbal techniques of therapy.

——, *Social Learning and Imitation*, Yale University Press, 1941. Official statement of the "learning theory" of the Yale group of behaviorists.

*Doob, Leonard W., *Public Opinion and Propaganda*, Holt, 1948. Theoretic and practical aspects, including polls and media, by an OWI official and Yale professor.

——, *Social Psychology: An Analysis of Human Behavior*, Holt, 1952. Includes useful material on language, groups, communication, mass media.

Fansler, Thomas, *Creative Power Through Discussion*, Harper, 1950. Conference techniques.

Fenton, J. C., *A Practical Psychology of Babyhood*, Houghton Mifflin, 1925.

Ferguson, Charles W., *A Little Democracy Is a Dangerous Thing*, Association Press, 1948. Grass-roots influence through discussion groups to solve public problems.

Flesch, Rudolf, *The Art of Plain Talk*, Harper, 1946. Report on the author's statistical "readability formula."

Follett, Mary P., *Creative Experience*, Longmans, Green, 1924. A classic by one of the pioneers in conference techniques.

Frank, Lawrence K., *Society As the Patient: Essays on Culture and Personality*, Rutgers University Press, 1948.

Frank, Lawrence K., *Nature and Human Nature: Man's New Image of Himself*, Rutgers University Press, 1951.

*Fries, Charles Carpenter, *The Structure of English: An Introduction to the Construction of English Sentences*, Harcourt, Brace, 1952. A Michigan professor "presents an alternative to traditional grammar based upon the methods of modern linguistics."

*Frisch, Karl von, *Bees, Their Vision, Chemical Senses, and Language*, Cornell University Press, 1950. A clear, short, readable account of some famous experiments in animal communication.

Galbraith, J. K., *American Capitalism*, Houghton Mifflin, 1952. Sound semantic analysis of present economic trends.

Gallup, George, *A Guide to Public Opinion Polls*, Princeton University Press, 1944. Concise information in question-and-answer form.

*Gans, Roma, Stendler, C. B., and Almy, Millie, *Teaching Young Children*, World Book Co., 1952. Many useful sidelights on language teaching and development.

Gesell, Arnold, and Ilg, Frances, *Infant and Child in the Culture of Today*, Harper, 1943.

Grady, James F., and Hall, Milton, *How to Dictate Better Letters*, Harper, 1942. Antidotes for gobbledygook and business-ese.

*Hayakawa, S. I., *Language in Thought and Action*, Harcourt, Brace, 1949. One of the best general introductions to General Semantics, by the editor of *ETC*, the semantic quarterly.

———, editor, *Language Meaning and Maturity*, Harper, 1954. An anthology of articles from the first ten volumes of *ETC*.

Hoffer, Eric, *The True Believer: Thoughts on the Nature of Mass Movements*, Harper, 1951. Panaceas and their credulous seekers.

Hogben, Lancelot, *From Cave Painting to Comic Strip: A Kaleidoscope of Human Communication*, Chanticleer Press, 1949. Many fine illustrations selected by Marie Neurath, with text intended for the "middlebrow."

Homans, George C., *The Human Group*, Harcourt, Brace, 1950. Analyzing group interaction as reported in five independent case studies.

Hovland, Carl I., Janis, Irving L., and Kelley, Harold H., *Communication and Persuasion*, Yale University Press, 1953. Psychological studies of opinion change.

Hovland, Carl I., Lumsdaine, Arthur A., and Sheffield, Fred D., *Experiments on Mass Communication*, Vol. 3 of *Studies in Social Psychology in World War II*, Princeton University Press, 1949.

Howe, Quincy, *The News and How to Understand It, In Spite of the Newspapers, In Spite of the Magazines, In Spite of the Radio*, Simon and Schuster, 1940. How a publicist and journalist selects his news sources and interprets and discounts what he reads and hears.

Huxley, Julian, *Evolution in Action,* Harper, 1953. See especially chapter 4, "The Development of Mental Activity."

Inkeles, Alex, *Public Opinion in Soviet Russia: A Study in Mass Persuasion,* Harvard University Press, 1950. First report published by the Russian Research Center at Harvard. Introduction by Clyde Kluckhohn.

Institute of Radio Engineers, *Convention Record,* I.R.E., 1953. See especially part 8, "Information Theory."

Jennings, Helen Hall, *Leadership and Isolation,* Longmans, Green, 1943, 1950. Classic studies in group interaction.

Jesperson, Otto, *Language, Its Nature, Development and Origin,* Holt, 1922; Macmillan, 1949. A Danish scholar formulates a broad theory of linguistic development, through communities and individuals, beginning in childhood.

Johnson, Wendell, *People in Quandaries, The Semantics of Personal Adjustment,* Harper, 1946. Describes the author's use of General Semantics in guidance and clinical work with stutterers at Iowa State.

Kelley, E. C., *Education for What Is Real,* Harper, 1947. Pedagogical implications of the perception studies at Hanover and Princeton.

Keyes, Kenneth S., Jr., *How to Develop Your Thinking Ability,* McGraw-Hill, 1950. Another introduction to General Semantics, describing "six tools for thinking."

*Kilpatrick, Franklin P., editor, *Human Behavior from the Transactional Point of View,* Princeton, Institute for Associated Research, 1952. "A first attempt at giving an overall view of the implications of the visual demonstrations and the perceptual theory which have originated at the Institute for Associated Research."

*Korzybski, Alfred, *Science and Sanity: An Introduction to Non-Aristotelian Systems and General Semantics,* International Non-Aristotelian Library Publishing Co., 1933, 1941, 1948. Distributed by Institute of General Semantics, Lakeville, Conn. Monumental, stimulating, difficult work by the founder of General Semantics. The bible of the orthodox semanticists.

———, *Selections from Science and Sanity,* International Non-Aristotelian Library Publishing Co., 1948. Distributed by Institute of General Semantics, Lakeville, Conn. A skillful piece of editing by Guthrie E. Janssen, which includes a new six-page Author's Note by Korzybski.

———, *The Manhood of Humanity,* International Non-Aristotelian Library Publishing Co., 1921, 1950. Distributed by Institute of General Semantics, Lakeville, Conn. Thesis parallels in many ways the culture concept in anthropology. For comment, see chapter 12 of the present book.

LaBrant, Lou, *We Teach English,* Harcourt, Brace, 1951.

Laird, Charlton, *The Miracle of Language*, World Publishing Co., 1953. A professor at the University of Nevada conceals great scholarship in a popular volume. "I tried to ask myself all the most important questions about language."

Langer, Susanne K., *Philosophy in a New Key: A Study in the Symbolism of Reason, Rite and Art*, Harvard University Press, 1942. How symbols and meaning offer a new and fertile starting point for philosophy. Influenced by Whitehead, Cassirer.

Lasswell, Harold, editor, *Language of Politics: Studies in Quantitative Semantics*, George W. Stewart, 1949. A collection of analyses of wartime propaganda.

Lazarsfeld, Paul F., and Field, Harry, *The People Look at Radio*, University of North Carolina Press, 1946. Reporting a survey taken by the National Opinion Research Center, and sponsored by the National Association of Broadcasters.

Lazarsfeld, Paul F., and Kendall, Patricia, *Radio Listening in America: The People Look at Radio—Again*, Prentice-Hall, 1948. A second survey under the same auspices.

Lee, Alfred McClung, *How to Understand Propaganda*, Rinehart, 1952.

——, and Lee, Elizabeth Briant, editors, *The Fine Art of Propaganda: A Study of Father Coughlin's Speeches*, Harcourt, Brace, 1939. Illustrates the method of the useful though short-lived Institute for Propaganda Analysis, with a foreword by its secretary, Clyde R. Miller.

*Lee, Irving J., *Language Habits in Human Affairs: An Introduction to General Semantics*, Harper, 1941. The author is one of the most successful teachers of General Semantics, and this work is widely used as a textbook.

——, *The Language of Wisdom and Folly: Background Readings in Semantics*, Harper, 1949.

*Lewin, Kurt, *Field Theory in Social Science: Selected Theoretical Papers*, edited by Dorwin Cartwright, Harper, 1951. By a noted Gestalt psychologist, leader of the school labeled "Group Dynamics."

——, *Resolving Social Conflicts: Selected Papers on Group Dynamics*, Harper, 1948.

Lieber, Lillian R., and Lieber, Hugh Gray, *Mits, Wits and Logic*, Norton, 1947. A light and amusing presentation of the elements of logic by a mathematics teacher, with sketches by her husband.

Lindeman, Eduard C., *Social Education*, New Republic, 1933. By an early student of group action.

Linebarger, Paul M. A., *Psychological Warfare*, Infantry Journal Press, 1948. Textbook on propaganda for army specialists.

Lippitt, Ronald, *Training in Community Relations*, Harper, 1949. An early field study in group dynamics, described by one of Lewin's associates.

Lippmann, Walter, *Public Opinion*, Harcourt, Brace, 1922. A classic work on communication and propaganda which still has current relevance.

Lydgate, William A., *What Our People Think*, Crowell, 1944. Opinion formation discussed by an associate of Dr. Gallup's.

*Mandelbaum, David G., editor, *Selected Writings of Edward Sapir in Language, Culture and Personality*, University of California Press, 1949. Dates go back as far as 1911, and titles include: "Language and Environment," "Time Perspective in Aboriginal American Culture," "Grading: A Study in Semantics."

*Mayo, Elton, *The Social Problems of an Industrial Civilization*, Harvard Graduate School of Business Administration, 1945. By a great social scientist and student of communication in industry, sponsor of the famous Hawthorne experiments.

Markey, John F., *The Symbolic Process and Its Integration in Children: A Study in Social Psychology*, Harcourt, Brace, 1928. A learned study of communication at its beginnings.

McBurney, James H., and Hance, Kenneth G., *Discussion in Human Affairs*, Harper, 1939, 1950. Textbook by two professors in the School of Speech at Northwestern.

Miel, Alice, and associates, *Cooperative Procedures in Learning*, Teachers College of Columbia University, 1952. Examples of planning and initiative by class groups.

*Miller, George A., *Language and Communication*, McGraw-Hill, 1951. Lacking a textbook that would integrate the various aspects of communication for his course at M.I.T., the author wrote this one.

Minteer, Catherine, *Words and What They Do to You: Beginning Lessons in General Semantics for Junior and Senior High School*, Row Peterson, 1953. An adaptation of some teaching methods of Irving Lee.

Morris, Charles, *Signs, Language and Behavior*, Prentice-Hall, 1946. A philosopher at the University of Chicago undertakes to provide semantics with a new set of scientific terms.

Mowrer, O. H., *Learning Theory and Personality Dynamics*, Ronald Press, 1950. Contains an interesting chapter on "The Speech of Birds and Babies."

Murray, Elwood, *The Speech Personality*, Lippincott, 1937, 1944. Textbook by the director of the School of Speech of Denver University.

——, Barnard, Raymond H., and Garland, Jasper V., *Integrative Speech*, Dryden Press, 1953. Textbook which attempts to relate speech to social problems, through psychology, group dynamics, General Semantics, etc.

Ogden, C. K., *The General Basic English Dictionary*, Norton, 1942. Translates more than 20,000 words, with more than twice as many meanings, into the 900 words of Basic.

*Ogden, C. K., and Richards, I. A., *The Meaning of Meaning*, Harcourt, Brace, 1923, 1936. A semantic classic of great importance and influence.

Pei, Mario, *The Story of English*, Lippincott, 1952. An objective attempt "to describe what has happened and is happening to a language," in this case our own.

———, *The Story of Language*, Lippincott, 1949. Analyzes relationships among Western and Indo-European languages.

Peters, Raymond Wendell, *Communication Within Industry*, Harper, 1949. Research in labor-management communication, done as a survey for Standard Oil of New Jersey.

Philbrick, F. A., *Understanding English: An Introduction to Semantics*, Macmillan, 1942. Textbook by one of the faculty at Phillips Exeter Academy, chiefly influenced by I. A. Richards.

Piaget, Jean, *The Language and Thought of the Child*, Harcourt, Brace, 2nd edition, 1932. Records and analysis of spontaneous questions of a Swiss six-year-old.

Pillsbury, Walter B., and Meader, Clarence L., *The Psychology of Language*, Appleton, 1928.

*Rapaport, Anatol, *Science and the Goals of Man: A Study in Semantic Orientation*, Harper, 1950. By the associate editor of *ETC*, a mathematical biologist at the University of Chicago.

Richards, I. A., *Interpretation in Teaching*, Harcourt, Brace, 1938. A classic for teachers of English.

———, *Practical Criticism*, Harcourt, Brace, 1935. Describes the author's famous field study in the comprehension of poems.

———, *Principles of Literary Criticism*, Harcourt, Brace, 1924, 1928.

———, *The Philosophy of Rhetoric*, Oxford University Press, 1935.

*Rogers, Carl R., *Counseling and Psychotherapy*, Houghton Mifflin, 1942. "Non-directive counseling" described by its inventor.

Ruesch, Jurgen, and Bateson, Gregory, *Communication, the Social Matrix of Psychiatry*, Norton, 1951. A psychiatrist and an anthropologist contribute essays at a rather high level of abstraction.

Russell, David H., *Children Learn to Read*, Ginn, 1949.

Sapir, Edward, *Language: An Introduction to the Study of Speech*, Harcourt, Brace, 1921. A clear, nontechnical work that "aims to give a certain perspective on the subject of language rather than to assemble facts about it."

Schiller, F. C. S., *Formal Logic*, Macmillan, 1931. A critical analysis.

Schlauch, Margaret, *The Gift of Tongues*, Viking, 1942. Discussion of language and communication for the general reader, by a professor of English at New York University.

Schramm, Wilbur, editor, *Communications in Modern Society*, University of Illinois Press, 1948. Fifteen studies of the mass media, one hundred titles for further reading.

Seldes, Gilbert, *The Great Audience*, Viking, 1950. Movies, radio, and television discussed by an authority on the "lively arts."

*Shannon, Claude, and Weaver, Warren, *The Mathematical Theory of Communication*, University of Illinois Press, 1949. A theory for telephone engineers, of the first importance to the whole study of communication.

Shenton, Herbert N., Sapir, Edward, and Jesperson, Otto, *International Communication*, Kegan Paul, 1931.

Siepmann, Charles A., *Radio, Television and Society*, Oxford, 1950. By the author of *Radio's Second Chance* (Little, Brown, 1946). Leans on Lazarsfeld.

Smith, Bruce Lannes, Lasswell, Harold D., and Casey, Ralph D., *Propaganda, Communication and Public Opinion: A Comprehensive Reference Guide*, Princeton University Press, 1946. Continuing an earlier bibliography (1935), with the addition of more than 2,500 titles; also essays on channels, contents, effects of communication, and political specialists.

Snygg, Donald, and Combs, Arthur W., *Individual Behavior: A New Frame of Reference for Psychology*, Harper, 1949. Linked with Rogers and with the Gestaltists, the authors' theory analyzes experience in terms of each individual's "phenomenal world."

Stern, Catherine, *Children Discover Arithmetic: An Introduction to Structural Arithmetic*, Harper, 1949. A new teaching method with semantic value, developed by a Gestalt psychologist and educator.

Stevenson, Charles L., *Ethics and Language*, Yale University Press, 1944. An attempt to clarify the meaning of ethical terms.

Sturtevant, Edgar H., *An Introduction to Linguistic Science*, Yale University Press, 1947. Contains chapters on phonetics and phonemics, the relation of writing and speech, origin of language, etc.

Thelen, Herbert A., *Effective Group Operation, Principles and Practices*, University of Chicago Press, 1954. Fresh analysis and practical demonstrations, by the head of the Chicago Training Laboratory in Group Development.

Thorner, Melvin W., *Advertising and Propaganda, A Communication Theory*. Unpublished manuscript. A neurologist-psychiatrist discusses both advertising and propaganda as experiments with "purposeful communiqués" and measurable results.

Upward, Allen, *The New Word*, Mitchell Kennerley, 1910. An independent student's early approach to semantics.

Walpole, Hugh R., *Semantics*, Norton, 1941. Praises Ogden and Richards as against Korzybski. Introduction by Richards.

Warner, W. Lloyd, *American Life, Dream and Reality*, University of Chicago Press, 1953. Contains useful material on radio and other media.

Warner, W. Lloyd, and Lunt, Paul S., *The Social Life of a Modern Community*, Yale University Press, 1941. Group interaction in "Yankee City."

Whitehead, Alfred North, *The Aims of Education*, Macmillan, 1929. A classic with the theme: "The students are alive. . . ."

Whyte, William F., Jr., *Is Anybody Listening?* Simon and Schuster, 1952. Numerous examples of gobbledygook in business.

*Wiener, Norbert, *Cybernetics*, Technology Press, 1949. Robot computers described by the distinguished mathematician who invented and improved them.

*———, *The Human Use of Human Beings: Cybernetics and Society*. Houghton Mifflin, 1950.

Wolff, Werner, *The Personality of the Preschool Child: The Child's Search for His Self*, Grune and Stratton, 1947. Observation and experiment in Germany, at Vassar and Bard College.

*Young, J. Z., *Doubt and Certainty in Science: A Biologist's Reflections on the Brain*, Clarendon Press, 1951. BBC lectures which demonstrate how "the necessity to communicate . . . dominates all our actions."

Zipf, G. K., *Human Behavior and the Principle of Least Effort: An Introduction to Human Ecology*, Addison-Wesley Press, 1949. Highly technical attempt to quantify behavior through statistics on vocabularies of individuals and groups in different cultures. Continues the method of his earlier work.

———, *The Psycho-Biology of Language*, Houghton Mifflin, 1935.

PAMPHLETS

Barth, Alan, *The Government and the Press*, University of Minnesota School of Journalism, 1952. 14 pages. Sixth Annual Newspaper Guild Memorial Lecture.

Birdwhistell, Ray L., *Introduction to Kinesics*, Washington, Foreign Service Institute, 1952. 75 pages.

Bloch, Bernard, and Trager, George L., *Outline of Linguistic Analysis*, Baltimore, Linguistic Society of America, 1942. 82 pages.

Chisholm, Francis P., *Introductory Lectures on General Semantics*, Lakeville, Conn., Institute of General Semantics, 1944. 126 pages. Lithoprinted text with blackboard diagrams, prepared for a study group.

Gowers, Sir Ernest, *Plain Words: A Guide to the Use of English*, London, His Majesty's Stationery Office, 1948. 94 pages.

Hall, Edward T., and Trager, George L., *The Analysis of Culture*, Washington, Foreign Service Institute, 1953. 62 pages.

Hall, Milton, *Getting Your Ideas Across Through Writing*, Washington, Federal Security Agency, Training Manual No. 7, 1950. 44 pages. Borrows various practical suggestions from other publications by the author in collaboration with James F. Grady.

*Kendig, M. M., editor, *General Semantics Bulletin*, Lakeville, Conn., Institute of General Semantics, 1950 and later. Listed here as a pamphlet series because it appears irregularly, this bulletin contains stimulating and important material.

Lorge, Irving, *The Semantic Count of the 570 Commonest English Words*, Teachers College of Columbia University, 1949. 186 pages.

May, Mark A., and associates, *Seventh Semi-annual Report of U.S. Advisory Committee on Information*, House Document 94 of 83rd Congress, 1953. 23 pages. Analyzes major propaganda issues in the world today and offers recommendations for Voice of America, etc.

Trager, George L., *The Field of Linguistics*, Battenburg Press, 1949; Foreign Service Institute, 1952. 8 pages. Number 1 of "Occasional Papers," issued as a supplement to the journal, *Studies in Linguistics*.

*——, and Smith, Henry Lee, Jr., *An Outline of English Structure*, Battenburg Press, 1951. 92 pages. Number 3 of the "Occasional Papers."

*Whorf, Benjamin Lee, *Four Articles on Metalinguistics*, Washington, Foreign Service Institute, 1949. Reprints of three articles from the *Technology Review* and one from the Sapir memorial volume, *Language, Culture and Personality*.

ARTICLES

Bavelas, Alex, "Communication Patterns in Task-Oriented Groups," *Journal of the Acoustical Society of America*, November, 1950.

Bernays, Edward L., "The Engineering of Consent," in *Annals*, American Academy of Political and Social Science, March, 1947. A special issue on "Communication and Social Action."

Bird, Donald E., "Teaching Listening Comprehension," *Journal of Communication*, November, 1953.

Chafee, Zechariah, Jr., "The Disorderly Conduct of Words," *Columbia Law Review*, March, 1941.

Chase, Stuart, "Communication—Up, Down and Sideways," *Reader's Digest*, September, 1952. Describes two-way communication in a small, integrated factory.

Eliot, Thomas D., "Science and Silence," *Friends Intelligencer*, sixth month, 1943.

Estes, Charles T., "The Place of Communication in Maintaining Labor-Management Peace," *Personnel Administration*, September, 1949.

Kawai, Kazuo, "*Mokusatsu*, Japan's Response to the Potsdam Declaration," *Pacific Historical Review*, November, 1950.

Kelley, Douglas M., "The Use of General Semantics and Korzybskian Principles as an Extensional Method of Group Psychotherapy in Traumatic Neuroses," *Journal of Nervous and Mental Disease*, September, 1951.

Kirk, John R., "Communication Theory and Methods of Fixing Belief," *ETC*, Summer, 1953. In a special issue on Information; less technical than most of the contributions.

Konvitz, Milton R., "Justice and the Communist Teacher," *The New Leader*, April 20, 1953. By a professor of law at Cornell.

Lee, D. D., "Linguistic Reflection of Wintu Thought," *International Journal of American Linguistics*, October, 1944.

Loomis, Charles P., "Tapping Human Power Lines," *Adult Leadership*, February, 1953.

McCulloch, W. S., and Pitts, W., "A Logical Calculus of the Ideas Immanent in Nervous Activity," *Bulletin of Mathematical Biophysics*, December, 1943.

MacKay, D. M., "The Nomenclature of Information Theory," in *Symposium on Information Theory*, London, Ministry of Supply, 1950.

Minnick, Wayne C., "Graduate Study and Research in Propaganda," *Southern Speech Journal*, September, 1952.

Paul, Wilson B., Sorensen, Frederick, and Murray, Elwood, "A Functional Core for the Basic Communications Course," *Quarterly Journal of Speech*, April, 1946.

Read, Allen Walker, "An Account of the Word 'Semantics.'" *Word*, August, 1948.

Ridenour, Louis N., "The Role of the Computer," *Scientific American*, September, 1952. See also the rest of this issue on cybernetics and automatic control.

Whorf, Benjamin Lee, "An American Indian Model of the Universe," *International Journal of American Linguistics*, April, 1950.

———, "Language, Mind, and Reality," *ETC*, Spring, 1952. *ETC*'s special issue on metalinguistics includes also a Whorf bibliography by Herbert Hackett listing articles on the Hopi, Aztec, Maya, Shawnee, Sonoran languages, and the English of Eastern Massachusetts.

———, "Languages and Logic," *Technology Review*, Cambridge, Massachusetts Institute of Technology, April, 1941.

———, "Linguistics as an Exact Science," *Technology Review*, December, 1940.

———, "Science and Linguistics," *Technology Review*, April, 1940. This article and the two preceding ones are reprinted in the Foreign Service Institute's pamphlet on Whorf.

Ziebarth, E. W., "The Mass Media in International Communication," *Journal of Communication*, May, 1952.

Index